A BUDGET QUARTET

Critical Policy and Management Issues

Donald Axelrod

Professor Emeritus
of Public Administration

Nelson A. Rockefeller College
of Public Affairs and Policy
State University of New York at Albany

St. Martin's Press
New York

To My Wife Selma

Acquiring Editor: Larry Swanson
Project Management: Publication Services, Inc.
Cover Design: Ben Santora

Library of Congress Catalog Card Number: 88-61940
Copyright © 1989 by St. Martin's Press, Inc.

Manufactured in the United States of America.
32109
fedcba

For information, write
St. Martin's Press, Inc.
175 Fifth Avenue
New York, NY 10010

ISBN 0–312–02386–3

ACKNOWLEDGMENTS

Roy Bahl, "The Design of Intergovernmental Transfers in Industrialized
Countries," *Public Budgeting and Finance*, Vol. 6, No. 4 (Winter 1986).

National Academy of Public Administration, *Report on Government
Corporations, Vol. 1* (Washington, D.C.: 1981). Adapted by permission of National
Academy of Public Administration.

Larry Berman, *The Office of Management and Budget and the Presidency, 1921–
1979.* Copyright © 1979 by Princeton University Press. Adapted by permission of
Princeton University Press.

PREFACE

Since the early 1980s, budget issues have dominated policymaking in government as never before. Several recent books on budgeting reflect this emphasis as well as the urgency and the dynamism of the budget process. Yet, so complex is the modern budget process that few, if any, books on budgeting capture its many dimensions. As a result, some of the most significant forces that shape budgets are given short shrift.

The current budgetary literature admirably covers fiscal and economic policy. It is especially strong on the political framework of budgeting. It also treats budget formulation and implementation adequately. Nevertheless, it either ignores or gives but minimal attention to such increasingly important issues as the reliance of government on public authorities and government corporations and their impact on the budget process; the role of the courts in budgeting and policy development; the leverage of the budget process to achieve management improvements; and the effect of ever changing intergovernmental financing on the budgets of various levels of government. (Some impressive monographs cover intergovernmental relations, but the focus is not necessarily on budget decisionmaking.)

This book grew out of the writer's frustration in attempting to consider these four issues adequately in his recently published *Budgeting for Modern Government* (St. Martin's Press, 1988). This, then, is the genesis of *A Budget Quartet*, which covers more completely the policy and management dimensions of four major movements in budgeting. Because of their controversial nature, the reader will find as much cacophony as harmony in these movements.

The four critical issues discussed here in some detail make this slender volume a useful supplement not only to the literature on contemporary budgeting, but also on domestic policy development, public management and intergovernmental relations. It can therefore be used as an additional resource, coupled with a basic text, in graduate and advanced undergraduate courses in these fields. Instructors may also find that the book will serve to highlight strategic issues in introductory and capstone or end-of-program courses in MPA programs in public administration. The exploration of these issues may also appeal to public administrators and interested citizens generally.

Some features of this book merit emphasis. It is based in large part on the writer's many years of experience as a practitioner, consultant and teacher of budgeting in the United States and other countries. It deals with all levels of government in the United States. At the same time, it has a comparative perspective and highlights relevant budget practices and related policy issues in other countries. Such comparisons remind us that budget problems are global phenomena and may serve to identify workable solutions.

The book assumes no previous background in budgeting on the reader's part. It endeavors to explain simply such technicalities as arise. In keeping with its focus, the issues are taken up in four separate sections:

Section I, "Off-Budget Budgets: Financing Public Enterprises," highlights the growing reliance on public authorities and government corporations to conduct and finance major governmental projects and programs. Since many such enterprises are off-budget, they raise important questions of control, oversight and accountability.

Section II, "The Judicial Power of the Purse," emphasizes that budgeting is not the sole prerogative of chief executives and legislatures and that federal and state courts are also major players in the process. Through hundreds of court decisions, they have compelled governments to change policies and increase costs significantly.

Section III, "The Leverage of the Budget Process to Improve Governmental Management," focuses on a perennial theme that has been an inextricable part of budgeting from the very beginning: the use of the power of the purse to improve operating programs and capital projects. It examines attempts over the last fifty years by federal, state and local governments to effect management improvements through the budget process.

Section IV, "Intergovernmental Budgeting," deals with a crucial dimension of budgeting: the dependence of state and local governments on the federal government for financial assistance and the even greater dependence of local governments on state governments for grants, subsidies and loans. In this complex relationship, controversial issues arise, such as the declining amount of federal aid; the use of federal and state aid to correct disparities in fiscal resources between rich and poor local governments; and the controls exercised by donor governments over receiving governments on the theory that he who pays the piper calls the tune.

In preparing this book, I benefitted from the advice and assistance of many organizations and individuals. I should like to acknowledge in particular the help of the National Association of State Budget Officers; the U.S. General Accounting Office; the U.S. Office of Management and Budget; the British Treasury; the United Nations; former colleagues in the New York State Division of the Budget, especially Robert Kerker, Janet Butlin, Harold Rubin and Harold Juhre; T.N. Hurd, former Budget Director and Secretary to the Governor of New York State; Digambar Bhouraskar, a senior official of the United Nations; A. Premchand of the International Monetary Fund; Richard D. Irving, bibliographer of the Library of the State University of New York at Albany; Frederick C. Mosher of the University of Virgina; Roger Brown of the University of North Carolina in Charlotte; and Catherine Albright of Publication Services, Inc.

I owe a particular debt of gratitude to Michael J. White of the University of Southern California, and to my wife, Selma. Both patiently reviewed several drafts of this book and made numerous suggestions that, I hope, have resulted in a better structured and clearer text. Needless to say, I alone bear the responsibility for any errors of fact or misinterpretation of data. Finally, I should like to express my thanks to Maxine H. Morman, who typed and retyped the several drafts of this book.

CONTENTS

≡ 1 OFF-BUDGET BUDGETS: FINANCING PUBLIC ENTERPRISES

The fastest growing parts of the public sector in the United States and other countries are thousands of public enterprises.[1] In the United States, the better known enterprises include the Postal Service, the Government National Mortgage Association (GNMA) and the Tennessee Valley Authority at the federal level; the Port Authority of New York and New Jersey, the State of Washington Public Power Supply System and the Massachusetts Bay Transportation Authority at the state level; and housing, water supply, waste disposal and transportation authorities at the local level. In other countries, equally well known large public enterprises engage in virtually every type of economic activity.

Each government has its own favorite label for public enterprises. Hence, they are variously termed public authorities, government corporations, public benefit corporations, special districts, off-budget enterprises (OBEs), parastatal organizations, state-owned enterprises (SOEs), special funds, commissions, revolving funds and development banks. Despite differences in terminology, public enterprises everywhere have much in common. For the most part they are autonomous corporate bodies outside the regular government structure. Also, with some exceptions, they are "off-budget"—that is, they are exempt from review by the central budget office and do not appear in budget totals or documents. Similarly, they are not generally subject to the legislative appropriation process. Yet, they

1

account for a significant share—and in some governments a major share—of public expenditures, revenue, debt and employment. To the extent that budgets omit public enterprises, they understate the size and growth of public spending.[2]

Created by special or general statutes, public enterprises engage in commercial-type revenue producing activities and are intended to be substantially self-sustaining. They are generally free to use their own revenue for operating expenses and capital investment, to borrow funds in capital markets, and to control their own assets. To give them the flexibility and autonomy of business enterprises, governments have set them up as corporate bodies with the power of self-governance through boards of directors (or occasionally single administrators). As such, they are usually more or less exempt not only from central controls over budgets, but also staff appointments, procurement, and contracting.[3]

Despite their autonomous corporate status, public enterprises are fundamentally instruments of public policy. To carry out these policies, governments could have turned to regular operating agencies or to the private sector instead of creating public enterprises. Yet, for a variety of reasons discussed below, they have chosen to rely on public enterprises. For example, in recommending the creation of the Tennessee Valley Authority in 1933, President Roosevelt visualized it as "a corporation clothed with the power of government but possessed of the flexibility and initiative of private enterprise."[4] This has been the guiding spirit behind the creation of many public enterprises in the United States.

Owned in whole or large part by governments, public enterprises depend on governments for their startup capital in the form of advances, loans, grants or the purchase of shares of equity (where the public enterprises issue stock). They count on governments to guarantee, explicitly or implicitly, loans from investors in domestic and foreign capital markets. Where public enterprises issue bonds for the construction of capital facilities, investors look to governments, again either explicitly or implicitly, to back up the payment of principal and interest. Should public enterprises fail to be self-supporting, governments assist them with subsidies or bail them out if they default in paying their obligations. Conversely, in a minority of cases, public enterprises actually contribute to public revenue.

Despite their profound and obvious impact on budgets, public enterprises have remained substantially off-budget. Hence, in most governments, public sector budgeting is fragmented. The official budget covers the programs and projects of operating agencies plus subsidies, loans and grants to public enterprises. For the most part, budgets of public enterprises are excluded. Often the twain do not meet, complicating the problems of formulating a coherent budget policy.

Notwithstanding the importance of public enterprises, only sketchy information exists on their activities, financing and performance. No precise data are even available on the actual numbers of public enterprises. In effect, they are the "underground" or "hidden" government, the *terra incognita* of public administration. Except for a few pioneering studies cited in this section, most budgetary literature, surprisingly, is silent on the linkages of budgets and public enterprises.[5]

To shed some light on the impact of public enterprises on budgeting, this section focuses on several major issues: the number and types of public enterprises; their functions; their economic and fiscal effect; the rationale for creating them and placing them off-budget; the extent of control by chief executives and legislatures over their finances and performance; mechanisms designed to enforce accountability for results; the major fiscal and operating problems of public enterprises; attempts to strengthen budget control over public enterprises without crippling their flexibility and autonomy (if this is not a contradiction in terms); and current attempts to divest governments of some enterprises by "privatizing" them. While the section deals primarily with public authorities and government corporations in the United States, it also highlights the relevant experience of other countries where public enterprises play a major role in the economy.

THE ANATOMY OF PUBLIC ENTERPRISES: THEIR NUMBERS, STRUCTURE, AND FUNCTIONS

☰ How many public enterprises do we have?

In the number of public enterprises, the "free enterprise" United States leads the world outside the communist bloc (where nearly all enterprises are state-owned). This estimate is based on a variety of sources, since no precise data are available anywhere. Only the United States Bureau of the Census attempts to compile data on the number of public enterprises in the United States, primarily at state and local levels. Yet, at best, the information is limited. It comes out every five years and lumps some but not all state and local public enterprises with special districts which it defines as "limited purpose government units (other than school district governments) which exist as separate entities and have substantial fiscal and administrative independence from general purpose local governments."[6] In applying this definition the Bureau is often inconsistent and excludes from its compilation many of the largest and richest public authorities such as power authorities, housing finance agencies, economic development authorities and transportation authorities.[7]

In the latest Census of Governments in 1987, the Census Bureau counted 29,487 special district governments, of which about 94 percent performed a single function, such as protection of natural resources, fire protection, housing, community development, water supply, sewage disposal, utilities, or hospitals. Less than half of the special districts have the power to tax the property of users of their services. Hence, they are not public enterprises that charge for specific use of services and products. Presumably, the majority are revenue producing enterprises.[8] But the data are not clear on this point. Furthermore, because of the present criteria used by the Census Bureau, the data exclude about 1,000 state and interstate and at least 1,000 local public authorities.[9]

At best, informed estimates will have to do on the number of public enterprises in the United States. In the first authoritative study of state and local enterprises, Walsh estimated that in the late 1970s some 6,000 local and 1,000 state and interstate public authorities existed.[10] Later, the estimate for both categories was raised to 10,000.[11] New York led state governments with some forty-one public authorities, and local governments in Pennsylvania, with nearly 2,500 public authorities, topped local governments in other states.[12] Because of definitional problems, these figures may not be precise.

The federal government has far fewer public enterprises than state and local governments. Depending on the definitions and classifications employed, the number ranges from thirty-one to forty-seven.[13] In this case, though, small is big. Federal public enterprises are among the largest in the world in operating expenditures and the capacity to make and guarantee loans. As a result of their activities, the federal government is the largest insurer, lender, borrower, landlord, producer of electrical power, owner of grazing and timber lands, grain owner, warehouse operator, shipowner and truck fleet operator in the United States.[14]

Structurally, the federal government corporations are complex and diverse. Most are wholly owned by the government; some, in theory, combine public and private ownership; some are financed by the government but run as private entities; and some (the so-called government-sponsored enterprises [GSEs]) are chartered by the government, but privately owned and operated. A few examples will illustrate these categories. The Government National Mortgage Association (GNMA), which guarantees mortgage securities, is wholly owned by the federal government. The Rural Telephone Bank represents mixed public and private ownership. The Corporation for Public Broadcasting is financed by the federal government, but run as a private corporation. Typifying the GSEs, the Federal National Mortgage Association buys mortgages from banks to expand the credit market for housing.[15]

Even this summary of federal government and quasi-government corporations does not tell the whole story. In addition, the federal government operates four massive unincorporated enterprises such as the Bonneville Power Administration in the Northwest and hundreds of self-financed enterprises in the operating agencies (run. through revolving funds).[16]

Outside the United States, public enterprises loom especially large in the economies of developed and developing countries and in both centrally planned and market economies. As in the United States, it is difficult to obtain data on the number of public enterprises, especially at the local level, since such information is not systematically collected and consolidated.[17] Many of them depend heavily on government loans, subsidies and grants and are mainly off-budget. This is true in Britain, even though major public enterprises were denationalized by the Thatcher government in the 1980s; Japan, with over 3,000 off-budget public enterprises; Canada, with some 400 government-owned "crown corporations," including Air Canada and the Bank of Canada; France, with a large number of public enterprises that in 1982 employed 23 percent of the work force, only to be privatized in large part by the Chirac government; Italy, with two giant holding companies that control hundreds of firms in every economic sector; Brazil, with over 500 public enterprises at the federal level, including Petrobras, the national oil company; and Kenya, with over 300 major public enterprises.[18]

≡ Public enterprises come in various shapes and forms and perform virtually all economic functions

Depending on the statutes that create them, public enterprises come in various legal forms. A favorite structure is a government corporation or public authority set up by a special act with the board of directors appointed in the United States by the president, governor or mayor. The chief executives also influence the appointment of the top staff. At times the public enterprise may be a holding company with the power to establish subsidiary corporations, as is true of the Metropolitan Transportation Authority of New York State, the Massachusetts Bay Transportation Authority, the Tennessee Valley Authority and the Port Authority of New York and New Jersey.[19] In mixed public enterprises, the board of directors includes representatives of the private sector. Even though government-sponsored enterprises like the Federal National Mortgage Association are private organizations, they include government representatives on their boards.

The many diverse functions of public enterprises fall into five major categories:

1. *Development and rehabilitation of the infrastructure.* Nearly all governments in the United States rely on public authorities and special districts to finance, build and operate the infrastructure, including roads, bridges, tunnels, parkways, dams, ports, airports, public buildings, industrial parks, water supply systems and waste disposal systems. These are the traditional activities of public enterprises. With the deterioration of the infrastructure in the United States,

they have assumed new importance. As of 1982, 7,329 state and local public enterprises engaged in the construction and rehabilitation of the infrastructure. Another 3,089 also had this mission but were inactive during that period.[20]

2. *Construction, operation and maintenance of utility and transportation systems.* In most countries of the world it is commonplace for public enterprises to construct, operate and maintain mass transportation systems, telecommunications systems and utility systems to generate and distribute electricity and gas. The United States is different. With some major exceptions, the private sector dominates telecommunications and utilities. The exceptions include the TVA, the Power Authority of New York State, the Bonneville Power Administration and the State of Washington Public Power Supply System. At one time the private sector controlled the transportation of passengers on railroads and buses. With the bankruptcy and default of many of these systems, public enterprises became responsible for mass transportation through Amtrak (National Rail Passenger Corporation) and numerous public authorities among the states and cities, such as BART (Bay Area Rapid Transit) in the San Francisco area, and the Massachusetts Bay Transportation Authority, which serves some 152 communities. Similarly, as private railroad companies responsible for shipping freight went bankrupt in the Northeast, the federal government created CONRAIL, a public enterprise designed to revive and subsidize the ailing freight systems (privatized in 1986).

3. *Construction of facilities for health, education and housing programs.* The "baby boom" and population shifts in the United States in the 1950s and 1960s led to a large scale construction of schools, university buildings, dormitories, public hospitals, housing for low- and moderate-income groups and health centers. In most state and local governments, public enterprises were established to finance and construct these facilities.[21]

4. *Financial services.* In the sheer volume of financial transactions and expenditures, the financial services of public enterprises exceed those of other government corporations and public authorities. At the federal level, corporations provide insurance, loans and loan guarantees running into hundreds of billions of dollars to major sectors of the economy: banks, agriculture, investors, small business, home builders and home owners, university students and export firms.[22] Since the 1960s, state governments have created what in effect are hundreds of public investment banks to lend money to banks, real estate developers, small business, non-profit health care facilities, colleges and private utility firms. Variously termed housing finance agencies, mortgage agencies, industrial development author-

ities and health or environmental facility corporations, these public enterprises construct nothing. They are solely intermediaries. They borrow funds in the tax exempt bond market and relend them to private firms, non-profit organizations and individuals for mortgage loans, student loans, the establishment or expansion of business, the construction of health facilities and the purchase of pollution control equipment.[23]

5. *Manufacturing and trading enterprises.* More so than in the United States, public enterprises in other countries engage in manufacturing, trading, mining, marketing, banking, insurance and housing. In some countries they dominate key sectors of the economy, such as steel, coal and oil production, telecommunications and transportation. Only in war emergencies has the United States Government ventured into the ownership of manufacturing plants on a large scale. For example, during World War II it created several giant holding companies. One of them, the Defense Plant Corporation, owned over 2,000 factories engaged in the production of war materials. The Reconstruction Finance Corporation, established during the Depression in the 1930s to aid ailing businesses and governments, proved to be a handy vehicle during the war to set up subsidiary corporations to produce and distribute rubber, metals and petroleum. In the post-war period the government liquidated its manufacturing enterprises save for such activities as the production of fertilizer by the TVA and the generation of electrical power. It rescued ailing manufacturing plants such as the Lockheed and Chrysler Corporations through loans and loan guarantees and supported new ventures such as the synthetic fuels industry through grants, loans and guaranteed loans by the Synthetic Fuels Corporation.[24]

≡ Why create public enterprises and place them "off-budget"?

No overarching theory of public ownership explains the rise of public enterprises in the United States as it does in other countries. For a variety of pragmatic, fiscal and non-ideological reasons, federal, state and local governments have chosen to use public authorities and government corporations to carry out public policy instead of relying on conventional organizational structures, the marketplace, regulation, tax incentives and the budget system to fund additional expenditures.[25] If any normative beliefs influence the creation of public enterprises, it is the tendency to cloak public functions in the garb of a business enterprise in harmony with the values of the marketplace. Among the major forces which have led to the creation of public authorities and government corporations have been the following:

1. *Failings of the marketplace.* With the market unable to provide at a profit affordable housing to low- and moderate-income groups, hundreds of public enterprises at all levels of government loan funds at below-market interest rates; construct and operate public housing; guarantee loans for housing; insure mortgages; subsidize housing costs; and purchase mortgages from commercial lenders to provide additional funds to build single-family and multi-unit apartments. Among the major federal public enterprises engaged in mammoth housing credit programs are the Federal Housing Administration, which insures single-family mortgages; the Government National Mortgage Association (GNMA), which guarantees securities (backed up by insured mortgages) issued by private lenders; the Federal National Mortgage Association (a government sponsored enterprise), that purchases mortgages from banks and savings institutions; and the Farmers Home Administration, that loans funds to farmers. At the state level, housing and mortgage finance agencies loan funds at relatively low interest rates to banks, builders and homeowners. In many localities, public housing authorities provide low-cost housing to low-income groups. This is made possible by subsidies, loans and loan guarantees by the federal and state governments and tax exemptions by local governments.

Similar gaps and imperfections in the market have resulted in the establishment of public enterprises to subsidize and guarantee loans to college students, operate and subsidize mass transportation systems, support the prices paid to farmers and provide electricity to rural areas.

All of these programs have an impact on the budget. Subsidies increase operating costs. Should borrowers fail to repay loans, the defaults also increase expenditures. All guaranteed and insured loans constitute a contingent liability for government. If the loans are not repaid, governments are legally obligated to pay the creditors. Thus, a loan guarantee shifts the risk of default from the lender to the government.[26]

2. *Bypassing constitutional and legal limits on expenditures, taxes and debt.* Nearly all public enterprises, especially among state and local governments, have been off-budget. In many cases this has been a deliberate ploy to reduce budget totals and to bypass constitutional and legal limits on expenditures, taxes and debt. Beginning in the 1960s and continuing at an accelerated rate in the 1980s, state and local governments established thousands of public authorities to get around constitutional and statutory restrictions on debt financing and limits on taxing and spending.[27] One direct consequence of these actions has been the dramatic increase in non-guaranteed or moral obligation debt with public authorities the prime vechicle for debt financing through the use of revenue bonds. In the wake

of the taxpayer revolt in the late 1970s, dramatized by Proposition 13 in California and Proposition $2\frac{1}{2}$ in Massachusetts and lids on expenditures by local governments, many local governments created off-budget, self-financed public authorities. For example, following a tight expenditure limitation law in New Jersey, the number of local authorities increased to some 250.[28]

Attempts at federal expenditure control had a similar effect. Following the adoption of the unified budget in 1967 with the objective of incorporating in the budget virtually all expenditures in the public sector, the number of autonomous public enterprises increased. They and their sponsors wanted no part of a comprehensive budget which subjected them to budgetary controls. Similarly, the Congressional Budget Act of 1974, with its focus on aggregate and functional expenditure limits, was partially responsible for the creation of additional independent government corporations.[29]

3. *"Beating the system."* Quite apart from the perceived advantages of going off-budget, governments have also set up public enterprises to "beat the system" by exempting them from central controls over personnel ceilings, civil service salaries, budgets, audits, procurement, construction and other "red tape." Frequently, this motivation goes hand in hand with the impetus to finance the activities of the public enterprises outside the regular budget. It is argued that the traditional bureaucracy is slow, rigid and ill-equipped to administer high priority and novel programs. In contrast, supporters of autonomous public enterprises claim that they are fast-moving, flexible and creative and in a position to assemble a specialized and talented staff quickly to get the job done. The effect is to perpetuate alleged deficiencies in central control systems by going around them instead of meeting them head on and correcting them.[30]

4. *Aversion of private sector to risky and unprofitable ventures.* Without government loans, grants and loan guarantees, private entrepreneurs are reluctant to undertake possibly risky, uncertain and unprofitable ventures. Hence, in the energy crunch of the late 1970s the federal government established the Synthetic Fuels Corporation to underwrite the commercial production of synthetic fuels through various forms of financial assistance and price guarantees. The Small Business Administration was created to guarantee loans to small businesses which had no ready access to commercial credit.[31] Loans and guaranteed loans to exporters through Eximbank (Export-Import Bank) provide risk protection against possible defaults in the payment of bills. At the state and local levels, job development and industrial development authorities have issued tax exempt bonds in order to provide low cost loans to private firms.

5. *Regional and economic development.* Virtually all forms of public enterprise, including industrial and job development authorities, in theory, stimulate regional and economic development. For some public enterprises, this is one of their main missions, as is true of the Tennessee Valley Authority, the New Jersey Economic Development Authority, the Port Authority of New York and New Jersey, the Urban Development Corporation of New York State, the Delaware River Basin Commission and hundreds of local economic development authorities. These public authorities highlight the role of public ownership as a development strategy.[32]

6. *Rescue of ailing industries.* Unlike governments in other industrialized countries which frequently take over ailing firms in key economic sectors, governments in the United States have generally limited their rescue efforts to railroads, buslines and port terminals. Through Conrail and Amtrak the federal government acquired defunct railroads.[33] State and local governments have taken over bus lines. For example, the New Jersey Transit Corporation has purchased and operates the largest bus company in the state. The Port Authority of New York and New Jersey took over a failing commuter line serving New York and New Jersey (the PATH system), and port corporations in various parts of the United States acquired, rehabilitated and improved marine terminals. In the mid-1980s the federal government bailed out failing banks. Through the Federal Deposit Insurance Corporation (FDIC), the Federal Savings and Loan Insurance Corporation (FSLIC) and the Federal Reserve Board, it engineered, at considerable cost to the government, changes in management of the banks and transfers of ownership of defunct banks to more financially stable institutions.

7. *Political visibility of public enterprises.* Public enterprises are useful as political symbols. They give high political visibility to functions which otherwise might be subsumed in a regular operating agency. The creation of a public enterprise reminds the voters that the government is "doing something."[34]

8. *Insulation from political pressures.* Only sparse evidence suggests that this indeed is the case.[35]

9. *Increased access to the tax exempt bond market.* This has been a major development in recent years, especially because of implicit and explicit guarantees of the payment of debt service by state governments. In addition, public authorities are assured of dedicated and earmarked funding for high priority projects.[36]

10. *The only way to get the job done.* In complex policy areas where government has had little experience, the creation of public enterprises may be the only way to get the job done.

≡ The driving forces behind the creation of public enterprises in other countries

Many of the forces that led to the creation of public enterprises in the United States have also proved to be potent in other countries—both developed and developing.[37] But major differences exist. In these countries, public enterprises encompass nearly all economic sectors and, in many governments, are regarded as the key to economic development. To stabilize employment, governments are far less reluctant to take over ailing firms. This has been done extensively in Europe and Latin America. In various countries, such as Italy, India, Canada and Brazil, public enterprises have a significant role in regional economic development. In developing countries especially, public enterprises are created to offset the inadequacy of the marketplace. Little private capital is available for investment, and private enterpreneurs shrink from starting new firms in unstable economies.[38]

In contrast to the United States, ideological and political factors have led to a proliferation of public enterprises in other countries. To control their own economic destiny as they saw it, several governments nationalized large firms in key economic sectors. For example, the Labor Governments of Britain in 1945–51, 1967 and 1977 nationalized the coal, railway, electricity, gas, steel and ship-building industries.[39] In 1982 the Socialist government of France, headed by President Francois Mitterand, added to an already formidable list of state-owned companies major commercial and investment banks, manufacturing firms and producers of aluminum, steel, chemicals, glass and synthetic fibers. The effect was to create in France the largest public sector among non-communist industrialized countries.[40] In the mid-1980s, equally ideological conservative governments in France and Britain began to sell off nationalized firms to the private sector. Large scale nationalization of firms also took place in Argentina, Mexico and Egypt.[41]

Not all public enterprises are completely owned by the governments. Some enterprises are joint ventures with the private sector. In others the governments, through stock ownership, maintain majority control. As a result, nearly all countries outside the communist bloc have a mixed economy with varying combinations of public and private ownership.

A variety of other economic and social pressures has induced developing countries, in particular, to create public enterprises: maintenance of employment; the need for revenue from profitable public enterprises (especially monopolistic ones such as tobacco firms); substitution of national goods and services for imports; the need to control prices for goods and services; location of enterprises in various regions of the country; redistribution of income; and assistance to underprivileged ethnic groups (at times at the expense of other ethnic groups).[42] As much emphasis was placed on the non-commercial objectives of public enterprises as on their profitability. Often the two sets of goals were irreconcilable.

THE BUDGETARY AND ECONOMIC IMPACT OF PUBLIC ENTERPRISES IN THE UNITED STATES

Despite some similarities between federal and state/local public enterprises in the United States, major differences exist in size, scope of activity, expenditures, the amount of credit and loan guarantees extended to the private sector, the effect on budgets and the impact on the economy. Hence, public enterprises at each level of government merit separate analysis.

· ≡ Public enterprises in the federal government have been on- and off-budget in varying degrees

Budget policy with regard to federal public enterprises has been contradictory, inconsistent and frequently ambiguous. Of thirty-one government corporations analyzed by the Congressional Research Service in 1983, nineteen were on-budget in the sense that they appeared in the budget document and hence were part of a unified budget. The "on-budget" public enterprises included the Commodity Credit Corporation, which assists farmers through loan, purchase and payment programs; the Federal Deposit Insurance Corporation; and the Tennessee Valley Authority. On the other hand, twelve public enterprises were either totally or mainly "off-budget." This category included the Postal Service, the Federal Financing Bank (more later on this), the Synthetic Fuels Corporation, and the National Consumer Cooperative Bank.

Nearly half the public enterprises were more or less exempt from review and monitoring by OMB. The fact that data on a public enterprise appear in the federal budget does not necessarily mean that the enterprise is subject to budget review. Conversely, the omission of a public enterprise from the budget document does not automatically remove it from the budget process. For example, the Federal Deposit Insurance Corporation was "on-budget." Yet OMB did not review its budget estimates. On the other hand, the Rural Telephone Bank was "off-budget," but was completely subject to budgetary review.

In general, the estimates of public enterprises supported by appropriations or Treasury loans were reviewed by OMB. Even this policy was not consistent. Although the Legal Services Corporation and the Neighborhood Reinvestment Corporation received federal funds, they were insulated by statute from budget review. On the other hand, some self-sustaining public enterprises, such as the TVA and the Federal Home Loan Bank Board, were subject to budget review. Other self-supporting enterprises, such as the National Consumer Cooperative Bank and the Securities Investors Protection Corporation, were not.[43]

Budgeting, of course, encompasses more than budget review and includes implementation and monitoring of the approved budget. In this area, practices were equally murky and inconsistent. In a study by the National Academy of Public Administration for OMB in 1981, federal public enterprises that responded to a questionnaire reported the following budget controls:[44]

- ☐ *Lids on administrative expenses*   14 yes, 13 no
- ☐ *Limits on capital expenses*   11 yes, 14 no
- ☐ *Line item review*   12 yes, 13 no
- ☐ *OMB apportionment of funds*   17 yes, 13 no
- ☐ *Subject to all above controls*   8
- ☐ *Subject to none*   6
- ☐ *Pay scales*   GSEs and so-called "mixed ownership" and private corporations generally exempt from civil service limits. Separate personnel systems in TVA and Postal Service.

≡ Budget policies vis-à-vis public enterprises eroded the unified budget

The exemption of public enterprises in whole or part from central budget control resulted in an erosion of the unified budget. The effect was to exclude from the budget hundreds of billions of dollars of expenditures, loans, grants and loan guarantees. Every government corporation and GSE is an instrument of public policy. By omitting their loans, loan guarantees and expenditures from the budget, it became difficult to develop coherent and comprehensive budget policies covering the entire public sector. It deprived budget-makers of the opportunity to weigh explicitly the relative merits of expenditures, subsidies, loans and loan guarantees as a means of achieving public priorities. Each fiscal tool influences the allocation of public and private resources and, in conjunction with the others, has a profound effect on programs, the budget, the distribution of income, and the economy. Hence all fiscal instruments should be considered together in a unified budget. To leave any of them out is to understate budget totals and to undermine accountability.[45]

≡ Off-budget expenditures

Off-budget expenditures prior to 1985 highlight some of these problems. In the early 1980s off-budget outlays ranged from roughly $14 billion to $21 billion. While significant, they represented but a small part of the total budget.[46]

The Federal Financing Bank (FFB), which is an integral part of the

Treasury Department, accounted for about 90 percent of all off-budget expenditures.[47] Created in 1973 (87 Stat. 937, U.S.C. 2281-2296), FFB was intended to centralize borrowing for operating agencies and government corporations. Previously, agencies with authority to borrow funds to finance their activities competed with each other and the Treasury to obtain funds in capital markets. Now FFB borrows from the Treasury and, at a small charge, lends the money to such agencies as the Farmers Home Administration and the Rural Electrification Administration. In turn, these agencies use the funds for loans and loan guarantees to businesses and individuals.[48]

Later, the mission of FFB was broadened to authorize it to buy the loan assets of the various agencies and public enterprises. Loan assets are the loans made primarily to the private sector on which payments of principal and interest are due.[49] Purchases of existing loans by FFB permits the agencies and government corporations to make additional loans for farms, homes, utility services, public housing and even exports of weapons. Such purchases of loan assets by FFB increased the off-budget expenditures of the federal government.[50]

The present arrangement was unsatisfactory on two grounds. First, it weakened budget control. Second, it obfuscated the budget process. For example, the Farmers Home Administration (FMHA), which is on-budget, could borrow, say, $5 billion from FFB for loans to farmers and businesses. Ordinarily the transaction would be shown as a budget outlay by FHMA. FHMA, however, is free to sell its loan portfolio to FFB for $5 billion.[51] By budgetary legerdemain, a sale of this type cancels the outlay and results in showing zero expenditures by FHMA. What happened was that an on-budget loan was transferred to off-budget status. The loan did not vanish, even though it did not appear in the unified budget. It became part of the off-budget deficit, which the Treasury finances through additional borrowing.

This oversimplified example highlights the complexity and obscurity of off-budget spending. In 1985 Congress simplified the process by requiring that agencies include in their budgets all FFB transactions.[52]

≡ Off-budget loans and loan guarantees overshadow off-budget expenditures

Far more significant than off-budget expenditures are over 100 credit programs that include off-budget loans and loan guarantees. Through direct loan programs, the government, like a bank, loans funds directly to a variety of borrowers and collects the principal and interest payments over the life of the loans. Through loan guarantee programs, the government guarantees loans made by private lending institutions.[53] At the end of 1987, outstanding loans and loan guarantees advanced by on- and off-budget entities and GSEs approximated $1.3 trillion, as the following table shows.

Table 1-1
Outstanding federal loans and loan guarantees, 1984–1987 (in billions of dollars)

	1984	1985	1986	1987
Direct loans	$229.3	$257.4	$251.6	$234.2
Primary guaranteed loans	386.7	410.4	449.8	507.0
Loans by Government-Sponsored Enterprises	314.1	370.0	453.3	581.1
Total federal and federally-assisted loans	930.1	1,037.8	1,154.7	1,322.3

Source: Budget of the United States Government, Fiscal Year 1989, Special Analyses, "Special Analysis F, Federal Credit Programs," p. F-31; _____, Fiscal Year 1989, p. F40.

These figures highlight the role of the federal government as the nation's largest financial intermediary. The $257 billion in direct loans at the end of 1985 exceeded by 30 percent the combined loan assets of the two largest U.S. commercial banks. When added to outstanding loans by GSEs, the total loans outstanding were $627.4 billion. Outstanding loan guarantees of $410.4 billion represented nearly 40 percent of all credit extended or sponsored by the federal government. The beneficiaries of direct loans and loan guarantees are farmers, homeowners, small business, exporters, utilities, students, ship-builders and state, local and foreign governments.[54]

Looked at over a seven year period, 1981–1987, the trends in direct loans and loan guarantees are revealing. As Table 1-2 shows, federal lending for programs cited above ranged from 12.2 to 23.2 percent (the so-called participation rate) of all the credit advanced in the United States to the public and private sectors. (Actually the federal government borrows much more to finance its deficit. Hence federal and federally assisted borrowing accounted for 45.2 percent of all funds borrowed in U.S. credit markets in 1987.)[55] Most federal loans and loan guarantees originated in off-budget public enterprises or quasi-public enterprises.

In each of the seven years, actual loans and loan guarantees were greater than the figures shown in the table. The table is on a net basis. This means the government subtracts from new loans and loan guarantees loans that were repaid, written off or otherwise adjusted.[56]

Loan guarantees come in two forms: (1) federal guarantees of the repayment of the loan to private creditors in whole or part in the event of default by the borrowers, and (2) the use of insurance premiums such as mortgage insurance by the Federal Housing Administration (FHA) to protect lenders against default. Most of the loan guarantees secure housing loans by banks and other institutional lenders. The rest include loans to students, small businesses, farmers, foreign governments and exporters. As a result of these guarantees, the contingent liability of the federal government in the event of default is enormous, totaling about $419 billion in FY 1987.[57] Despite their importance, guaranteed loans did not appear in the unified budget until the early 1980s. Budget outlays included only funds to cover defaults and subsidies for interest and insurance premiums.[58]

☰ Loans by GSEs

By a large margin the five GSEs lend more and borrow more than public enterprises. In 1987, as Table 1-2 indicates, net lending amounted to $107.8 billion. At one time the GSEs were, in the main, wholly owned by the federal government as off-budget public enterprises. Since 1969 they have been "privatized," but continue to enjoy a "special relationship" that carries with it such financial benefits as: lower interest rates only marginally higher than those for Treasury bills and notes; lines of credit at the Treasury; exemption from corporate income tax (two of five); exemption of investor interest income from state and local taxes (three of five); and eligibility for Federal Reserve open market purchases.[59]

The federal government does not guarantee securities of the GSEs. Nevertheless, investors regard them as a "moral obligation" on the part of the government and, hence, as noted, are willing to accept lower interest rates.[60]

Table 1-2

Federal and federally assisted lending by amount and as a percent of domestic credit markets (in billions)

	1981	1982	1983	1984	1985	1986	1987
Total funds loaned in U.S. credit markets [1]	$410.5	$391.1	$547.6	$649.5	$687.5	$830.0	$642.7
Federal and federally assisted lending	86.5	87.6	86.5	79.5	110.3	129.1	149.2
Direct loans	26.1	23.4	15.3	6.3	28.0	11.2	−19.0
Guaranteed loans	28.0	20.9	34.1	20.1	21.6	34.6	60.4
GSE loans [2]	32.4	43.3	37.1	53.1	60.7	83.3	107.8
Federal lending as percent of total U.S. credit	22.1	22.4	15.8	12.2	16.0	15.6	23.2

[1]Funds loaned to and borrowed by non-financial sectors, excluding equities.

[2]The government sponsored enterprises (GSEs) are the Federal Home Loan Banks, the Federal Home Loan Mortgage Corporation, the Federal Mortgage Association, the Farm Credit System, the Student Loan Marketing Association.

Source: Federal Reserve Board Flow of Fund Accounts summarized in *Budget of the United States Government, FY 1989,* "Special Analysis F," p. F94.

Designed primarily to facilitate the financing of home mortgages, student loans and agricultural credit, the GSEs comprise the following entities:[61]

1. *Federal Home Loan Banks.* The Federal Home Loan Bank System promotes home ownership by extending credit to savings banks and other financial institutions. These advances are repaid.

2. *Federal Home Loan Mortgage Corporation (FHLMC, more familiarly known as "Freddie Mac").* A wholly owned subsidiary of the Federal Home Loan Banks, FHLMC raises money in the capital markets through the sale of equities and uses the funds to buy mortgages from banks, savings institutions and other primary lenders. This expands mortgage credit available for the purchase of homes. By buying mortgages from the originating lenders, FHLMC creates an active secondary market for mortgages. It gets its primary revenue from the repayment of principal and interest by borrowers.

3. *Federal National Mortgage Association (FNMA otherwise known as "Fannie Mae").* FNMA operates like FHLMC. Together with the Government National Mortgage Association (a government corporation), it dominates the secondary mortgage market and enlarges the pool of credit available for mortgages.

4. *Student Loan Marketing Association (SLMA, aka Sally Mae).* SLMA expands the credit pool for loans to college students by buying loans from banks and other primary lenders or lending additional funds to private lenders. It raises its funds by selling equities in the security market. From 1974 to 1980 SLMA borrowed exclusively from the Federal Financing Bank. Beginning in 1981, it turned to the private capital market for financial support.

5. *Farm Credit System (FCS).* FCS is a system of banking cooperatives that borrows funds from the financial markets and channels them to its component parts: the Federal Intermediate Credit Banks; the Federal Land Bank Associations; the Production Credit Associations; the Federal Land Banks; and the Banks for Cooperatives. In turn, these institutions lend funds to farmers, farm-related businesses, ranchers, commercial fishermen and rural homeowners. An independent government agency, the Farm Credit Administration, supervises the FCS. In the financial crisis that hit the farmers in the mid-1980s, FCS experienced severe losses (about $4.8 billion from 1985 to 1987). At the same time, it was unable to provide additional loans to thousands of hard-pressed farmers. To protect FCS and its constituent banks and cooperatives against insolvency, Congress in 1987 approved $6 billion in interest-free loans and a restructuring of the system.[62]

≡ Direct loans and loan guarantees have a direct and indirect effect on the budget and the economy

Because of the elusiveness and complexity of credit programs, it is difficult to get precise data on their budgetary and economic effect. The federal budget tells only part of the story. Direct loans are outlays and generally appear in the budget. So do interest subsidies for various programs. On the other hand, guaranteed loans, until the early 1980s, were excluded from the unified budget altogether, since they imposed no immediate cost. Only when borrowers defaulted on the repayment of loans did the budget provide the necessary funds to pay the creditors.[63] Potential defaults are an explosive ingredient in budgeting. In 1986, agencies reported over 1.8 million delinquent accounts valued at $89 billion and wrote off bad debts amounting to $3.4 billion.[64] In 1987, direct loan write-offs and defaults in guaranteed loans totaled about $11.6 billion.[65]

Other subsidies are hidden, and their costs can only be determined by elaborate and methodologically sophisticated studies. For example, borrowers fortunate enough to get direct loans enjoy several benefits. They get larger loans than private creditors would ordinarily make available to them; longer maturities than fully private loans; below market interest rates; waivers or reductions of loan fees; occasional deferrals of interest payments; grace periods to avoid foreclosure; and availability of funds for purposes that would be rejected by the private sector. The estimated value of such subsidies in 1985 was $9.8 billion. This was a minimum figure that does not measure the full benefit of the subsidy to the borrowers.[66]

Borrowers of guaranteed loans enjoy similar advantages. They benefit from low insurance rates; the availability of loans that the private sector might otherwise regard as risky; favorable interest rates; and virtually complete coverage of the loans by government guarantees. At a minimum, this subsidy was worth $8.7 billion in 1988–89.[67] Because of difficulties of gathering data, OMB has not estimated the undoubtedly large subsidies of programs administered by GSEs.[68]

No less than the government budget itself, the credit programs allocate resources and shape national priorities. As in the case of expenditures, the allocation of credit is influenced more by social objectives and political judgments than by market forces. In large part this is a legacy of the Depression and World War II. To protect homeowners, farmers, small businesses and veterans, the federal government gave them access to low-cost credit frequently denied by banks and other financial institutions. Later, other groups benefited from federal largess. The result is that in the allocation of credit, some sectors, such as housing, education, agriculture and small business, get more preferential treatment than other sectors in the economy. Not only do they secure credit on more favorable terms than private capital markets would provide, but they benefit, as noted, from direct and indirect subsidies. Conversely, less favored sectors are either crowded out of the credit market or obtain loans at high interest rates, with a variety of onerous conditions attached to the loans. The effect is to redistribute resources by channelling credit to preferred groups, with the taxpayers assuming all the risks. From an economic standpoint, the credit may be diverted from productive to less efficient uses.[69] As Ippolito reminds us, however, "when credit politics and economics collide, the former usually wins."[70]

☰ Controlling federal off-budget expenditures and credit programs

Since the end of World War II, the federal government has shifted its course several times in its attempts, through the budget process, to control public enterprises responsible for off-budget expenditures and credit programs. No consensus prevailed in the executive and legislative branches as to the desirable degree of control and oversight. The "integrationists" favored supervision and control of most public enterprises by federal departments and central review of enterprise budgets by OMB. The "autonomists" found such controls anathema and irreconcilable with the autonomy and flexibility essential to the effective operation of public enterprises. Between these extreme positions "pragmatists" regarded the dichotomy of control vs. no control as a false issue. In their view, oversight was essential. What really counted, though, was the quality and nature of central monitoring of plans, programs and budgets of public enterprises. They saw no problem in creating innovative government corporations, giving them flexibility to manage their programs without stifling day-to-day controls, and yet holding them accountable for results in terms of achieving governmental objectives and priorities.[71]

☰ A start on control—the Government Corporation Control Act of 1945

The first ambitious attempt to control public enterprises was the Government Corporation Control Act (GCCA) of 1945 (59 Stat. 597; 31 U.S.C. 841). The Act differentiated between "wholly owned" and "mixed ownership" corporations. For the former, the legislation required the annual submission to the Bureau of the Budget (later OMB) of a "business-type budget" including "a statement of income and expense, an analysis of surplus or deficit, a statement of sources and applications of funds, estimates of operations by major types of activities, together with estimates of administrative expenses; estimates of borrowings, and estimates of the amount of Government capital funds which shall be returned to the Treasury during the fiscal year or the appropriations required to provide for the restoration of capital impairment."[72] After review and, where appropriate, revisions of the budget, the President was to transmit the budget to Congress as part of the annual budget of the federal government.

While mixed ownership corporations were not subject to central budget review, the President was required to include in his budget any recommendations with regard to the return to the Treasury of capital given to such entities.[73] In this connection the legislation required the Secretary of the Treasury to approve the terms and conditions of all bonds, notes and other financial instruments issued by wholly owned and mixed ownership corporations.[74] The Act also required GAO to conduct commercial-type audits of all government corporations covering financial management, compliance with the law and internal controls.[75]

To implement the new legislation, the Bureau of the Budget and the GAO established special staffs to deal solely with government corporations. The House Appropriations Committee set up a new subcommittee to review corporation budgets. BOB and GAO joined in formulating criteria regarding the establishment and use of government corporations.[76]

The implementation of the Government Corporation Control Act fell far short of expectations. It turned out to be an inadequate instrument for controlling mixed ownership corporations that relied on federal funds. At various times in the 1950s, the Eisenhower administration vainly sought legislation to tighten controls, primarily budget review, over mixed corporations that used federal funds or whose obligations were federally guaranteed. The Farm Credit Banks successfully led the opposition to this move in a political climate increasingly hostile to the use of government corporations which were characterized either as inefficient or as unfairly competitive with private enterprise. Such controls as existed in the legislation proved to be too much for Congress. By 1981 it has gutted the GCCA by conferring off-budget status on twelve of thirty-five government corporations and exempted eighteen corporations from some or all of the provisions of the legislation. It had also created a new hybrid in the "twilight zone" of mixed public-private financial enterprises—the GSEs.[77]

In reviewing the budgets of public enterprises, the Bureau of the Budget veered from excessive line item control to indifference. At first it treated government corporations like regular operating agencies, contrary to the intent of the GCCA. Rather than focusing on the objectives, policies and results of programs and projects, BOB engaged in a detailed review of objects of expense, set personnel ceilings and limited corporate outlays.[78] By the 1960s, BOB had virtually ceased to monitor public enterprises and, by default, left much of the oversight and control to several uncoordinated congressional committees.[79] This was no accident. BOB mirrored the prevailing executive and congressional reluctance to control public enterprises.

On the eve of the first Reagan administration the National Academy of Public Administration (NAPA) was commissioned by OMB to assess the performance by and oversight of government corporations. After a comprehensive study, it concluded in 1981 that "no persuasive evidence has been presented to demonstrate that the GCCA failed either to provide effective accountability and control or impaired the capability of government corporations to function in a business-like manner." The problems resulted from the inept and indifferent administration of the legislation by OMB and Congress.[80] NAPA urged the adoption of the following steps:

1. Limit government corporations to those "which are revenue producing, potentially self-sustaining and which require a separate legal entity for effective operation."

2. Place government corporations "normally" in a cabinet department to assure compatability of policies with those of the administration, but separate them from the normal departmental structure.

3. Require a "business-type budget which after review by OMB should be submitted to Congress as part of the U.S. Budget," thus integrating the budgetary and financial policies of public enterprises with those of the administration.

4. Incorporate the financial data of government enterprises into the unified budget.

5. Relieve government corporations of fiscal year or line item limitations on expenditure, quarterly apportionments and personnel ceilings so as to permit them "to respond to changing market demands for their services."

6. Authorize corporations "to retain and use earnings without fiscal year limitations and to determine the character and necessity of their expenditure."

7. Report all credit financing guaranteed by the government in the budget.

8. Place on the corporations the "burden of proof of exemption from government personnel regulations and pay scales" since their employees should be unequivocally regarded as government employees.

9. Substitute advisory boards for governing boards so as to make clear the lines of authority running from the president or the cabinet secretary to the chief executive officer of the government corporation. (NAPA found that there were more drawbacks than advantages in following the private corporation model).

10. Require Treasury approval for the timing and terms of borrowing by government corporations and coordinate lending and loan guarantees with the government's fiscal and economic policies.[81]

Lamenting the erosion of OMB's controls over government corporation budgets, NAPA suggested that OMB take a two-pronged approach: (1) budget examination units should review the programs and projects of public enterprises and relate them to similar programs in other governmental agencies; and (2) OMB should recreate a specialized staff on public enterprises for policy advice to budget examiners, the OMB leadership and the administration. Similarly, NAPA urged GAO and the government operations committees of Congress to "maintain specialized staffs responsible for complete oversight of government corporation activities."[82]

≡ Budgeting public enterprises responsible for credit financing

Beginning in the late 1970s, the federal government moved slowly to control the burgeoning credit financing of public enterprises. The Congressional Budget Office spurred the debate by proposing in 1978 the preparation of a credit budget for all direct loans and guaranteed loans and the incorporation of the credit budget in the regular budget. Under the CBO concept, the President in the annual budget would recommend targets for the volume of credit to be extended under federal auspices during the next fiscal year. Congress would review the proposal together with the rest of the budget and, in its concurrent budget resolutions, establish aggregate ceilings by function for federal credit. The annual appropriation act for each program would provide the authority to make or guarantee loans, just as it sets the level of new budget authority for expenditure programs.

To implement the credit budget CBO suggested three possible approaches: amend the Budget and Accounting Act of 1921; amend the Congressional Budget Act of 1974; or use implied authority in the Congressional Budget Act. CBO argued that the adoption of its proposal would enable Congress to control aggregate credit activities "while respecting important differences between credit activities and direct expenditures." By meshing the credit budget with the regular budget, Congress and the president would have to choose between financing programs by direct spending or credit or both.[83]

The proposal was clearly an idea whose time had come. GAO, OMB, congressional committees and the Federal Reserve Board generally concurred with the CBO approach and recommended budgetary credit controls.[84] Finally, in its 1979–80 budget, the Carter administration, for the first time, included, if not a credit budget, at least proposed credit controls to limit new obligations and commitments for direct loans and loan guarantees. The controls extended to programs on and off the budget, and were incorporated in the appropriation acts in order to subject "credit programs to the same review process as the budget." Congress went along with this approach, and its second budget resolution for the 1980 fiscal year "set targets for new direct loan obligations, new primary loan guarantee commitments, and new secondary loan guarantee commitments."[85]

The Reagan administration even more severely controlled direct loans and loan guarantees and expenditures by government corporations on and off budget. In 1981 it cut back targets proposed by the outgoing Carter administration, reduced the scope of federal credit activities and successfully sought changes in the basic authorizing legislation.[86] Congress supported the administration by incorporating caps for loans and loan guarantees in its concurrent resolution. These, however, were not binding on the authorizing and appropriation committees.[87]

In later years, Congress went through the motions of controlling credit financing through concurrent resolutions, although this was not required by the 1974 Congressional Budget Act. In most resolutions, targets approved by Congress were non-binding guidelines. Invariably, the aggregate loans and loan guarantees in the resolution were higher than those proposed by the President, and few reductions in lending took place. A fragmented Congress was mindful of important constituencies that benefitted from loan programs. It hesitated about making explicit the loans and loan guarantees which were diffused and hidden in substantive legislation and appropriation acts. Much of the lending (an estimated 45 percent) was "uncontrollable" in the sense that by statute it was open ended and without annual appropriation limits. And Congress was not about to control "uncontrollable" lending any more than it controlled "uncontrollable" spending. While the Budget Committees were sensitive to the need to discipline credit financing, they were fearful of antagonizing other committees by proposing tighter controls over federal credit.[88]

≡ Soaring deficits finally compel Congress to control off-budget spending and lending

Under the whiplash of soaring deficits, Congress adopted the Balanced Budget and Emergency Deficit Control Act of 1985 (PL 99-177, the so-called Gramm-Rudman-Hollings bill) to reduce deficits on a phased basis, culminating in a balanced budget in FY 1991. In addition, the legislation accomplished what the Government Corporation Control Act and the credit budgets of the 1980s failed to do. It mandated the incorporation of all off-budget outlays, receipts and credit activities, including those of the Federal Financing Bank, into the President's budget and in congressional concurrent resolutions on the budget. To achieve the latter, it amended the Congressional Budget Act of 1974 to provide: (1) including in the concurrent resolution all new direct loan obligations and loan guarantees as well as new budget authority, outlays, and entitlement authority; (2) incorporating all these components of the budget in the reconciliation procedures; and (3) allocating to the appropriation committees the responsibility of acting on loans and loan guarantees approved in the resolutions. Prior commitments for loans and loan guarantees were exempted from congressional actions.

In implementing the legislation, the President and Congress tightened controls over credit and established a comprehensive credit budget. For example, Table 1-3 shows actual and estimated credit budgets for FY 1984 through FY 1989:

Table 1-3
Credit budget totals, FY 1985–FY 1990 (in billions of dollars)

	Actual			Estimate		
	1985	1986	1987	1988	1989	1990
Direct loan obligations						
Farmers Home Administration	7.9	5.0	3.6	3.3	0.9	0.7
Foreign military sales	4.9	5.0	4.1	4.1	4.5	4.5
Commodity Credit Corporation	10.4	17.7	16.6	15.0	10.7	10.9
Rural Electrification Administration	4.0	3.1	1.2	2.0	0.2	0.2
Veterans Administration	1.0	1.0	1.0	1.1	1.0	0.7
Export-Import Bank	0.7	0.6	0.7	0.7	0.7	0.7
Low-rent public housing	14.1					
All other	9.6	8.9	2.6	2.6	2.0	2.2
Total obligations	52.6	41.3	29.8	28.8	20.0	19.9
Guaranteed loan commitments						
Federal Housing Administration	47.4	102.6	80.0	59.8	61.8	63.9
Veterans Administration housing	12.1	34.3	34.9	18.3	17.9	17.0
Guaranteed student loans	8.9	8.6	9.7	9.6	10.0	10.5
Export-Import Bank	7.8	5.5	6.8	14.6	10.2	10.4
Commodity Credit Corporation	2.7	2.5	3.0	5.5	3.5	3.5
Small Business Administration	2.8	2.8	3.4	3.7	3.6	3.6
Farmers Home Administration	1.2	1.6	1.7	2.9	3.7	3.9
Rural Electrification Administration			0.6	2.0	1.3	1.4
Foreign military sales				5.2	2.3	3.3
All other	1.8	1.3	2.0	1.6	1.0	0.6
Total commitments[1]	84.7	159.2	142.1	123.2	115.3	118.1
Total credit budget	137.6	200.6	172.1	147.2	135.6	138.0
MEMORANDUM						
Secondary guaranteed loan commitments	54.6	138.0	140.0	83.4	83.6	84.5

[1]Excludes commitments for guarantees of loans previously guaranteed (secondary guarantees) and commitments for guarantees by one Government account of direct loans made by another Government account. Totals for the former are shown in the memorandum. Totals for the latter are included as direct loans.

Source: Budget of the United States Government, Fiscal Year 1989, Special Analyses, "Special Analysis F", p. F-11.

As an additional step, the administration proposed in 1988 that agencies should request general fund appropriations for the present value of subsidies of new direct loan obligations and guaranteed loan commitments. The amounts appropriated by Congress would be channeled to a central fund in the Treasury to serve, among other things, as a reserve against potential defaults of guaranteed loans.[89]

Congress also set aggregate and functional credit targets in the concurrent resolution and reconciliation bill. This affected appropriation acts and legislation authorizing credit programs.[90] At long last, credit financing was subject to the budget process in a meaningful way. In theory, the administration and Congress could now weigh more explicitly the relative advantages of expenditures, credit and tax expenditures (tax breaks for special groups) to achieve policy goals.

As part of the congressional compromise that led to the Balanced Budget Act, Congress, in a startling reversal of policy, excluded from the budget the outlays and revenues of the Social Security trust funds. This change was intended to remove the Social Security program from budget review and protect it against possible cuts. But it had the effect of dismantling the unified budget established in 1967. What Congress accomplished in placing public enterprises on-budget, it more than offset by excluding even larger expenditures and revenues from the budget. The effect on budget totals was dramatic. Previously off-budget expenditures rarely exceeded $21 billion. As a result of the new legislation, off-budget expenditures in FY 1985 soared to $176.8 billion, or nearly 19 percent of outlays, because of the exclusion of Social Security payments.[91] And government corporations, including the United States Postal Service, were now subject to budget cuts under the GRH formula.

≡ The Government-Sponsored Enterprises (GSEs) still remain in budget limbo

Whether or not the budget should include GSEs has been a vexing problem for nearly thirty years. When the President's Commission on Budget Concepts in 1967 successfully urged the adoption of a unified budget, it found itself unable to make a clear recommendation on the budgetary treatment of loans and loan guarantees by such entities as GSEs because of the hazy borderline between public and private transactions. It took refuge in the following possibly equivocal language:

> To work well, the governmental budget process should encompass the full scope of programs and transactions within the Federal sector and not subject to the economic disciplines of the marketplace.[92]

Elmer B. Staats, then Comptroller General of the United States, advised the Commission that an enterprise should be excluded from the budget when it meets all of the following criteria:

1. The planned ownership of the enterprise is private.
2. Its current ownership is more than 50 percent private.
3. It is not subject to the budgetary control provisions of the Government Corporation Control Act, and
4. It is not otherwise subject to action on its budget by Congress in the appropriations process.[93]

These views were possibly understandable in the late 1960s before GSE loans mushroomed to the point where they exceeded other credit programs. They still remain major instruments of federal policy, and investors regard GSE debt as virtually the same as Treasury bills and notes. As emphasized above, GSEs enjoy a number of other profitable financial advantages not available to other private institutions. Without such advantages, they would be compelled to pay higher interest rates. Furthermore, in the event of financial difficulties, the government leaps to the rescue with loans and subsidies, as it did for the Farm Credit System and the Federal Home Loan Banks in the late 1980s.[94]

Because of the linkage between the government and the GSEs, CBO has raised for consideration several alternatives to their present status: explicit, rather than implicit, governmental guarantees of GSE debt to remove uncertainty on the part of investors; regulation by the Securities Exchange Commission and other agencies to control risky investments; nationalization to convert GSEs into government-owned and operated agencies; or, conversely, full privatization with an end of governmental guarantees by a specified date; and conversion of implied governmental guarantees into self-financed unsubsidized insurance with the GSEs and borrowers bearing the risks. In 1988, the Reagan administration opted for full privatization.[95]

Should GSEs be fully "privatized", no budget controls will be needed. As long as they have actual or potential claims on the Treasury and enjoy a privileged financial status, they should be held fully accountable for the results of their operations through the budget process. This can be done without jeopardizing their autonomy and flexibility. At present, the government merely includes the financial statements of GSEs in the Budget Appendix and summarizes their borrowing and lending transactions in the budget document, *Special Analyses*. In a crisis, however, Congress and the administration subject their finances to a searching review.

Given the political will, it is not beyond the government's talents to devise budget reviews of GSEs that will focus on program objectives, fiscal and economic policy and financial performance objectives, fiscal and economic policy and financial performance rather than on staffing controls, objects of expense and the details of operations.

≡ Divestiture and "privatization" of federal public enterprises and loans

As CBO pointed out, the government has the option of selling public enterprises to the private sector. It exercised this choice in part in the quasi-privatization of the GSEs. By the mid-1980s, the Reagan administration recommended the dismantling of the Synthetic Fuels Corporation and the sale of Conrail, the largest freight system in the Northeast and Midwest, in which the government had invested more thatn $7 billion.[96] It also considered the sale, for $8.85 billion, of the Bonneville Power Administration, that generates more than half the power in the Pacific Northwest. Except for the Synthetic Fuels Corporation, which had few supporters, the administration ran into congressional opposition to the privatization of the other public enterprises for a variety of interrelated financial, economic, political, regional and service reasons.[97] Turned profitable, Conrail was the most likely candidate for divestiture. Through the sale of shares, it was converted into a private corporation in 1986.

In 1987 the government began to divest itself of loans by selling loan assets to investors through brokerage firms and investment banks. OMB's target was the sale of loans with a face value of $6.7 billion for $4.8 billion in FY 1987, and loans with a face value of $10.8 billion for $5.8 billion in FY 1988. From the government's standpoint, the sales had three advantages despite the losses incurred: (1) they eliminated both delinquent and good loans in one fell swoop; (2) they resulted in one-time revenue gains that could be used to cut the deficits; and (3) they were first steps in privatizing the servicing of loans. From the investor's standpoint, the deep discounts and the availability of collateral in the event of default made the purchase of the loan assets an acceptable risk. Through these steps, however, the administration foreclosed the possibility of gaining future revenue.

Going further, the Reagan administration in 1987 proposed the sale of all new direct loans without federal guarantees. The purchasers "would assume all of the responsibilities and costs of servicing the loans." The budget would include any subsidies representing the difference between the sale proceeds and the face value of the loans. For loan guarantee programs, the government would purchase insurance covering potential liabilities. This would transfer the contingent liability of the guarantees from the government to the private insurers. Any net costs incurred by the government would be included in the budget as a subsidy.[98]

≡ The budgetary and economic effect of state and local government public enterprises

In the absence of precise data on the budgetary and economic effect of public enterprises in state and local governments, it is necessary, with caution, to use some crude assumptions and estimates. Bennett and DiLorenzo estimated in 1983 that off-budget spending by state public authorities totaled about $100 billion annually.[99] With state expenditures approximating $310 billion in 1981–82, spending by public authorities equaled about one-third of state outlays. Unfortunately, it is not currently possible to combine on and off-budget spending to arrive at a ratio of expenditures by off-budget public authorities in relation to total outlays by the state public sector. Too many data gaps and murky classifications exist. Hence, the available information can do no more than highlight trends.

According to the Institute of Public Administration, the forty-nine largest public authorities and special districts in FY 1986 collected $20.8 billion in revenue; spent $16.6 billion for operating expenditures and $7.9 billion for capital expenditures; and had an outstanding long-term debt of $43.7 billion.[100]

In analyzing the outstanding debt of state and local governments, a clearer picture emerges. As the following table shows, most long-term debt as of FY 1985 was "non-guaranteed" (without voter approval) rather than guaranteed "full faith and credit" (with voter approval) debt.

Off-budget public authorities incurred most of the non-guaranteed debt through "moral obligation" bonds and assorted revenue bonds which did not require a voter referendum. Prior to the proliferation of off-budget public authorities in the 1960s and thereafter, the amount of full faith and credit debt exceeded non-guaranteed debt. In 1960, the ratios of full faith and credit and non-guaranteed debt at the state level were about even, 49.2 percent and 50.8 percent respectively. Then non-guaranteed debt took off to the point where it exceeded two-thirds of all debt. Local governments were somewhat slower in resorting to non-guaranteed bonding. In 1960, non-guaranteed debt was about one-third of all debt, and in 1978 about 47 percent. Thereafter, it climbed to levels exceeding full faith and credit debt.[101] Even the debt figures can be misleading. Some states pay for facilities constructed by public authorities through long term lease payments. The payments appear in the budget, but are not counted as part of the debt.[102]

Table 1-4
Outstanding long-term debt of state and local governments, FY 1985

Outstanding long-term debt	Amount (billions)	Percent
Total	640.6	100.0
Full faith and credit	190.1	29.7
Non-guaranteed	450.5	70.3

Source: U.S. Department of Commerce, Bureau of the Census, *Government Finances in 1985–86* (Washington, D.C. 1987), Table 25, p. 37.

User charges and fees by off-budget public enterprises have grown much faster than tax revenue. For example, during the 1970s, non-tax revenue, mainly receipts by public enterprises, climbed 1.5 times faster than tax revenue.

≡ Governors and legislatures are reluctant to control public enterprises unless scandals and crises erupt

Despite the impact of off-budget public enterprises on state and local finances and economies, governors and legislatures are, in the main, reluctant to control them unless scandals and fiscal crises erupt. They generally limit themselves to policy direction. In the first place, they created public authorities to reduce or curb the size of the budget; to circumvent constitutional and statutory restrictions on expenditures, taxes and debt; and to override controls over budgets, procurement and staff appointments and salaries.[104] Hence, in most states they rarely turn on their own statutory creatures and subject them to routine and detailed oversight and review of their financial performance, programmatic results and budgets. They intervene in the affairs of public authorities only when the following conditions arise:

1. A fiscal crisis occurs, bringing with it the spectre of default in the payment of debt, as was true of the Urban Development Corporation of New York State, the Public Power Supply System of the state of Washington and housing agencies in Massachusetts and Pennsylvania.[105]
2. Public authorities are unable to market bonds, as was the case in Massachusetts in 1975 when the Housing Finance Agency could not sell $78 million in bonds, and in North Carolina when the Housing Corporation in 1970–1972 failed to sell any bonds.[106]
3. Scandals, corruption, and mismanagement arouse the voters. These resulted in lurid headlines in several states. For example, Walsh found a "persistent pattern" of misallocated resources, waste, confusion of public and private interests and failure to take into account the social implications of projects.[107]
4. Public authorities require increased subsidies for mass transportation and housing. This is a commonplace in many states.
5. Poor investment practices lead to heavy financial losses of the kind experienced by the New York State Dormitory Authority in 1983.[108]
6. Low credit ratings of the bonds of public authorities endanger the creditworthiness of state and local governments.
7. Public authorities develop tempting surpluses that might be

diverted to state programs. Thus, New York and New Jersey pressured the Port Authority to buy buses and an unprofitable private commuter railroad.[109]

8. Public authorities seek an expansion of their bonding capacity for a variety of construction projects.

9. Financial problems of privately owned transportation facilities and utilities lead to proposals for a state takeover, using public authorities as the instruments.

Many state and local public authorities avoid these problems and are self-sustaining. Some, like the Port Authority of New York and New Jersey, are models of public management. Should major crises occur, however, governors and legislatures will subject public enterprises to budget controls. In this respect, the experience of New York State is revealing and may foreshadow future developments in other state governments that are concerned about the growth of public authorities and the seeming lack of adequate controls over them.

≡ New York State leads all other states in the number, size of budgets and problems of off-budget state public authorities

New York State public authorities are in a class by themselves, especially after their proliferation during the Rockefeller years (1959–1973). In 1981 they borrowed more, spent more and employed more staff than twenty-five state governments.[110] No public authorities in other states come even close to the combined expenditures, revenue and debt of public enterprises in New York state.

In FY 1987, the twenty-nine largest public authorities planned to spend over $10 billion for operating expenses and capital programs and $5.6 billion for debt service. This was equal to about 61 percent of the governor's proposed general fund budget for 1987–88. Public authorities are a major vehicle for capital construction, with a debt of about $40 billion that exceeds the state debt per se.[111]

Until 1975, the controls exercised over public authorities were tenuous and sporadic. Like other state governors, the governors of New York appointed members of authority boards and approved the minutes (in effect, the decisions and budgets) of some of them. They sought legislative approval of bond issues and subsidies in behalf of the public authorities.

This off-hand approach came to an abrupt end in February 1975 when, as previously noted, the Urban Development Corporation (UDC), a state public authority that was the nation's largest developer of subsidized low-cost housing, failed to meet its current financial obligations, particularly the repayment of short-term notes. At that time it was responsible for over $1 billion in outstanding moral obligation bonds and about the same amount in partially completed construction. During the same year, New York City defaulted on the payment of short-term notes that had become due. Both the state and the city faced an unprecedented credit crisis and effectively were barred from the credit markets. It took several emergency measures, including budgetary controls, before the confidence of investors could be restored.[112]

The post-mortem of the entire affair, which had national repercussions, was conducted by a special inquiry commission, the Moreland Act Commission on the Urban Development Corporation and Other State Financing Agencies, established by Governor Carey in 1975. The Commission found that many of the problems arose from the fact that authorities were a separate rather than an integral part of government. It was critical of the lack of executive and legislative controls over public authorities. It saw the UDC crisis not as an isolated phenomenon, but "as a reflection of State fiscal policies and as a symptom of deeper economic and governmental issues." It castigated the moral obligation bond designed to "avoid the referendum requirement" as a "dangerous and misleading illusion and now a totally discredited device."[113] Finally, it proposed a series of controls, some of which were adopted in whole or part.

The combined effect of the Commission's recommendations, actions by the governor and legislature and later developments (including heavy losses by the Dormitory Authority) was to establish for the first time the following unprecedented and sweeping controls over public authorities in New York State (unmatched by any other state):[114]

1. *Creating a State Public Authorities Control Board (PACB).* In 1976, legislation (plus later amendments) established the board to regulate public authorities funded primarily by moral obligation debt (but excepting the Municipal Assistance Corporation, which is responsible for restructuring the debt of New York City.) Composed of the director of the budget, who serves as chairman (if appointed by the governor), the chairmen of the two legislative fiscal committees and two non-voting members recommended by the minority leaders in each house, the Board reviews and controls proposed financing and construction commitments. No additional moral obligation debt can be issued without its approval.

2. *Capping moral obligation debt.* Except for debt incurred by the Municipal Assistance Corporations in behalf of New York City, the state capped all moral obligation debt. Only PACB can exceed the ceiling.

3. *Salvaging the Urban Development Corporation.* The state clamped

a lid on future commitments by UDC and established a Project Finance Agency to redeem all UDC notes within ninety days of the default, and authorized PACB to approve the funding necessary to complete projects under construction. In 1985, a rehabilitated UDC became the vehicle for prison construction by issuing moral obligation debt.

4. *Coordinating the sale of securities.* Through executive orders, the State created a State Securities Coordinating Committee to control the timing of bonds and notes issued by the State and the major public authorities.

5. *Submitting annual reports.* The authorities were compelled to prepare more comprehensive and meaningful annual reports covering operations, accomplishments, revenues, expenditures, assets and liabilities, outstanding bonds and notes and obligations issued and redeemed in the course of the year.

6. *Reporting the results of external audits.* In addition to comprehensive audits by the State Comptroller, public authorities were also required to report the results of any additional external examinations by private audit firms and other groups.

7. *Telling the whole story.* Because of the increasing wariness of investors and rating organizations, the state issues a prospectus, a so-called "official statement" on state finances, when it goes through the annual ritual of selling short term tax and revenue anticipation notes. Prepared with the aid of brokerage firms, the "official statement" is a hard-hitting and objective analysis of the state's budget problems. One section deals comprehensively with public authorities on the assumption that the "fiscal stability of the state is related to the fiscal stability of the authorities."[115] In admirable detail, the section lays out the problems of the various authorities, specifies the state's obligations and summarizes the extent of state subsidies to authorities.

8. *Centralizing oversight of authorities in the budget office.* The patent need for intensified oversight by the budget office led to the creation of a special unit responsible for monitoring authorities continuously and preparing detailed analyses of their operations and finances in behalf of the governor and legislature. However, this is done for informational purposes and does not constitute detailed budget analysis. Budget examination units review some authority budgets.

9. *Changing the format of the budget document.* The annual budget now includes a special section devoted to public authorities. The section provides summary data on all authorities as well as more detailed information on each authority.

10. *Establishing investment guidelines.* Public authorities must submit to the Division of the Budget, the Comptroller and legislative fiscal committee guidelines on investment standards and policies.

11. *Formulating "rolling" five-year capital plans.* Every public authority must develop annually and send to the governor a rolling five-year capital plan which identifies the estimated costs of projects and the sources of funding.

From an attitude of almost casual indifference to public authorities, the New York State government, under duress, swung to the point where it imposed some of the most comprehensive controls in the United States over them. In this respect, it established, at least on paper, something of a model for other state and local governments as well as the federal government. The effectiveness of these controls, however, has yet to be evaluated. Despite these changes, public authorities are still off-budget in the sense that they are not part of budget totals. But their capital plans, financing and budgets are subject to a broad review by the central budget office. Moral obligation bonds still remain the chief source of funds for public authorities. Only infrequently do the governor and legislature chance a voter referendum on a proposed bond issue for capital construction.

Considering the experience of New York State, other states and local governments, the Institute of Public Administration proposed the following steps to enforce fiscal, legal, political, policy and performance accountability:

1. Information and reporting: defining content of required reports or annual business plans.
2. State approval and coordination of borrowing proposals for form, legality, timing and credit capacity.
3. Capital planning and budgeting at the state level, including investment plans of authorities and districts.
4. Overlapping directorships, putting city, county or state officials on authority and district boards.
5. Requiring financial and performance audits.
6. Grouping special districts and authorities under sectoral umbrella districts or metropolitan coordinating commissions or general purpose governments.
7. Regulation by sectoral state agencies or by regional agencies.
8. Application of sunshine and freedom of information laws.
9. Change in state law or constitutional provisions to enhance the capability of cities and counties to establish dependent service districts, to issue revenue bonds, to manage construction efficiently.
10. Reform of the processes for forming new districts, adding criteria and consultation, and in some cases special legislation.[116]

IN SHEER NUMBERS, LOCAL GOVERNMENT PUBLIC AUTHORITIES PREDOMINATE IN THE UNITED STATES

Over 6,000 regional and local government public authorities in this country raise their funds primarily through revenue bonds, with user fees and charges serving as security for repayment of the debt. In varying degrees, federal, state and local grants, loans and loan guarantees augment authority revenue. Pennsylvania, as noted, heads the list with about 2,500 municipal authorities, which by 1976 had run up about $5 billion in debt.[117] The chief rationale for creating many of them was to construct school buildings under lease purchase plans. In New York State, nearly 1,000 local public authorities are responsible for housing, industrial development, community development, parking, sports facilities, sewers, water supply, solid waste disposal and hospital care.[118] At present, the major emphasis is on the improvement of the infrastructure.

Virtually every state has created local authorities or special districts to handle similar functions. Large regional and metropolitan authorities deal primarily with transportation, water supply and waste disposal. The state of Washington is typical in this respect. Under a state law authorizing the formation of metropolitan municipal corporations, King County, in which Seattle is located, created METRO, which provides public transportation and waste/water treatment for the entire county.[119]

Always significant, local public authorities are assuming even more importance because of tax and expenditure limits. They have become major vehicles for infrastructure construction and maintenance, environmental management and economic development.

The local public authorities are creatures of the state. They derive their existence from general state law or specific statutes and are subject to state audit and oversight. They are mainly off-budget and are administered by a board of directors appointed by local chief executives. Because of their structure, they have achieved "substantial administrative and fiscal independence from general purpose local governments."[120]

THE BUDGETARY AND ECONOMIC IMPACT OF PUBLIC ENTERPRISES IN OTHER COUNTRIES

Public enterprises in other countries perform more functions than those in the United States. What they do or fail to do holds important lessons for us in terms of oversight and budget control. Not only do they encompass the economic activities carried on by government corporations/public authorities in this country but, as discussed above, they are also heavily involved in manufacturing, banking, trading, insurance, transportation, energy production and distribution and telecommunications. This, of course, is the norm in the communist bloc, which relies almost exclusively on public enterprises for all economic activities. But even developed and developing countries committed to a market economy depend heavily on public enterprises in key economic sectors. In this respect, until the mid-1980s, France led all other industrialized nations outside centrally planned economies, with public enterprises in 1984 responsible for 30 percent of industrial output.[121] With the assumption of power by the Chirac government in 1986, this trend was reversed. Nevertheless, in France and other non-communist countries, the impact of public enterprises on the economy and government budgets is still sharp and direct.

As in the United States, it is difficult to get precise data on the economic performance and budgetary impact of public enterprises. Much of the data assembled by national statistical bodies and international organizations are fragmentary, inconsistent and often contradictory.[122] As crude indicators, they, nevertheless, highlight the significance of public enterprises in three critical economic areas: contribution to Gross Domestic Product (GDP), share of gross fixed capital formation, and share of non-agriculture employment and public sector employment.

Public enterprises are key factors in economic growth. According to 1983 estimates, they accounted for about 10 percent of GDP in developed and developing countries.[123] At the high end of the scale were France, Egypt (over 30 percent), Venezuela (27.5 percent) and Britain (10.9 percent).[124] Public enterprises are especially significant in capital investment. In the late 1970s and early 1980s they were responsible, on the average, for over 11 percent of capital formation in industrialized countries and 27 percent in developing countries. Among industrialized countries, public enterprises in France, Britain, Italy and Spain accounted for 15 to 40 percent of national capital formation. Far higher ratios prevailed in developing countries: for example, Egypt, 47.8 percent; Venezuela, 36.3 percent; India, 41 percent; and Kenya, 26 percent.[125]

In all countries, public enterprises are major employers in the public sector. For example, in Britain, Ireland and West Germany, the share of public sector employment ranges from 21.3 percent to 33 percent. Similar rates prevail in various developing countries, with a high of 50 percent in Brazil.[126] In several countries, public enterprises account for a significant proportion of all non-agricultural employment as well, for example, nearly 9 percent in Britain and Ireland and nearly 18 percent in India.[127]

Where public enterprises contribute markedly to economic growth and are financially self-sufficient, governments tend to keep them at a distance. At best, they make certain that the firms' production, marketing and investment policies accord with national and social objectives. They expect profitable firms, it at all possible, to provide a return on the government's original investments, share surpluses with them and repay governmental and international loans for startup capital. For public enterprises, the price of autonomy is fiscal independence.

Rarely do such positive results occur. In many countries, especially developing countries, public enterprises are losers rather than winners. Rather than experiencing profits, they incur losses and deficits. Rather than contributing to governmental revenue and repaying governmental loans, they require continuing financial assistance and are a chronic drain on budgets. To be sure, exceptions exist in various countries, but, in the aggregate, the financial results are negative. Among developing countries, the financial outlook is especially bleak, with the exception of India, where public enterprises in 1983 showed a 16 percent profit on invested capital.[128] Various studies in the late 1970s demonstrated that, in the main, public enterprises operated in the red. They could not finance their own investment programs, let alone repay loans to the government and foreign creditors.[129]

A variety of complex factors accounts for the dismal financial performance of many enterprises. In various countries, the enterprises suffer from waste, mismanagement, and inefficiency, as evidenced by the poor quality of merchandise, underutilization of capacity, excess inventories, shipping delays, power outages, equipment breakdowns, redundant staff, delays in implementing schedules and lack of adequate financial controls.[130] At times, political interference in day-to-day operations cripples the performance of public enterprises. Conversely, governments may ignore them altogether, with little pretense of guidance or oversight.[131]

For this sad state of affairs, the public enterprises and the governments that, in theory, oversee them have no one but themselves to blame. On the other hand, several critical external factors that adversely affect profitability are beyond their control. Among them are the world price of the commodities they export; currency devaluations that raise the costs of imports and reduce the price of exports; and limited supplies of foreign currency for the purchase of supplies and equipment abroad. Equally significant are the non-commercial objectives of governments which adversely affect the profitability of public enterprises: government subsidized prices for low income groups, special price breaks for depressed regions and price freezes to combat inflation.[132] In the clash between the firm's objectives to maximize profits and social and economic policies of the government, the firm frequently loses out.

This is not to say that financial results are the sole measures of the efficiency of public enterprises. Even unprofitable firms may meet important social and economic objectives and, in that sense, may be "socially profitable." In fact, many public enterprises were established in the first place to correct the failings of the marketplace and to serve as instruments of development without any assurance of profitability. As Self reminds us, "a government is not a firm whose output should necessarily be optimised."[133] Social needs often override the imperatives of the profit and loss statement at considerable cost to public enterprises and governments.

Regardless of the reasons for poor performance of public enterprises, the impact of unprofitability on budgets is unmistakeable. Frequently the public enterprises require heavy infusions of subsidies to meet operating and capital costs. Rarely do they repay the government or central banks for initial loans to start the enterprise. For the most part, the loans are interest-free, even though governments may have borrowed the funds in the capital markets at prevailing rates of interest. At times, governments have no choice but to write off the loans. In the main, they can not count on public enterprises for revenue (except for a few monopolistic firms), dividends, or for the timely payment of taxes in whole or part. (In many countries, government corporations are required to pay taxes and dividends). As noted, the return on government investments is minor or negative. Public enterprises have been responsible for significant increases in foreign and domestic debt and, on occasion, can not pay the debt service. As a result, governments often assume the debts and the responsibility for paying the principal and interest. The combined effect of these developments is to increase annual budgets drastically and to raise national deficits and debt.[134]

≡ Several governments have taken significant steps to monitor and control public enterprises

To ignore the budgetary effect of public enterprises is to lose control over fiscal policy. As a result, governments have been searching for an appropriate mix of budgetary and policy controls over public enterprises to facilitate accountability and yet not stifle necessary autonomy and flexibility. At the same time, several governments have begun to liquidate unprofitable public enterprises and to sell off ("privatize") others. Some of the measures are similar to belated controls by federal and state governments in the United States. Others have not as yet been applied here and may serve as useful models. Among the major developments are the following:

1. *Central review of the performance and budgets of public enterprises.* Increasingly, central budget offices and special units in ministries of finance have intensified their review of the finances, budgets, and performance of public enterprises. This takes place whether or not the budgets of the enterprises appear in national budgets. Some examples illustrate this growing trend:

   a. *India.* An influential Bureau of Public Enterprises in the Ministry of Finance monitors public enterprises continuously and advises the enterprises, the Ministry and Parliament on appropriate corrective measures.[135]

b. *Britain.* In Britain as in other countries, public enterprises operate under the wing of "sponsoring" ministries that are formally responsible for oversight. Nevertheless, the Treasury (Britain's budget office), as the banker, makes the important financial decisions affecting public enterprises with the ministries, though influential, serving as a conduit for Treasury policy. Little contact takes place between the Treasury and the public enterprises.

The focal point for the coordination of Treasury policy with regard to the public enterprises is the Public Enterprises Group—very much akin in the scope of its responsibilities to similar units in OMB and the New York State Division of the Budget. The Treasury participates in a wide range of decisions: borrowing and expenditure limits; the economic impact of borrowing; major investments; appropriate interest charges; the rate of return on the government's investments; the effect of pricing policy on profitability, inflation and economic policy generally; financial targets and measures of financial performance; strategic options available to public enterprises; the desirability of outright subsidies for services deliberately run at a loss, such as bus and train routes; productivity and efficiency. (A growing literature and a series of government White Papers deal with these and related issues.)[136]

c. *Mexico.* The Secretary of Programming and Budgeting, who heads a combined planning and budgeting office, authorizes, in conformity with the National Development Plan and governmental fiscal policy, aggregate expenditures, investments, loans and subsidies for 903 public enterprises. Another office, headed by the Secretary of Finance and Public Credit, borrows funds and allocates credit to public enterprises.[137]

2. *Expansion of the breadth and coverage of budget review of public enterprises.* Belatedly and under the pressure of fiscal stress, governments have recognized that the budget process is the one focal decision-making point for relating the fiscal and economic policies of public enterprises to those of the public sector as a whole.

3. *Reliance on contracts between governments and public enterprises as a framework for oversight and accountability.* To avoid stifling line-item review of public enterprise budgets, several governments, as in France, Senegal and Pakistan, have developed comprehensive contracts with public enterprises. The contract spells out mutual-

ly agreed-upon performance and financial targets and serves as a framework for accountability in general and budget review in particular, thus blending autonomy and central control. For example, the French government consults with the largest public enterprises in drafting the contracts and attempts to reconcile corporate plans with the economic policies and development plans of the government. Once the performance targets are quantified and accepted, the Ministry of Economy and Finance monitors the results, but does not intervene in the activities of the public enterprises unless the contractual terms are breached. Should unforeseen developments occur, it may be necessary to renegotiate the contract. The French government has found the contract less important than the consultative process of identifying and quantifying the goals of the public enterprises.[138]

4. *Establishing financial and performance targets without the use of formal contracts.* Concerned about low profitability or chronic losses of public enterprises, Britain, India and several Latin American countries have imposed financial targets on them without using contracts as a mechanism. For Britain, this represents a major switch in policy, considering its previous reliance on "arm's length" oversight. Since the late 1970s it has set for public enterprises, primarily nationalized industries, an EFL (external financial limit), which sets an annual ceiling for grants and loans, and RRR (required rate of return), which specifies the expected real rate of return (adjusted for inflation) on the government's investments. (In 1978, the RRR was 5 percent, which turned out to be lower than the rate of return in the private sector.) In addition, the Treasury establishes ceilings on investments (similar to caps on public authorities in New York State), controls domestic and foreign borrowing (similar to the credit budgets in the U.S. federal government) and, in its rolling three-year financial plans (PES—public expenditure survey) fixes expenditure limits for public enterprises as well as national and local governments.[139]

5. *Making subsidies explicit in the budget.* Several governments, as in Italy, openly compensate public enterprises in the budget for the losses they incur in complying with non-commercial objectives such as establishing unprofitable prices for goods and services, propping up failing firms and opening plants in economically depressed areas. The government's budget includes specific subsidies for this purpose. In some respects this is similar to practices in the United States in providing subsidies in the budget for transportation, housing and student loans.[140]

6. *Incorporating public enterprises into the budget.* Few governments are consistent in keeping the budgets of public authorities in or out of the main budget. Many include subsidies, loans, grants and equity capital in the budget, as previously noted. Some, as in Britain and West Germany, encompass in their multi-year financial plans the revenues and expenditures of public authorities. Others, as in France, Egypt and the Philippines, provide comprehensive data on the budgets of public authorities in the main budget or annexes to the main budget.[141]

7. *Taking account of public enterprises in capital planning and budgeting.* As in the United States, many governments have medium-term capital development plans, which include the capital projects of public enterprises. They either stand by themselves, as in Portugal and Spain, or are part of a comprehensive development plan, as in France, Japan and most developing countries. In many countries the budget decision-making process with regard to capital projects is frayed because of split jurisdiction between budget and planning offices.[142]

8. *Developing methods of evaluating the performance of public enterprises.* Without a flow of adequate data on the performance of public enterprises, no meaningful budgetary and other policy decisions can be made. On this point all government agree and are searching for management information and accounting systems that will measure results against expected performance.[143]

9. *Restructuring debt.* Nearly all developing countries are in the throes of a debt crisis. Because of excessive and, in retrospect, possibly imprudent domestic and foreign borrowing, public enterprises are responsible for a significant part of the overall debt. Several countries, including Kenya and Peru, have written off the debt and assumed it in whole or in part or, in consultation with creditors, have restructured the debt.[144]

10. *Reconciling oversight by ministries and the central budget office.* In most countries, "sponsoring" ministries provide broad policy direction to the public enterprises under their wing in addition to monitoring their activities. This is somewhat akin to practices in the United States, where the Department of Housing and Urban Development oversees GNMA (the Government National Mortgage Association) and the Department of Transportation does likewise for the St. Lawrence Seaway Corporation. Mexico takes the process further by designating one ministry as the lead agency for coordinating all public enterprises in a specific sector. Thus, the Secretary of Energy, Mines and Parastatal Industry monitors the

activities and approves the policies and budgets of all public enterprises in the energy and mineral sectors. The Secretary of Agriculture and Hydraulic Resources coordinates and controls public sector firms in the agro-industry. The central budget office, however, determines the aggregate expenditures, investments, loans and subsidies in each sector.[145]

11. *Exercising fiscal and policy control through the boards of directors of public enterprises.* By appointing members of boards of directors and influencing the selection of chief executive officers, governments frequently control the management and financial policies of public enterprises.[146]

12. *Overseeing the performance of public enterprises through comprehensive post-audits.* Following the approach of the U.S. General Accounting Office, independent auditors in many governments audit the performance and finances of public enterprises. The results of the audit have proved to be invaluable in budgeting.[147]

13. *Exercising legislative oversight of public enterprises.* In the United States, legislative oversight of public enterprises is unstructured and spotty except for GAO audits. In the rest of the world, it is virtually non-existent except for a handful of legislatures and, of course, reports by independent auditors responsible to parliament. The experience of Britain and France is revealing in this respect. In Britain, Parliament attempted to achieve a crude accountability of the performance of public enterprises by establishing a Select Committee on Nationalized Industries. Lacking staff, it relied on a variety of means to focus public debate on the financing, policies and performance of public enterprises: review of reports by the public enterprises; testimony by senior civil servants and representatives of the enterprises; and "question time" in Parliament. In this manner it covered major industries about every four or five years. The Committee's reports were penetrating, went to the heart of the major policy and technical issues affecting nationalized industries and occasionally influenced government policies.

In a shakeup of the committee structure in the 1980s, the Select Committee was abolished. Instead, two key committees delved into the affairs of public enterprises and ministries: the Treasury and Civil Service Committee, and the Committee on Accounts, which reviews audits by the independent comptroller and auditor general. Other standing committees monitor the activities of the ministries.[148]

≡ Governments are privatizing public enterprises for fiscal
   and ideological reasons

Various industrialized and developing countries have begun to eliminate some of their public enterprises by selling them off or liquidating them
altogether. In a few instances, governments have encouraged private firms
to compete with public enterprises that had previously enjoyed a virtual
monopoly.[149] Through such competition, public enterprises may improve
their economic performance. The emphasis on privatization has both fiscal
and ideological roots.

Fiscal problems have prompted governments in Latin America with
large deficits and debts to liquidate some public enterprises, sell others and, while retaining ownership, sell non-voting shares in profitable
enterprises. This has been the policy in Brazil, Mexico, Argentina, Colom-
bia, Chile and Venezuela. To a lesser degree, several countries in Africa
(for example Kenya, the Ivory Coast and Egypt) and Asia (for example
Malaysia, Thailand, Bangladesh, South Korea and Sri Lanka) have followed
this approach.[150]

The path toward privatization is a rocky one in these countries. If the
public enterprises are profitable, the governments are reluctant to lose
them. If the enterprises are consistently in the red, few potential buyers
are interested.[151] Furthermore, no strong capital market exists in many
developing countries. Hence, governments must look to foreign purchasers
to take over enterprises, buy shares in them or enter into joint ventures
as more or less equal partners. This, however, raises the spectre of foreign control. Governments try to guard against such domination by either
retaining public enterprises in key economic sectors or holding the majority
share of stock. On the other hand, would-be foreign buyers are fearful of
political instability and shifts in policy. What one government privatizes, a
succeeding government may nationalize. To protect themselves, they seek
investment guarantees, tax breaks and the opportunity to take their profits
home.[152]

In recent years, Britain and France among the industrialized countries and Chile among the developing countries have led the rest of the
non-communist world in the ideological fervor with which they denationalized industries previously nationalized by socialist governments. Under the
banner of economic efficiency and "popular capitalism" (widespread ownership of company shares), the Thatcher government in Britain from 1980 to
1987 privatized fourteen large companies and many smaller ones with about
600,000 employees. The government gained about $18 billion from the sale
of its assets. Among the large public enterprises that were sold were British
Telecom, British Gas, British Oil, the British Airports Authority, and British
Aerospace.[153]

Following the defeat of the Mitterrand government in France in 1986, the new conservative coalition government, headed by Jacques Chirac, committed itself to selling to private investors by 1991 sixty-five publicly owned banks and industrial firms worth $50 billion. As of June 1987 the government had sold off ten of the largest firms, including Compagnie Generale dElectricite ($8.5 billion in sales), Rhone-Poulenc (a chemical company with $5.8 billion sales), Saint-Gobain, a large conglomerate with $7 billion sales) and several banks. As in Britain, millions of shares were sold to small investors.[154] The French Government symbolized its determination to privatize the nationalized sector by giving the Minister of Economy and Finance a new title—the Minister of Economy, Finance and Privatization.

Nationalization and denationalization in Chile have occurred under harrowing and unstable political conditions. From 1970 to 1973, the Allende government expropriated 259 private firms to bring the total of public enterprises to 527. The Pinochet government denationalized the same firms and sold others. At the same time, to guide the economy it kept some of the largest firms in the public sector.[155]

□ □ □

Despite various forms of privatization in vogue in some governments because of economic, budgetary and ideological factors, public enterprises in this and other countries will continue to constitute a major segment of the public sector. They will remain major instruments of public policy and invaluable mechanisms for debt financing. As such, they should be subject to the discipline of the budget process if governments are not to lose control over fiscal policy and the achievement of policy goals. Old line budget systems, however, with emphasis on routine line item controls, are self-defeating. What is needed is a broad and creative approach such as is practiced by several governments discussed in this section, one that focuses on significant economic, management, social and fiscal issues and provides for a periodic review of performance.

≡ 2　THE JUDICIAL POWER OF THE PURSE[1]

No longer is budget decisionmaking the sole prerogative of chief executives and legislatures in the United States. Since the early 1950s, federal and state courts have participated in budgeting on an unprecedented scale. Through their decisions and orders, they have intervened in every phase of the budget process at all levels of government. Hundreds, if not thousands, of decisions affect budget formulation; the appropriation of funds for major programs; budget implementation; capital construction; the issuance of bonds; intergovernmental grants; legislative-executive relations in budgeting; taxation; and the financing of public authorities.

Few aspects of budgeting are beyond the reach of the courts. Their decisions determine not only funding levels, but standards of service, staffing patterns, salaries and even executive and legislative budget procedures. Not content with decisions alone, courts in many cases oversee the implementation of their orders by appointing monitors, committees, special masters and, at times, receivers to administer programs.[2]

While judicial decrees affect nearly all government programs, their most profound impact has been on programs and policies in mental health and retardation, correctional services for adult and youthful offenders, education, welfare and environmental protection. In many states, court orders have drastically altered the financing and operation of these programs and sharply increased state budgets. Even the threat of a court challenge can result in significant programmatic and budgetary changes.[3]

These developments have occurred even though courts have no direct role in the budget process. Their point of entry is litigation initiated by an aggrieved plaintiff in the federal courts (518 district courts, twelve circuit courts of appeal, and the United States Supreme Court) or state courts [also with three levels of adjudication from the lowest to the highest court]. In seeking the protection of the courts, plaintiffs typically assert that existing programs deprive them of their individual rights guaranteed by federal and state constitutions and laws. In much of the litigation, they invoke the protection of the Eighth Amendment of the United States Constitution, which prohibits "cruel and unusual punishment" and the Fourteenth Amendment, which guarantees equal protection of the laws and due process in all issues affecting life, liberty and property. (Similar clauses exist in the constitutions of state governments.) Should the courts provide relief by ordering modification of programs and policies, they generally (with some exceptions) ignore the impact on budgets. In fact, state governments cannot plead lack of funds as a basis for non-compliance with decisions. As one federal judge put it, "the decisions of the courts are legion that cost burden is not a defense to the deprivation of individual rights." [4]

THE COURTS IN THE UNITED STATES ARE DIFFERENT

In the sweep of their decisions covering public policy and budgets, the courts in the United States are unique among world courts.[5] High courts in federal systems such as Australia, Canada, India and West Germany on occasion adjudicate disputes between national and state or provincial governments on taxation and expenditures. For example, the high court of Australia ruled that, under the constitution, only the federal government and not the states could levy indirect taxes such as sales and excise taxes.[6] With mixed results, the states also challenged grants by the federal government for road construction and maintenance, regional development and the dispensing of drugs as intrusions on their power.[7] In one landmark case, the state of Victoria unsuccessfully attempted to upset legislation which provided grants only on the condition that the states would not levy taxes during the year in which they received the grants.[8]

Even in unitary systems of government such as Britain and France, the courts determine the power of local governments to tax and spend and appropriate compensation for private firms taken over by the government. For example, the highest court in Britain, the Court of Appeals (the House of Lords sits as this court), prohibited the Greater London Council from ordering a borough to raise taxes so that it could reduce fares for mass transportation by 25 percent.[9] In another case, a lower court cancelled a wage settlement by the Borough of Camden in London on the grounds that it exceeded the national rate of wage increases and violated the Local Government Act of 1982.[10]

Judicial intervention in the budget process is thus not limited to the United States. But no courts in other countries adjudicate all phases of budgeting on the scale they do here. No courts anywhere have greater responsibilities in this respect.[11] How did this come about?

THE SEEDS OF JUDICIAL ACTIVISM IN BUDGETING

The fact that courts make policy and influence budgets by their interpretation of constitutions, statutes, regulations and executive orders is neither new nor startling. In fact, it is an inherent part of the judicial function.[12] Starting in 1803, when the U.S. Supreme Court, in *Marbury v. Madison*, declared an act of Congress unconstitutional, both federal and state courts have over the years determined the constitutionality of statutes.[13]

Similarly, courts have the last word on the meaning of constitutional and statutory provisions. This holds not only for provisions which affect individual rights, but also for sections of constitutions and laws that deal directly with the budget process. At all levels of government, constitutions and financial laws govern the major phases of budgeting. While the U.S. Constitution is somewhat general in this respect, the constitutions of state governments are detailed and restrictive. Supplementing the constitutions, an extensive body of law prescribes the budget process for federal, state and local governments. As long as these laws exist, the courts will interpret them.

Since the 1800s, several controversial court decisions have affected the budget process directly and indirectly. Nevertheless, none of these developments foreshadowed the explosion of judicial decisions in the 1950s and thereafter that gave the courts the *de facto* power of the purse. Several factors account for this burst of judicial activism. At least three cases (not directly related to budgeting) signalled the start of the era of intervention and initiated a momentum in judicial decision-making that persists to this day. One was the decision by the Supreme Court, *Brown v. the Board of Education*, 377 U.S. 533 (1954), that led to racial desegregation in elementary and secondary education. The others were two reapportionment cases also decided by the Supreme Court: *Baker v. Carr*, 369 U.S. 186 (1962), and *Reynolds v. Sims*, 377 U.S. 533 (1964).[14] These and related cases brought about more equitable redistribution of congressional and state legislative seats on the basis of population and relevant social, economic, political and geographical factors.

What distinguished these cases is that the courts decided controversial social and political issues rather than leaving them to be settled by legislatures and chief executives as "political questions." Their decisions were based on a broad interpretation of the due process and equal protection clauses of the Fourteenth Amendment. In the wake of the decisions, lower federal courts established standards for desegregation and reapportionment and, where necessary, developed their own desegregation plans and reapportionment orders.[15] The basis was laid for a similar approach to budgetary issues.

The decisions came at a time when governmental functions expanded, budgets soared, and social legislation (with thousands of regulations implementing the legislation) reached a new high. The welfare state and the Great Society were well on their way. Nevertheless, intractable problems still remained, and legislatures continued to procrastinate on policies affecting sizable groups of the population.

In this impasse, aggrieved individuals turned to interest and advocacy groups and centers of public law that flourished in Washington, D.C., and state capitals. Encouraged by the decisions on desegregation and reapportionment, these groups now looked to the courts to settle policy and budgetary problems in mental health, mental retardation, correctional services, education and other governmental functions. In the new climate of judicial activism, the courts were ready to provide a forum for the resolution of complex social problems.[16] As a result, the volume of civil cases in the U.S. district courts alone rose from 60,000 in 1960 to 155,000 in 1979.[17]

In virtually every state, judicial decisions affected the allocation of resources; capital construction; debt financing and intergovernmental grants; budget implementation; taxation; the financing of public authorities; and the budget process itself.

THE COURTS DETERMINE THE ALLOCATION OF RESOURCES FOR A VARIETY OF PROGRAMS

By the end of the 1970s, many states had overhauled their programs and capital facilities and sharply expanded their appropriations for mental health, mental retardation, correctional services, education and welfare. This was due to the direct and indirect effect of a string of landmark court decisions.[18] The momentum generated by these cases persists to this day.

≡ The effect of court decisions on programs for the mentally ill and mentally retarded

A series of court decisions dramatically changed the scope and financing of programs for the mentally ill and mentally retarded in state governments. The turnabout came in 1966, when the Federal District Court in Washington, D.C., in *Rouse v. Cameron*, asserted that mentally ill patients had a constitutional "right to treatment."[19] Otherwise, they could not be held in hospitals against their will. This case set in motion still other decisions by federal courts in various states, some broad, some narrow.[20]

The precedent-making Wyatt v. Stickney case

Several precedent-making decisions, originally in Alabama and then in other states, spelled out the meaning of the "right to treatment." In *Wyatt v. Stickney*, Judge Frank Johnson Jr. of the Federal District Court in Alabama ordered the Mental Health Board in 1971 to provide within six months the required level of care for the mentally ill in a large institution.[21] When the state failed to comply with the decision, Judge Johnson issued a broad decree affecting all mental hospitals and prescribing "minimum constitutional standards."[22] In an appendix to the decision, he laid down the standards which included the amount of square feet of space per patient, provisions for privacy, furniture per patient, toilet and washing facilities, individual treatment plans and staffing ratios that provided for every 250 patients two psychiatrists, four other physicians, twelve registered nurses, seven social workers (with two having an M.S.W. degree) and other categories of professional and paraprofessional personnel. In effect, Judge Johnson had revised the Alabama mental health budget.

He made it clear that the lack of funds, staff and facilities was no defense and, in the event of failure to comply with its decree, threatened the state as follows:

> In the event, though, that the Legislature fails to satisfy its well-defined obligation, and the Mental Health Board, because of lack of funding or any other legally insufficient reason, fails to implement fully the standards herein ordered, it will be necessary for the Court to take affirmative steps, including appointing a master, to ensure that proper funding is realized and that adequate treatment is available for the mentally ill of Alabama.

While the governor and the state legislature were free to appeal the court's decision to the federal circuit court and, if necessary, to the Supreme Court, they decided, in the face of political pressures, to go along with it by allocating $11 million from federal revenue sharing funds in 1972 to the State Mental Health Board and raising the appropriation from $14 million in 1971 to $58 million in 1973.[23] The cost per patient day jumped from $6.40 in 1974 to $28 in 1977.[24]

The federal court and the Alabama state government tangled once again in 1972 with regard to the care and treatment of mentally retarded individuals.[25] This time the court imposed standards for medical, educational, nutritional, therapeutic and recreational services. These were essential, the court asserted, to protect the inviolable constitutional rights of the mentally retarded to "habilitation." The court defined "habilitation" as the acquisition and maintenance of those life skills which enable a patient "to cope more effectively with the demands of his own person and of his environment and to raise the level of his physical, mental and social efficiency."

The state, however, appealed to the federal circuit court and asserted that compliance with the decision would result in substantial outlays at the expense of other state programs. Brushing aside this argument, the court stated categorically that the legislature is not free to deny an individual's constitutional rights for "budgetary or any other reasons." It recognized that it could not mandate appropriations. On the other hand, it could compel the governor to propose methods for meeting the state's constitutional obligations with regard to the mentally retarded.[26] If this is not a mandate, it has a curious resemblance to one. In any event, Alabama did not contest this ruling by appealing to the Supreme Court.

The effect of the Alabama cases on other states

The ripples started by the Alabama cases reached into virtually every state. Where the issue of the quality and financing of state programs for the mentally ill and retarded was adjudicated, the federal courts invariably echoed the Alabama decisions. Some other prominent cases highlight this trend. For example, in 1977 the federal court in Minnesota agreed that compliance with its decree would cost the state an additional $10–12 million a year. Nonetheless, it issued the following by now familiar dictum:

> . . . if Minnesota chooses to operate hospitals for the mentally retarded, the operation must meet minimal constitutional standards, and that operation may not be permitted to yield to financial considerations.[27]

A similar ruling in Louisiana had a major impact on budgets for the care and treatment of mentally retarded individuals in and out of state institutions. A broad decree issued by the Court in *Gary W. et al. v. State of Louisiana* in 1976 covered literally every aspect of a child's life.[28] It was up to the state legislature to provide the necessary funds, like it or not. In Pennsylvania, the federal court in 1977 mandated community placement for the mentally retarded and fined the Department of Public Welfare for failing to pay the costs of a special master and a hearing master appointed by the court to oversee implementation of the decree.[29] In continuing litigation on the same case, the Supreme Court in 1981 displayed some sensitivity to the effect of decisions on state costs. Reversing earlier decisions by federal district and circuit courts, it held that the state could not be forced to comply with the federal Developmentally Disabled Assistance and Bill of Rights Act of 1975 since it was not the intent of Congress to "impose massive financial obligations on the states."[30]

Going beyond the rulings in Alabama and other states, the federal courts in New York State over more than a ten year period, beginning in 1973, controlled the programs and budgets for the mentally retarded, especially in a mammoth state institution in New York City, the Willowbrook Developmental Center for the Mentally Retarded, with some 5,000 patients. The courts mandated a drastic shift from institutionalization to community care, larger state and local budgets and implementation of revised standards for the care and treatment of patients. In the first of a series of cases, *New York State Association for Retarded Children Inc. and Patricia Parisi et al. v. Nelson A. Rockefeller*, the federal district court in 1973, as a start, ordered the immediate hiring of 85 more nurses and thirty more physical therapists.[31] To put teeth in its decision, the court, two years later, in 1975, issued a consent decree covering the level of appropriations, staffing ratios, the level of service, the rate of deinstitutionalization and space standards. These were embodied in some thirty-five standards for the mentally ill and forty-nine standards for the mentally retarded.[32]

In 1975, Governor Hugh A. Carey signed the decree with some reluctance in view of the heavy fiscal implications. Beginning in 1976-77, successive budgets sharply increased state aid for community mental health programs as well as state programs for the mentally retarded so that they rose from $243 million to over $1 billion in 1985-86.[33] The number of residents at Willowbrook declined to about 2,000, but the state failed to meet the court-imposed deadline of April 31, 1978, to reduce the population to 250. Sufficient community-based programs simply did not exist. With the decline in the number of residents, the cost per patient sharply increased from $4,600 to $26,300. At the same time, capital budgets for reconstructed facilities climbed.[34]

For the federal courts, the Willowbrook decision was not a one-time decree. As in Alabama, they maintained continuing jurisdiction over the implementation of the order through human rights committees, review panels, visits to institutions by attorneys for the plaintiffs, and reports on compliance with the standards in the consent decree.[35]

≡ The effect of court decisions on appropriations for correctional services

Court decisions have led to a restructuring of prison systems for adult and youthful offenders and a sharp increase in operating and capital budgets for correctional services in many states and cities. The states of Alabama, Arkansas, Florida, Maryland, Massachusetts, Mississippi, New Hampshire, and especially New York, Ohio, Oklahoma and Rhode Island bore the brunt of judicial decrees. In various cities, including Baltimore, St. Louis, New Orleans, Toledo, New York City and Boston, federal and state courts actually took over the operation of jails.[36] These trends persist to this day.

In virtually every case the plaintiffs attacked the conditions of confinement as "cruel and unusual punishment" proscribed by the Eighth Amendment of the Constitution. For example, a federal court in Texas in 1974, in *Morales v. Turman*, found that conditions in certain facilities for youthful offenders were unconstitutional because of brutality, poor living conditions and indifference to the rehabilitation of the inmates.[37] In a decree encompassing every phase of the program, it ordered the closing of some institutions and extensive improvements in others.

Judge Frank M. Johnson, Jr., who had presided over the cases on mental health and mental retardation in Alabama, also took on the prison system. In a sweeping ruling sustained by the circuit court of appeals, he determined that the staffing and sanitary conditions of the main hospital of the prison system were inadequate to the point where they constituted cruel and unusual punishment. To overcome these deficiencies, he issued an order prescribing detailed standards, policies and procedures covering staffing, facilities and treatment.[38] Later, an even broader decision, in *James V. Wallace v. State of Alabama*, covered the entire prison system of Alabama and resulted in an immediate increase of $35 million in the budget for correctional services for FY 1976.[39]

As in the cases affecting the mentally ill and the mentally retarded, the courts made short shrift of state pleas about the lack of funds for prisons. In a ruling reminiscent of the decision in the Minnesota case with regard to mentally retarded individuals, the court warned Arkansas as follows:

> Let there be no mistake in the matter; the obligation of the Respondents to eliminate existing unconstitutionalities does not depend upon what the Legislature may do or upon what the Governor may do, or indeed, upon what Respondents may be able to accomplish. If Arkansas is going to operate a penitentiary system, it is going to have to be a system that is countenanced by the Constitution of the United States.[40]

When Oklahoma in 1978 balked at implementing a court-approved plan of changes and a timetable for instituting the changes, the federal court threatened the state with mandatory closing of facilities and fines up to $50,000 a day.[41]

In most cases, the orders of the federal district courts and courts of appeals stood. Few cases reached the Supreme Court. When they did, the Court followed what appears to be an ambivalent policy. On the one hand, it did little to curb the rulings of the lower courts. On the other, it emphasized the limited role of the courts and cautioned the lower courts against "excessive intrusiveness" in state and local programs.[42] It decided two cases on prison systems on fairly narrow grounds without ruling on the constitutionality of the programs or imposing financial obligations on the states. In one case, it found "double celling" was not unconstitutional. In another, it acknowledged the existence of "inadequate treatment," but saw no constitutional problem unless the state was "deliberately indifferent."[43] In reviewing the prison system in Alabama, however, the court took an unequivocal position. It ruled that the entire system was unconstitutional.[44]

The budgetary impact of decisions by the lower courts has been widespread. One estimate suggested that the cost of implementing court orders ranged "from as little as $5 million for some county governments to as much as $1 billion or more for some state governments."[45] An analysis of the budgetary effect of court-mandated reforms prior to 1979 in fourteen state governments compared spending for operating and capital expenditures before and after the decisions. Except for those in two states, capital expenditures went up markedly. Similarly, capital expenditures as a proportion of total state spending increased. The number of planned cells also increased. On the other hand, the impact on operating expenditures was minimal, suggesting that capital spending constituted a higher priority. Using expenditures per prisoner as a measure, states under the shadow of litigation spent less than other states, but were moving closer to the level of states with acceptable systems.[46] One possible explanation for the divergent trends in operating and capital expenditures may be the long lead time required to complete a capital facility. Once the project is operational, costs for staffing and maintenance begin to mount.

≡ The effect of court decisions on educational financing

Decisions by federal and state courts have affected all levels of education and have had a far-reaching impact on state and local education budgets. Even when plaintiffs lost a lawsuit, the litigation process itself has served as a catalyst to initiate changes in policies and budgets.[47] Litigation in education has covered such broad issues as racial segregation in schools; discriminatory practices in the allocation of resources to schools and universities with large minority groups; the education of physically handicapped children; state and local financing of elementary and secondary education; and the distribution of state aid to parochial schools and school districts. In terms of their fiscal effect judicial decisions on desegregation, handicapped children and school financing have been the most significant.

The desegregation issue

Beginning with the landmark decisions of the U.S. Supreme Court in 1954 and 1955 in *Brown v. Board of Education*, dozens of court decisions on desegregation have drastically changed school policies and budgets.[48] Court orders and decrees (primarily by federal courts) have led to reassignment of students to schools to rectify racial and ethnic imbalances; the expansion of bus fleets to facilitate desegregation; increased staffs; the stepped-up hiring of professionals in minority groups; the closing of schools; the repair of existing schools and the construction of new ones; the purchase of supplies and equipment deemed essential by the courts; and the appointment of agents of the courts to monitor judicial decrees.[49]

In a by no means atypical case, the Boston school system was in virtual receivership for several years and directed by United States District Judge W. Arthur Garrity. As *de facto* administrator, Judge Garrity specified expenditures for the repair of individual schools.[50] Only in 1985 was Judge Garrity satisfied that desegregation at long last had been accomplished and returned the schools to the control of the local authorities.

The Supreme Court recognized that desegregation through busing and other means imposed heavy costs on school districts. But the price had to be paid to comply with the Fourteenth Amendment of the Constitution.[51]

Reallocating resources to schools and universities with large minority groups

In several cases the courts have concluded that inequality in resources among schools with minority groups was *prima facie* evidence of racial discrimination. For example, noting the disparity in Washington, D.C., between per-pupil cost in schools attended by white and black students, a federal district court in 1971 ordered the school system to equalize the per-pupil expenditures for teachers' salaries and related benefits. It did not, however, go the whole way and mandate the equalization of all expenditures per pupil.[52] In North Carolina, the federal court took a similar approach in equalizing resources in colleges with a predominantly black student body with those in colleges attended mainly by white students. It initiated a consent decree in 1979 which not only mandated the equalization of financial support for all senior colleges, but ordered the colleges in the state to initiate several programs in behalf of black students: increased enrollment and employment; a variety of financial aids; expansion of opportunities in professional schools; comparable student-faculty ratios in all schools; parity in faculty salaries; and necessary capital imprisonments.[53]

Providing resources for the education of physically handicapped children

Through interpretations of the Fourteenth Amendment, the federal Rehabilitation Act of 1973, and the federal Education for All Handicapped Children Act of 1975, federal courts have compelled school districts to establish appropriate programs for handicapped children. While expressing concern about the fiscal effect of their decisions, federal judges have nonetheless issued decrees for individualized programs that cost state and local governments and school districts billions of dollars.[54]

Typical of dozens of cases is a class action suit that was initiated in the U.S. District Court of Eastern Wisconsin in 1972 on behalf of a blind and mentally retarded child and all handicapped children between the ages of four and twenty in the state of Wisconsin. The plaintiffs charged that the state deprived them of their constitutional right to equal protection by failing to provide an appropriate education at public expense. Under pressure of the litigation, the Wisconsin Legislature enacted in 1973 Chapter 115 of the Wisconsin Statutes, which compelled all school districts to furnish a free and appropriate education to all handicapped children. Pending the implementation of the legislation, the court stayed any further proceedings. When delays bogged down the start of the program, an exasperated court ordered the State Superintendent of Public Schools in August 1978 to enforce the law promptly and to file periodic progress reports demonstrating the extent of compliance with the legislation. As a direct result of such judicial intervention, the state increased aid to school districts for handicapped children from $29.5 million in FY 1974 to $117.4 million in FY 1982.[55]

Financing elementary and secondary education

Between 1971 and 1982, twenty-eight states, which accounted for about three-fourths of all students enrolled in the elementary and secondary schools in the United States, enacted, at high cost, fundamental changes in their methods of financing public education. In a minority of the states, actions resulted directly from court decisions upsetting the existing methods of financing education. Even when states won cases challenging their policies governing state and local aid to education, however, the momentum generated by the litigation led to sharp increases in state aid in nearly all states.[56]

The support of elementary and secondary education represents the largest single component of state and local government budgets. To finance these programs, local governments and school districts rely heavily on local property taxes augmented by state and federal grants. The effect has been that school districts with a substantial local tax base (because of affluent individual and corporate taxpayers) spend more for education than those with skimpy tax resources. While the states have attempted to equalize opportunities for children in all school districts by granting relatively more funds to poorer districts, sharp disparities between districts in expenditures per pupil persisted. Beginning in 1971, this method of financing education was attacked as a violation of the equal protection clauses in the U.S. and state constitutions.

At least thirty lawsuits took this position over a ten-year period in addition to relying on provisions of state constitutions which guarantee a "thorough and efficient system" of public schools.[57] Contrary to cases affecting other governmental functions, only one case was decided by the federal courts. The others were settled by the highest state courts, with mixed results. In seventeen cases which had been adjudicated by 1987, ten state courts rejected the assertion that existing systems of elementary and secondary education violated the equal protection clauses and state constitutional articles on education. The courts found that education financing was minimally adequate. In seven states, the courts took an opposite view. They mandated increased resources for the poorest districts, but did not cap expenditures in the richest districts. Nor did they require full equalization of resources.[58]

The most significant cases which influenced decisions in other states were *Serrano v. Priest* in California, *San Antonio School District v. Rodriguez* in Texas, *Robinson v. Cahill* in New Jersey and *Board of Education, Levittown Union Free School District v. Nyquist* in New York. Each affected state budgets significantly.

The first successful judicial challenge to existing systems of financing elementary and secondary education took place in California in 1971, when the highest state court determined that disparities in per-pupil revenue among school districts, ranging from $577 to $1,232, discriminated against the poor and violated the equal protection clauses of the federal and state constitutions. In *Serrano v. Priest*, the court stated categorically:

> This funding scheme invidiously discriminates against the poor because it makes the quality of a child's education a function of the wealth of his parents and neighbors. Recognizing as we must that the right to an education in our public schools is a fundamental interest which can not be conditioned on wealth, we can discern no compelling state purpose necessitating the present method of financing.[59]

Appreciating that it had raised complex issues of the quality of education, school financing, property tax relief, and the equity of formulas for distributing state grants, the Court laid down standards for compliance with its decree, but fixed no time limit.[60] After the legislature enacted some positive reforms designed to reduce interdistrict inequity in educational resources, the Court, reasonably satisfied, affirmed its original decree. It, however, insisted upon full compliance by September 1980.[61]

In Texas, a federal district court took a position similar to that of *Serrano* and found the state system for financing elementary and secondary education unconstitutional. It based its decision on glaring interdistrict disparities in per-pupil expenditures stemming from differences in the yield of property taxes. By a 5-4 vote in *San Antonio Independent School District v. Rodriguez*, the United States Supreme Court in 1973 reversed the decision on these grounds: (1) the equal protection clause "does not require absolute equality or precisely equal advantages"; (2) the present method of financing public education is not "suspect since the thrust of the Texas system is affirmative and reformatory"; (3) the court lacks expertise and familiarity with local conditions and, therefore, should defer to the legislature; and (4) education is not a "fundamental interest" under the federal constitution.[62]

Despite the ruling, the Rodriguez case turned out to be a catalyst for change. In the session that followed the Supreme Court decision, the legislature in 1975 approved major revisions in methods of financing, designed to equalize resources among school districts. A senior legislator explained the abrupt shift in policy in these terms: "The legislature will respond only when confronted with a situation of crisis proportions. The lower court decision in Rodriguez created just such a crisis."[63]

In a far reaching decision, the Supreme Court of New Jersey categorically outlawed existing methods of funding public schools which, in its view, not only violated the equal protection clauses, but also the requirement in the state constitution for a "thorough and efficient system of elementary and secondary education." In *Robinson v. Cahill*, it first called upon the state in 1973 to "finance a . . . system of education out of state revenues raised by levies imposed uniformly on taxpayers of the same class." Dissatisfied with the sluggish pace of change, the Court, in four subsequent decisions based on *Robinson v. Cahill*, took a series of drastic actions. It imposed deadlines on the state to come up with appropriate legislation. It ordered provisional relief for poor school districts. In 1975, it enjoined the state from distributing aid to school districts altogether and did not lift the injunction until 1976, when the legislature passed the state's first personal income tax to fund public education equitably.[64]

The highest court of New York State, the Court of Appeals, moved in an opposite direction. In 1982, it decided, in *Levittown*, that the state's system for financing elementary and secondary education was constitutional. This decision reversed earlier rulings by the state supreme court (the lowest court) in 1978 and the Appellate Division in 1981.[65] Joined by four large cities in the state (New York City, Buffalo, Rochester and Syracuse), the Levittown Board of Education had argued that fiscal disparities among school districts were unconstitutional (essentially the focus of *Serrano* and *Robinson*). The cities injected the further complaint that they were fiscally "overburdened" in view of their many functions and costly welfare programs for the poor. Hence, the quality of education suffered, and they should be compensated with additional aid because of the "municipal overburden." The lower courts concurred with these positions and found the state aid formulas unconstitutional and discriminatory.

In overturning these decisions, the Court of Appeals agreed that financial disparities existed among school districts. It was satisfied, however, that the state was meeting its constitutional obligations in providing a "sound basic education" to children. Any reforms of the present system designed to equalize expenditures should be the responsibility of the legislature and the executive. It would be "inappropriate . . . for the courts to intrude upon such decision-making." The Court rejected the argument that "municipal overburden" was unconstitutional and viewed local fiscal problems as a "product of demographic, economic and political factors intrinsic to the cities themselves." Hence, decisions on priorities in expenditures should remain a local responsibility.

As in Texas, the Court's negative decisions still had a positive effect. Following the ruling, the legislature and the governor in successive budgets significantly increased state aid for elementary and secondary education to reduce disparities in funding among school districts.[66]

Litigation on school financing continues to this day. For example, in a far-reaching decision reminiscent of the Robinson cases in New Jersey, a federal district court judge in Kansas City, Missouri, ordered nearly a doubling of the school property tax and a 25 percent increase in the income tax to wipe out the last remains of segregation in the school system.[67]

☰ The effect of court decisions on welfare costs

Several decisions, primarily by federal courts, have had a direct impact on federal, state and local welfare costs and on the management of welfare programs. The rulings deal with such issues as residency requirements for welfare; the attempts of states to place a ceiling on welfare costs; eligibility for food stamps; the funding of abortions; the adequacy of procedures for denying benefits; and state welfare administration. In many of the cases, the plaintiffs invoked the equal protection and due process clauses of the U.S. Constitution. In others, they challenged the legality of state and local actions. No clear trend is apparent in decisions by the federal courts. In some cases, they gave more weight to constitutional guarantees than to costs. In others, the reverse was true.[68]

The courts strike down residency requirements as a condition for welfare benefits

Beginning in 1969, the Supreme Court in several cases struck down residence qualifications (usually one year) as a condition for welfare benefits. In a landmark case, *Shapiro v. Thompson*, the court gave short shrift to states' concern about the impact of its decisions on budgets:

> We recognize that a state has a valid interest in preserving the fiscal integrity of its programs. It may legitimately attempt to limit its expenditures, whether for public assistance, public education or any other program. But a State may not accomplish such a purpose by invidious distinctions between classes of its citizens. It could not, for example, reduce expenditures for education by barring indigent children from its schools. Similarly, in the cases before us, appellants must do more than show that denying welfare benefits to new residents saves money. The saving of welfare costs cannot justify an otherwise invidious classification.[69]

In a similar ruling, the Court invalidated a one-year residency requirement for non-emergency hospitalization. Although the Court recognized that governments had a legitimate concern in curbing expenditures, it would not permit that interest to override constitutional rights.[70]

The courts rule on proposed ceilings on welfare costs

At various times, several states have attempted to reduce welfare costs by fixing a maximum allowance per family based on the number of family members. In 1969, New York State took this approach instead of using such criteria as "basic needs" and "special needs" which varied with the circumstances of each family. This change would have saved about $40 million. In *Rosado v. Wyman*, the U.S. Supreme Court ruled in 1970 that this policy conflicted with federal legislation.[71] Yet, in a later but similar case, *Jefferson v. Hackney*, the Court reversed itself in 1972 by upholding a reduced cost standard. It was not persuaded by the previous interpretation of the federal statute.[72] Confounding the states still further, the Court upheld Maryland's maximum welfare grant provision in *Dandridge v. Williams*.[73] This time the Court refused to "second-guess state officials charged with the difficult responsibility of allocating limited public welfare funds among a myriad of potential recipients." What's a poor state to do?

Who has a right to food stamps?

Outraged by what it regarded as an abuse of the expensive food stamp program by middle-class college students and "hippies," Congress inserted language in an appropriation act to make them ineligible. Only the deserving poor had a right to food stamps. The Supreme Court decided in 1977 that such legislation made "arbitrary distinctions between particular classes of potential recipients." Hence, it could not be tolerated under the equal protection and due process clauses.[74] Similarly, the Supreme Court blocked Illinois from disqualifying college students for benefits in the AFDC program (Aid for Families with Dependent Children).[75]

Who has a right to federally funded abortions?

Reacting to a highly charged emotional issue, the federal courts decided whether funds appropriated for Medicaid (combined federal-state-local programs of medical care for the poor) could be used to pay for abortions. In a controversial decision, the Supreme Court upheld the constitutionality of the denial of Medicaid funds only for non-therapeutic abortions. On the other hand, it agreed that therapeutic abortions could still be funded (abortions for mothers endangered by the continuation of pregnancy or for victims of rape and incest).[76] This time the court majority did not raise issues of equal protection and due process for poor pregnant women. On relatively narrow grounds, it defended administrative actions as rational and argued that women still had a constitutional right to an abortion, but no constitutional right to federal funds for non-therapeutic abortions.[77]

Even this narrow decision was too broad to satisfy members of Congress who wanted to bar federal funds for all abortions. On three separate occasions, from 1976 to 1979, Congress approved amendments to the appropriation act for the Department of Health, Education and Welfare severely limiting Medicaid funding for therapeutic abortions.[78] This immediately started widespread litigation. By April 1, 1980, fourteen federal courts which had considered the problem were split and issued conflicting decisions. And the litigation still continues. So uncertain is federal policy at this point that "a poor woman's access to a therapeutic abortion may well be dependent on the fiscal year in which she becomes pregnant."[79]

The effect of judicial decisions on welfare systems and administrative costs

Some states have attempted to realign and simplify their welfare systems in order to reduce administrative costs, even to the point of denying hearings before terminating welfare benefits. In *Goldberg v. Kelly* in 1970, the Supreme Court, however, ruled that benefits can not be ended without a hearing and an opportunity for the welfare recipient to consider the evidence.[80] While the court majority appreciated the fiscal implications of its decision, it urged the states to cut costs by better planning of hearings and more skillful use of personnel. Dissenting from this position, Chief Justice Burger warned that "new layers of procedural protection may become an intolerable drain on the very funds earmarked for food, clothing and other living essentials."[81]

In subsequent years the Supreme Court backed away from *Goldberg* and began to consider the trade-off between procedural safeguards and administrative costs. For example, because of cost factors, it concurred with a policy to limit the need for physicians to testify at disability hearings.[82] In *Mathews v. Eldridge*, the Court held that hearings were not constitutionally required before Social Security benefits could be terminated. It expressed concern about "the incremental cost resulting from the increased numbers of hearings and the expense of providing benefits to ineligible recipients pending decisions."[83] It did not dismiss the need for procedural safeguards required by due process. But it argued that such constitutional protection should be weighed against the need to conserve "scarce fiscal and administrative resources." The Court, however, has not determined how much weight should be accorded to each factor.[84]

THE COURTS DETERMINE THE SIZE OF PAYROLLS FOR STATE AND LOCAL GOVERNMENTS

Both federal and state courts have intervened in virtually every aspect of personnel administration, including pay levels, minimum wages, overtime pay, collective bargaining, position classification, alleged inequity in salaries for women and pension benefits. Among numerous cases, several stand out because of their widespread impact and fiscal implications for state and local governments.

≡ The application of the Federal Fair Labor Standards Act to state and local governments

In recent years, one of the more dramatic federal-state conflicts has resulted from attempts of the U.S. Department of Labor to impose on state and local governments the wage and hour provisions of the Fair Labor Standards Act (FLSA), especially requirements governing overtime pay. To the great relief of state and local officials, the Supreme Court in 1976 ruled in *National League of Cities v. Usery* that, in regulating commerce under the Tenth Amendment of the Constitution, Congress could not force on the states its choices "regarding the conduct of integral governmental functions."[85] The relief proved to be short-lived. In several cases involving transportation employees, the Supreme Court later decided that mass transportation was not an "integral" and "traditional" function of state and local governments. Hence, transportation systems were subject to the Fair Labor Standards Act and to federal laws governing strikes by public employees.[86]

The final blow came in *Garcia v. San Antonio Metropolitan Transportation Authority* in 1985, when the Supreme Court, by a 5-4 vote, reversed the *NLC v. Usery* decision and decided that the Fair Labor Standards Act controlled overtime pay and minimum wages of employees of state and local governments.[87] Rough estimates indicated that the ruling might cost state and local governments an additional $2 to $4 billion annually, primarily for overtime pay. It had long been a practice among these governments to give firefighters, police, transportation workers and other employees with flexible work shifts compensating time off in lieu of overtime pay. Now they were faced with the prospect of paying time and a half for hours worked beyond the normal work week. Following the Supreme Court decision, state and local government officials successfully pressed Congress to exempt them from provisions of FLSA. In November 1985, legislation approved by the President (PL 99-150) effectively overturned *Garcia*. Beginning on April 15, 1986, state and local governments could continue to substitute compensating time off for overtime pay. The time equivalent, however, could not be less than one and a half hours off for each hour of overtime.[88]

≡ Equal pay for jobs of comparable worth

In the 1980s, a new equal rights issue surfaced in the courts—equal pay for jobs of comparable worth. Previously, pay plans had emphasized equal pay for equal work. Now, women contended this was not enough, since jobs held predominantly by women were undervalued in governmental pay plans. Charging sex discrimination, they demanded equal pay for dissimilar jobs of comparable economic value.

In one of several suits charging sex discrimination, female prison guards in Washington City, Oregon, claimed that in violation of the United States Civil Rights Act of 1964 they received less pay than their male counterparts. Without coming to grips with this issue, a federal district court ruled that the jobs were not substantially equal, obviating any legal requirements for equal pay. The Supreme Court concurred with this in 1981.[89]

This case was a mere curtain raiser. In 1983, the American Federation of State, County and Municipal Employees claimed that the state of Washington discriminated against women employees in violation of the federal Civil Rights Act. On the whole, it argued, women received less pay than men in jobs of comparable worth. The federal district court found that this was indeed the case. Faced with an estimated cost of $400 million in back pay for approximately 15,000 employees, the state appealed to the federal court of appeals. Reversing the decision of the lower court, the court of appeals supported the state's policy of basing compensation on the marketplace rather than on complex theories of comparable worth. Nevertheless, the state and the union reached agreement on a $404 million pay package for jobs held primarily by women that would be phased in from 1966 to 1991.[90]

In the aftermath of the Washington decision, the future of pay plans based on comparable worth was uncertain. Nonetheless, several state governments implemented such plans and others rejected them as they contemplated additional costs for state and local governments ranging from an estimated $11-$14 billion. Where employees were turned down, they initiated lawsuits, as in California.[91]

As part of their retirement policy, many state and local governments had approved mandatory retirement of public safety officers at age 55. In 1983, the federal government challenged this position in *Equal Opportunity Commission v. Wyoming* as a violation of the federal Age Discrimination Employment Act (ADEA) of 1974. The amendment to the federal statute had broadened the definition of employer to include state and local governments. Hence, these governments could not distriminate against employees between the ages of 40 and 70 solely because of age except where age is a "bona fide occupational qualification." This meant that state and local governments could not adopt an across-the-board retirement policy, but had to make decisions to retire employees on a case-by-case basis. Wyoming contended that the extension of ADEA to state government was an unconstitutional application of the "commerce clause" of the Tenth Amendment and regulated states contrary to constitutional guarantees of a federal system. The United States District Court of Wyoming concurred with the state, only to be overruled by a 5-4 decision of the Supreme Court, which held that the extension of ADEA to the states was a valid exercise of congressional power.[92]

THE COURTS MONITOR THE IMPLEMENTATION OF THE BUDGET

The courts have been equally active in monitoring the implementation of the budget at all levels of government in the United States. In this context they have grappled with such issues as the power of presidents and governors to impound funds appropriated by the legislature; the use of legislative vetoes by Congress and state legislatures to turn down expenditures previously approved in appropriation acts; the startup of construction projects for which funds were appropriated, but which might conflict with other legislation; and the need for administrations to comply with nonbinding expressions of legislative intent.

☰ The courts pound the impoundment of funds

In an unparalleled intervention in the process of budget implementation, the federal courts, beginning in 1971 in some 100 cases, reviewed the impoundment of funds by the Nixon administration from 1969 to 1973. Prior to 1971, no federal courts had dealt with the issue. By 1973, over sixty cases were before the courts, with more to come.[93] What triggered this burst of judicial activity was the refusal of President Nixon to allot $14.5 to $28 billion (estimates differ) from appropriations for more than 110 programs previously approved by Congress.[94]

State and local governments and public interest groups promptly sued the appropriate cabinet officers to release the appropriated funds. In justification of its actions, the Nixon administration tried a variety of defenses: the President's statutory power under the Anti-Deficiency Act (31 U.S.C. 665) to withhold allotments so as to reduce the need for deficiency and supplemental appropriations; his constitutional duty to execute the laws "faithfully," including control of the national debt and promotion of economic stability; the immunity of a sovereign government to suits without its consent; the lack of jurisdiction of the courts over "political questions"; the ambiguous language in appropriation acts which did not necessarily mandate expenditures; an inherent constitutional power to impound funds under the doctrine of separation of powers; the broad powers of the President as commander in chief; the President's obligation to implement the budget as presented by him; and the lack of standing of the plaintiffs.[95] Except in two or three cases, the federal courts gave short shrift to these arguments. All cases but one were decided by federal district and circuit courts (courts of appeal). In the one case that reached the Supreme Court, it, like the lower courts, ordered the administration to allot to states funds for water pollution control appropriated by Congress.[96]

Even though the impoundments led to a constitutional confrontation between the President and Congress, the courts shied away from constitutional issues. They preferred to base their decisions mainly on the interpretation of existing statutes. With this approach, they concluded that the President, notwithstanding his arguments, lacked the discretion to impound funds in the absence of statutory authority.[97]

Two examples may capture the flavor of the tensions and problems surrounding the impoundment issue. Several court decisions compelled a reluctant Secretary of Agriculture to allocate funds to local clinics for the Special Supplemental Food Program for Women, Infants and Children (WIC), enacted by Congress in 1972 (PL 92-433) and designed to prevent birth defects and mental retardation in infants and young children. When the Secretary failed to implement the program during the 1972–73 fiscal year, the federal district court ordered him to "promulgate regulations and process applications for funding until the sum of $40 million was expended." During each of the next three fiscal years, the Secretary continued to withhold appropriated funds for WIC. On each occasion, the courts intervened and directed him to follow a clear congressional intent and to spend funds not only appropriated for the current fiscal year, but all unspent monies from previous fiscal years.[98]

The other example concerns funds for water pollution control programs. In October 1972, President Nixon vetoed an authorization bill that would have provided over three fiscal years $18 billion to the Environmental Protection Agency for grants to state and local governments, primarily for sewage treatment plants. Congress promptly overrode the veto (PL 92-500). Nevertheless, the President impounded about $13 billion. New York City successfully brought suit in the federal district court in Washington, D.C., which ruled that "the language of the pertinent sections of the act clearly indicated the intent of Congress to require the Administrator to allot, at the appropriate times, the full sums authorized to be appropriated." The court ordered the Administrator to allow from previously withheld funds $5 billion for FY 1973 and $6 billion for FY 1974, respectively, instead of the $2 billion and $3 billion the Administrator had scheduled for allotment. In the court's view, the money was enough to cover approved applications from states and municipalities. Hence, it did not compel the Administrator to allot the entire authorized amount. Both the Court of Appeals and the Supreme Court concurred with this decision.[99]

As the following table shows, the impact on two states—New York and New Jersey—was dramatic.[100]

State	FY 1972–73	FY 1973–74
		(in millions)
New York		
E.P.A. original allotment	$221.1	$332.7
Court-ordered allotment	552.1	663.7
New Jersey		
E.P.A. original allotment	154.0	231.1
Court-ordered allotment	385.2	462.2

By the mid-1980s still another form of impoundment emerged—sequestration. Under the Balanced Budget and Emergency Deficit Control Act of 1985 (PL 99-177), Congress set up annual deficit reduction targets. In the event the President and Congress reached an impasse on the budget, automatic cuts or sequestration would take place. Using this procedure, the Reagan administration, among other things, sequestered in 1987 about $180 million in revenue sharing funds for local governments. It did this by transferring the monies from the revenue sharing trust fund to the general fund. Claiming that the sequestration was illegal, several public interest groups representing local governments successfully sued in the federal district court only to lose in the Court of Appeals.[101]

≡ Courts erode the powers of governors to allot funds

The issues settled by federal litigation also came to a head in at least four states, and, for the first time, governors encountered serious challenges to the exercise of their powers to allot appropriated funds. Confronted by a projected deficit of $145.4 million in FY 1980–81, the Wisconsin State Secretary of Administration, among other cutbacks, ordered all agencies, including the Department of Instruction, to reduce allotments by 4.4 percent for FY 1980–81. As a result, the Department of Instruction notified school districts that state aid would be cut. While the court agreed that the Secretary of Administration had the statutory power to reduce allotments for operating agencies and programs, it did not regard state aid as part of the appropriations subject to allotment. Hence, it enjoined the Secretary from reducing payments to school districts. On the other hand, the court recognized that the state government must be in a position to deal with financial crises resulting from revenue shortfalls. The solution lay, however, in getting the legislature to revise statutes and readjust appropriations, not in an abuse of discretion by the state budget office.[102]

In a directly opposite ruling, the courts in Hawaii upheld the governor's impoundment of part of the general fund appropriations because of a shortfall in revenue. The ruling stressed that neither the constitution nor the statutes mandated the expenditures of an appropriation in whole or part.[103]

Rejecting this view, the New York State Court of Appeals ordered the governor of New York to release to local governments $7 million which he had impounded from a $26 million appropriation for local sewage treatment plants. In taking these actions, the governor had invoked the need for fiscal restraint and a balanced budget. This was not persuasive to the court, which stated flatly:

> ... under the state constitution, the executive possesses no express or inherent power—based upon its view of sound fiscal policy—to impound funds which have been appropriated by the Legislature.[104]

Part of the court's decisions turned on the language of the appropriation act, which provided "the moneys hereby appropriated shall be available and shall be apportioned as approved by the director of the budget." The court interpreted this to mean that the budget director could regulate the allocation of funds, but had no discretion to withhold them. Had the legislature chosen the word "may" instead of "shall," the results might have been different. This choice confronts future legislatures in determining the extent of discretion they wish to give governors and budget directors in implementing the budget.

≡ The legislative vetoes of proposed expenditures

The power of the executive to veto proposed legislation, including appropriation acts, is well known. What is relatively obscure is the power of legislatures to veto the use of appropriated funds or to give prior approval to the executive for the release of funds for contracts, construction projects and specified programs. Mainly a congressional prerogative, the legislative veto was challenged in the courts.

Starting in the 1930s, Congress exercised the veto power largely over reorganization plans proposed by the President. By the 1970s, this power of prior approval of executive actions had mushroomed to the point where Congress applied it to proposed projects, contracts, allotments, grants, loans, regulations, tariffs, defense policy, foreign policy, foreign trade and the use of atomic energy. Legislative vetoes became a significant instrument of budget implementation. Of some 500 veto provisions inserted in legislation from the 1930s to the mid-1980s, three-fourths originated in the 1970s alone. By 1985, some 200 statutory provisions for legislative veto were still extant.[105]

During the four-year period 1979–1982, new statutory provisions gave veto powers (without the need for presidential approval) to the following congressional entities:[106]

One house	24
Two houses	23
Committees	26
Other (committee chairman etc.)	5
	78

The growing use of the legislative veto as a major policymaking and budgetary tool received a blow in 1983 when the U.S. Supreme Court, in *Immigration and Naturalization Service v. Chadha*, struck down one-house vetoes of administrative actions as unconstitutional.[107] Later, it also rejected two-house vetoes or the use of concurrent resolutions as tantamount to vetoes.[108] The court majority held that the exercise of congressional vetoes by one or two houses without presidential approval constituted lawmaking and hence was unconstitutional. The court stressed that under Article I of the Constitution, laws could be passed only by both houses and presented to the president for approval or veto. Congress was still free to veto proposed administrative acts. But it could do it only through joint resolutions or bills subject to presidential approval.[109]

One of the central issues has been the impact of the *Chadha* decision and the related rulings on the role of Congress in budget implementation. Could one house of Congress continue to veto proposed deferrals of expenditures, as is provided in the impoundment control provisions of the Budget Act of 1974? Could both houses still turn down by joint resolution proposed rescissions of appropriations? In neither case did these actions require presidential approval. Could Congress still insist on prior approval of projects, grants, contracts, transfers of funds and the like before OMB, on behalf of the President, released funds? Could it, as in the past, exercise such veto powers through committees, subcommittees, committee chairmen, one house or two houses? Plainly, Congress concluded that the Court's decisions did not reject the use of such options as instruments of legislative control and oversight. In the sixteen months following *Chadha*, Congress relied on the legislative veto fifty-three times, mainly to reprogram the use of appropriated funds.[110]

Some examples highlight the continued potency of the legislative veto. In 1983 the President approved an appropriation bill that subjected the release of construction grants by the Environmental Protection Agency to prior committee approval, primarily the appropriations committees. The same act required the National Aeronautical and Space Administration (NASA) to get committee approval before authorizing the leasing or construction of facilities. A supplemental appropriations bill, also approved in 1983, compelled the Department of Interior and the Army Corps of Engineers to obtain committee approval before terminating specified programs and approving the payment of certain funds. In a continuing resolution providing stopgap funding, Congress prohibited the transfer of funds for foreign assistance between categories without prior concurrence by committees.[111]

Despite *Chadha*, then, the legislative veto still persists. This is not the result of congressional perversity, defiance of the courts, or a breakdown of the separation of powers. The fact is that, pragmatically, the legislative veto serves the needs of the President and Congress. In a complex society, Congress will continue to pass legislation, including appropriation acts, that confer broad discretion on the executive. At the same time, it insists on retaining control over the exercise of the discretion. One major means of control is the legislative veto. Deprived of this power, Congress could stud appropriation bills with line items instead of lump sums. It could refuse to delegate broad powers to administrative agencies. It could in legislation specify administrative activities in detail. These steps could lead to paralysis of the budgetary and administrative processes. The legislative veto avoids such deadlocks.[112]

Only a sprinking of cases illustrates the use of the veto by state legislatures. For example, the Supreme Judiciary Court of Massachusetts struck down a legislative veto of the hiring of new employees. The court regarded this as an encroachment of executive power.[113] In Montana, the Supreme Court held that the Legislative Finance Committee could not amend the budget. Only the full legislature or executive could do that.[114]

≡ The courts turn down major construction projects that conflict with other legislation

Even though funds have been appropriated for major construction projects, the courts, on occasion, have prevented the implementation of the projects because of conflict with other legislation. They have stopped the construction of dams, power plants, prisons and highways because the projects ran afoul of statutory standards for the protection of the environment, protection of endangered species and preservation of historic sites. Several cases underscore the courts' power.

In 1978, in the so-called snail darter case, the Supreme Court enjoined the Tennessee Valley Authority from spending funds for the construction of the Tellico Dam on the grounds that the appropriation conflicted with the Endangered Species Act which protected, among other wildlife, the snail darter, whose survival might be endangered.[115] It also took into account congressional rules which prohibited substantive amendments through appropriation acts and the lack of any clear intent by Congress to repeal the Endangered Species Act.[116]

After ten years of litigation, a federal appeals court in 1985 finally barred the construction of the Westway, a controversial multi-billion dollar highway project in New York City. The Court's ruling was based in large part on the failure of the Army Corps of Engineers to prepare an acceptable environmental impact statement as required by other statutes. The court was especially critical of the inadequate analyses by the Corps of the impact of the project on the survival of striped bass in the Hudson River.[117]

When Virginia attempted to build a prison with federal funds provided by the Law Enforcement Assistance Administration (LEAA), it ran into several legal challenges. A federal court of appeals ultimately found that the site selected for the project did not meet the standards of the National Environmental Policy Act and the National Historic Preservation Act.[118]

≡ The courts interpret the meaning of legislative intent in executive implementation of the budget

To what extent should a governor in implementing the budget follow non-statutory expressions of legislative intent? This issue surfaced in New York State when the fiscal committees of the legislature recommended the deletion of specific positions in their report on the governor's budget. In enacting the appropriation bills, however, the legislature eliminated many, but not all, the positions specified in the committees' report. Subsequent allotments by the budget office similarly cut only positions itemized in the appropriation act. A public interest group challenged the action in the state courts on the ground that the governor did not comply with legislative intent as reflected in the report of the fiscal committees. The court ruled that the committees' report was not legally binding and that the governor was free to authorize any expenditures approved by the legislature, the report notwithstanding. For the court, the appropriation act was the ultimate expression of legislative intent.[119]

THE COURTS REFEREE THE DISTRIBUTION OF INTERGOVERNMENTAL GRANTS

State and local governments depend on federal grants as a major source of revenue. In addition, local governments also count heavily on state assistance. The funds go directly to the governments for numerous programs and projects, and to individual beneficiaries, as in welfare programs. In the distribution of the grants, sharp conflicts have arisen between grantors, beneficiaries and would-be beneficiaries. In hundreds, if not thousands, of cases, the adversaries have turned to the courts for relief. The result has been the development of a formidable body of case law encompassing virtually every aspect of intergovernmental financing.[120]

In adjudicating the issues, the courts interpret the statutes authorizing the grants; determine, in some instances, the constitutionality of the grants; and look for compliance with across-the-board or so-called "cross-cutting" statutory provisions that affect all grants regardless of source. These requirements include standards for civil rights, anti-discrimination in employment, environmental protection, flood control, survival of endangered species, facilities for the disabled and preservation of historic sites.[121]

Several examples, in addition to cases previously cited, will illustrate the approach taken by the courts in ruling on eligibility for grants. In general, the courts have rejected the allocation of any grants that do not comply with the requirements in statutes authorizing the grants. A tale of three cities—Atlanta, Chicago, and Hartford—is revealing in this respect. In one financial move, Atlanta attempted to placate taxpayers and restless firemen. It used federal revenue sharing funds for a rebate to taxpayers for water and sewer charges and for salary increases for firemen. In *Matthews v. Mossell*, a federal district court ruled in 1973 that the rebate was not a statutory priority in the revenue sharing legislation, and hence was illegal. It therefore enjoined the mayor and city council from allocating federal funds for such purpose.[122]

Chicago also ran afoul of provisions in the revenue sharing act, which, among other things, prohibits discrimination in employment. The U.S. Department of Justice, black policemen and civil rights organizations sued in the federal court to enjoin Chicago from using federal revenue sharing funds for the Chicago police department on the ground that its employment policy discriminated against minority groups and women. Concurring with this position, the federal court of appeals found the city had violated the anti-discrimination provisions of the federal legislation in spending $135 million and enjoined the expenditures of any additional funds until it complied with the law.[123]

The Hartford case involved block grants for community development. In block grants, as in revenue sharing, state and local governments have a good deal of flexibility in contrast to categorical grants with rigid requirements. Yet, the exercise of such discretion must conform to statutory standards. The city of Hartford took this position when it argued in the federal district court that the Department of Housing and Urban Development should have allotted funds for community development to it rather than to seven adjoining suburban towns. The city claimed that the towns, in applying for funds, had not assessed the housing needs of low and moderate income groups as required by law. While the court agreed with Hartford, it gave the towns an opportunity to submit a revised application for grants instead of ordering a reallocation of funds to the city.[124]

Cases focusing on "cross-cutting" and constitutional provisions with regard to grants are legion. Yet, a small sample may capture their flavor. In *Dopico v. Goldschmidt*, a federal court of appeals in 1982 ordered federal, state and local governments to provide disabled individuals with access to mass transportation as required by the Rehabilitation Act of 1973. As a start, the court proposed the implementation of modest affirmative steps such as ramps for wheelchairs.[125] In 1982, the courts held Pennsylvania officials in contempt for failing to implement car inspection and maintenance programs to control pollution from car exhausts. The courts found that the state had violated the Clean Air Act Amendments of 1970 in administering a program funded in part by the federal government.[126]

In several cases, the courts have leaned on the equal protection clause of the Fourteenth Amendment to adjudicate conflicts in intergovernmental financing. Thus, in *Fullilove v. Klutzick*, the Supreme Court in 1980 turned aside challenges by state and local governments to the requirement that they set aside 10 percent of funds for federally financed public works projects for minority businesses.[127] Another case hinged on the rights of beneficiaries under the federal Comprehensive Employment and Training Act (CETA) designed to provide training and jobs for low income groups. The Act gave individuals no rights to employment. Yet, in *Hudson Valley Freedom Theater v. Heimbach*, the Supreme Court ruled in 1982 that under the Fourteenth Amendment and civil rights laws county officials could be sued by applicants for CETA funds if they were denied employment.[128]

In numerous cases cited in this section, state law has yielded to federal law. Despite lip service to state sovereignty and cooperative federalism, the federal courts have time and again asserted the supremacy of federal statutes. One of the most dramatic examples is *Garcia* on overtime pay. Among many other similar decisions is *North Carolina v. Califano*, in which the Supreme Court in 1978 upheld federal, rather than state, requirements for certification of need for new health care facilities as a prerequisite for federal assistance.[129]

THE COURTS RULE ON VOTER REFERENDA TO INCUR DEBT AND IMPLEMENT OTHER BUDGET POLICY

Public referenda on bond issues for capital construction and on other changes in budget policy are an integral part of the budget process in U.S. state and local governments. Such ultimate expressions of democratic rule would appear to be beyond the reach of the courts. Yet, on occasion, state courts, on constitutional grounds, have removed measures from the ballot, blocked their use and even nullified referenda after voter approval. From 1980 to 1984, the courts aborted ten referenda and initiatives covering a variety of issues.[130] Conversely, the courts have permitted state legislatures and governors to issue bonds for capital construction without a referendum despite constitutional requirements for voter approval.

Two cases in New Jersey and New York illustrate the courts' power to reject the results of public referenda. In 1978, the voters in New Jersey approved a $100 million bond issue for a variety of public works projects. Nevertheless, the state Supreme Court ruled in 1979 that the referendum was unconstitutional since the state constitution required bond issues to be devoted to a single purpose (for example, transportation) and not multiple purposes.[131] In New York State, the Court of Appeals came close to this position in 1977 when, on the eve of a general election, it refused to remove a $750 million bond issue from the ballot. In its decision it implied, however, that its action was dictated solely by time pressures and that the measure was suspect. Even if the voters approved the bond issue, the court hinted it was unconstitutional on the ground that it was not limited to a single work or purpose as mandated by the state constitution. The issue became moot, however, when the voters rejected the proposal by a large majority.[132]

On other budget issues, the courts have similarly turned down initiatives and referenda. For example, the highest court in Florida in 1984 removed from the ballot a measure that would have limited tax increases in state and local governments and would have required a referendum on revenues in excess of the proposed ceilings. Some $1.2 billion was involved. The court found that, contrary to the state constitution, the measure was not devoted to a "single subject" and was so broad as to be ambiguous.[133]

In California, the Supreme Court refused to give the voters an opportunity to act on an initiative calling for a balanced federal budget. Under the terms of the initiative, the legislature would be compelled to petition Congress for a constitutional convention that would adopt a constitutional amendment mandating a balanced budget. Legislators who refused to approve the petition would forfeit their salaries and other benefits. The court ruled that such compulsion on the legislature was unconstitutional since the state constitution envisaged that the legislature would use its best judgment on issues of public policy.[134]

The judicial position on the exercise of the initiative troubled at least one specialist who suggested that the decisions might "open justices to charges of arrogating to themselves the power to override legislation proposed by or enacted by the people . . . in the name of what?"[135] Presumably, those more sympathetic to the courts' views find that the courts acted in defense of specific constitutional provisions and would not be swayed by temporary voter majorities at odds with constitutions as interpreted by the courts.

One can find little trace of judicial activism, however, in cases involving "moral obligation" bonding. Time and again, state courts have avoided confrontation with governors and legislatures who, in seeming defiance of constitutions, have approved bond issues without voter referenda. In Wisconsin, for example, the legislature sidestepped the problem by creating a Housing Finance Authority to sell bonds for the construction of public and private housing. The Wisconsin Supreme Court ruled in 1973 that the bonds were revenue bonds and hence were not part of the state's debt. Constitutional restrictions, therefore, did not apply to them.[136] When a similar case reached the Court of Appeals in New York State, it refused to deal with the issue altogether on the ground that the plaintiffs had no standing to sue. The genesis of the case was voter disapproval of a bond issue in 1983 for the construction of prisons. Undaunted by this action, the legislature and governor designated a public authority, the Urban Development Corporation, to sell the bonds without another voter referendum. By taking refuge in dubious procedural grounds, the court avoided an interpretation of constitutional provisions on bond issues.[137]

No matter how debts are incurred, the courts generally protect the rights of holders of government bonds and notes. When New York City reached the verge of bankruptcy in 1975 and was unable to repay creditors about $5 billion in short-term notes due that year, the legislature and the governor approved a three-year moratorium on the repayment of the notes and gave creditors an opportunity to substitute their notes for longer-term bond issues at lower interest rates (Chapter 874 of the Laws of 1975). This was a holding action designed to restructure the finances of New York City by setting up the New York State Municipal Assistance Corporation to sell bonds for New York City and the Emergency Financial Control Board to monitor the city's budgets. Predictably, outraged creditors brought suit, claiming that the moratorium violated contractual obligations guaranteed by the federal and state constitutions. They won handily in the Court of Appeals in 1976, which overruled decisions of lower courts.[138] In a sense, though, it was a pyrrhic victory, since the Court of Appeals did not render its decision until one and a half years after the moratorium. This gave the state and city the time they needed to restore fiscal discipline in New York City.

Institutions and individuals who had purchased bonds from the Washington Public Power Supply System (WPPSS) were less fortunate. Because of the failure of WPPSS to complete two major projects, it stopped the payment of interest on bonds for the projects, and the value of the bonds dropped precipitously. Bondholders initiated a series of lawsuits involving the state, the federal government, many public and private utilities, and several banks and brokerage houses, with inconclusive results by the mid-1980s.[139]

THE COURTS RULE ON THE CONSTITUTIONALITY AND LEGALITY OF TAXES

Under federal and state constitutions in the United States, governments have concurrent taxing powers. The result is that nearly all levels of government impose income, corporation, sales, excise, gross receipts and energy taxes as well as a variety of user fees. Property taxes, however, are mainly the domain of local governments. In hundreds of cases over the years, taxpayers have challenged the constitutionality and legality of many of the taxes. In the process, federal and state courts have made some far-reaching decisions.[140]

In view of the plethora of judicial decisions, it is difficult to draw broad generalizations. One can, however, discern several trends. For example, federal courts have been vigilant under the commerce, supremacy and equal protection clauses in the U.S. Constitution in settling interstate conflicts and preventing states from imposing what it regarded as unfair tax burdens on non-residents. Thus, in a few states, the U.S. Supreme Court found unconstitutional a commuter tax levied against non-residents.[141] It declared invalid under the supremacy and commerce clauses a tax by Louisiana on natural gas distributed by pipeline companies to other states.[142] On the other hand, the Supreme Court approved a severance tax on coal by Montana, even though about 90 percent of the coal was shipped outside the state. In the case at issue, it found that residents and non-residents had similar tax burdens.[143] The Supreme Court also upheld a West Virginia wholesale gross receipts tax that the plaintiff charged interfered with interstate commerce.[144] But it refused to go along with a state tax in Hawaii that discriminated against products of other states in favor of local products.[145]

The U.S. Supreme Court has also adjudicated the legality of user fees that are now rising in popularity as a result of tax and expenditure limits. Should the fees for services or regulation be based on the cost to the government or the benefits to licensees and other recipients of governmental services? In *National Cable Television v. the Federal Communications Commission*, the Supreme Court held in 1976 that the FCC should base its fees on governmental costs, and not on the value of the license.[146] In *Federal Power Commission v. New England Power Co.*, the Supreme Court decreed in 1974 that FPC charges should be related to service given to a specific "identifiable recipient [who] derives a special benefit."[147]

For their part, state courts have adjudicated thousands of cases involving state and local taxes. Two of the most hotly contested issues have been the equity of local property taxation and property tax exemptions. Several major cases in Massachusetts, New York and other states illustrate the courts' concern about inadequate assessment practices, the lack of uniformity in valuation of property and the failure to assess property at full market value.[148] Cases on property tax exemptions for religious, educational, charitable, non-profit and art organizations are also legion. In the main, state courts throughout the country have upheld such exemptions.[149]

In addition to property taxes, the courts in various states have ruled on the validity of a differential tax on soft drinks; the equity of franchise taxes; and the collection of sales taxes based on estimates rather than actual receipts.[150]

One of the most controversial issues in taxation is so-called reciprocal immunity, whereby the federal government does not tax interest on municipal bonds and state and local governments don't tax interest on federal securities. While constitutional scholars disagree on the validity and impact of the doctrine of reciprocal immunity, it was more or less honored until the approval of the Tax Reform Act of 1986. For the first time, the Act set up categories of municipal bonds. Some continue to enjoy tax exemption on interest. For others, interest is taxable in whole or part. For still others, the interest is considered to be income possibly subject to the alternative minimum tax. In August 1987, several state and local governments and public interest groups challenged the constitutionality of the Act and claimed it violated the Tenth Amendment and constitutional guarantees of federalism. According to the plaintiffs, Congress asserted the right to tax interest paid by state and local governments while prohibiting state and local governments from taxing interest paid by the federal government.

In two major decision the federal courts virtually threw out the century-old doctrine of reciprocal immunity, according to the National Governor's Association. The Supreme Court ruled in *South Carolina v. Baker* that interest earned on unregistered municipal bonds is subject to taxation. In *Government Finance Officers Association et al. v. Baker* a U.S. District Court failed to rule on the constitutionality of the applicability of the alternative minimum tax (an integral part of the Tax Reform Act) to interest earned on state and local bonds.[151] By limiting the use of tax exempt bonds the decisions will raise the borrowing costs of state and local governments. Investors will insist on higher interest to compensate them for additional taxes.

THE COURTS OVERSEE THE BUDGET PROCESS

The courts have intervened in the budget process itself, as is evident from the previous discussion of budget formulation and implementation. Extending their reach, the courts have ruled on the requirements of governors to submit balanced budgets; the reduction of federal deficits; the format of the executive budget; the scope and format of appropriation bills; the exercise of item veto powers by the governors; and the funding of public authorities. In the volume of litigation on the budget process, New York State is second only to the federal government. While occasional cases in other states touch on budgetary systems and procedures, none come close to New York State in the number of decisions, which run into the dozens. This may foreshadow developments in other states and in the federal government as frustrated citizens and legislators seek to revise constitutions and statutes in order to control budgets. Once these changes occur, the cycle of litigation will begin with the courts called upon to interpret the new provisions.

≡ Submission and maintenance of a balanced budget

Like other governors, the governor of New York State must submit a balanced budget after taking into account estimated revenues and expenditures. A plaintiff argued, however, that it was unconstitutional to include estimated proceeds from tax and revenue anticipation notes in the financial plan. Being "iffy," they could not be used to balance the budget. Without coming to grips with this issue, the Court of Appeals approved the estimates as long as they were not "dishonest." Only when they were deliberately contrived to balance an unbalanced budget would they be unconstitutional. It is somewhat breathtaking to find courts scrutinizing revenue estimates for evidence of questionable manipulation.[152] The same court agreed in another case that the constitution required the governor to propose a balanced budget. But in the course of budget implementation, he is not compelled to keep the budget in balance. Therefore, he could not impound funds by citing the need to maintain a balanced budget.[153]

For the first time, federal courts dealt with the issue of balanced budgets after the passage of the Balanced Budget and Emergency Deficit Control Act of 1985 (PL 99-177) cited above. Among other things, the Act, as noted, mandates a phased reduction of federal deficits until the budget is balanced by 1991. A major participant in the process is the Comptroller General, who advises the President (after consultation with OMB and CBO) on the amounts that should be cut to meet the annual targets in the legislation. A three-judge district court ruled in 1986 that the Comptroller's role was unconstitutional and violated the separation of powers. Since the Comptroller General could be removed by Congress, it was "constitutionally improper" for an official of Congress to exercise an executive function of reporting expenditure cuts to the President. The court agreed, however, to stay its order pending an appeal to the U.S. Supreme Court. The latter went along with the decision.[154]

A major case in Mississippi also turned on the separation of powers.

In 1983 the Mississippi Supreme Court declared unconstitutional, among other issues, the execution of the budget by an executive-legislative Commission on Budget and Accounting. This was an unconstitutional violation of separation of powers. As a result two separate bodies were created—one dominated by the governor, and the other by the legislature.[155]

≡ The scope and format of appropriation bills

One of the major conflicts among state governments centered on the role of the legislature in appropriating federal funds. Many governors regarded the allotment of federal funds as an executive prerogative and rejected any legislative participation in the process. In settling this legislative-executive confrontation, several state courts took contradictory positions.[156] Now that nearly all state legislatures appropriate federal funds, the issue is moot.

An especially thorny problem in New York State with national implications is the format of the appropriation bill. Both governors and legislatures recognize the that this is not a mere technical issue, since the form of the appropriation bill determines the extent of legislative and executive control of the budget. Should the appropriation bill be itemized, as is required by constitutions in New York and other states? If so, what is the meaning of "itemization"? Does the growing use of lump sums in appropriation bills violate constitutional constraints?

After the 1969 session of the New York State Legislature, three legislators raised these questions and sought a court order declaring the appropriations unconstitutional in at least two respects: (1) the use of lump sums for general purposes did not constitute itemization required by the constitution, and (2) the power of the budget director to transfer funds between lump sums for programs negated legislative action. While a lower court ruled in favor of the legislators, the Court of Appeals sidestepped the issue on the ground that the plaintiffs had no standing to sue. On the other hand, it warned that lump sum appropriations should not be so broad as to nullify attempts by the legislature to reduce items.[157]

Finally, in two telling decisions, the Court of Appeals rejected attacks on lump sum appropriations. In *Hidley v. Rockefeller*, the Court asserted that critics are on weak ground in attacking lump sum appropriations as skimpy and inadequate. Appropriation bills don't stand by themselves. They should be read together with the executive budget, which runs to nearly 1,000 pages and is crammed with detailed information on expenditures and revenues. While budgets and appropriation acts are not exempt from "judicial scrutiny and review," the degree of itemization is a political issue that should be negotiated by the legislative and executive branches. The

Court reminded the legislature that it has the political and legal power to reject lump sum appropriations and budget bills.[158]

Taking a similar approach in *Saxton v. Carey*, the Court found that the appropriation bills were sufficiently itemized in a 1977-78 general fund budget exceeding $11.1 billion. A legislature dissatisfied with the appropriation bills could reject them or reduce them. It could insert restrictive language in the bills. It could not, however, substitute highly itemized appropriations for lump sum appropriations proposed by the governor. Its only recourse was to add new itemized appropriations to the governor's budget bills. In that event, the governor could exercise a line item veto subject to a legislative override of the veto.[159]

In Maryland, the highest court concurred with much of this reasoning. In *Bayne v. Secretary of State*, it approved the use of restrictive language in appropriation bills proposed by the governor as a means of controlling expenditures. The legislature could reject the restrictions; it could add its own. But it could not change the governor's wording.[160]

≡ Gubernatorial exercise of line item vetoes

So firmly implanted in most state constitutions is the governor's power to exercise line item vetoes over appropriations that legal attacks on this authority have been infrequent. Any challenges have been rejected by the courts. For example, in *Kleczka and Shabaz v. Conta*, the Wisconsin Supreme Court categorically upheld the item veto.[161]

≡ Funding public authorities and government corporations

State legislatures have been reluctant to encompass in the appropriation process the expenditures of public authorities and government corporations. Through appropriations, they have loaned funds to authorities, subsidized the weaker ones and bailed out those in financial distress. Nevertheless, they have preferred to keep them "off-budget" and "off-appropriations" on the ground that they are self-sustaining autonomous entities. In several cases in New York and other states, the courts have gone along with this position. For example, in 1971 the New York State Court of Appeals rejected the contention that the Metropolitan Transportation Authority, which manages the subway, bus system and commuter railroads in New York City, could not disburse revenues without a specific legislative appropriation. The Court decreed that the Authority's revenues did not constitute a fund subject to constitutional control by the state.[162] Whether this constitutes legal hair-splitting in view of heavy subsidies by the state and city is an arguable issue.

THE EXPLOSION OF COSTLY TORT SUITS AGAINST FEDERAL, STATE AND LOCAL GOVERNMENTS

A series of court decisions has led to an explosion of civil liability suits against federal, state and local governments for torts (or civil wrongs) committed by the governments or their employees. As a result, the scope of liability has broadened, monetary awards with a serious impact on budgets have escalated, and insurance rates have become so costly as to be prohibitive for many local governments.[163]

This is a far cry from the days when the federal and state governments, as sovereign bodies, enjoyed immunity from tort suits and local governments benefited from limited immunity. Several key court cases and legislation chipped away at that immunity. The federal Tort Claims Act of 1970 (28 U.S.C. 2674) authorizes individuals to sue the federal government for money damages arising out of common law torts. Federal officials are individually immune from suits for common law torts, provided (1) they act within the scope of their official duties, and (2) they do not violate the constitutional rights of citizens. Going further, the U.S. Supreme Court ruled in 1988 that all federal employees could be held personally responsible for certain common law torts. The House Committee on the Judiciary attempted to upset this decision by introducing legislation that would make the federal government the sole defendant.[164]

In general, state governments may not be sued without their consent even for alleged violations of the post–Civil War Civil Rights Act of 1871 (especially section 1983 of U.S.C. 42). The courts have ruled so because of the states' sovereign immunity under the Eleventh Amendment of the Constitution.[165] In self-denying legislation, nearly all state governments have waived their immunity in whole or part and virtually invited the financial burden of expanded tort liability.[166]

But it is local governments that are practically defenseless against the flow of thousands of tort suits as a result of four critical court decisions.[167] In *Monell v. the Department of Social Services of the City of New York*, the U.S. Supreme Court in 1978 stripped local governments of any sovereign immunity against civil litigation by injured parties.[168] Going further in *Owen v. City of Independence, Missouri* and in *Maine v. Thiboutot* in 1980, it held local governments responsible for violations of the Constitution and federal statutes.[169] As Justice Powell of the Court's minority put it, municipal governments were now given the impossible task of predicting the course of constitutional law if they want to avoid heavy money damages.[170] The Supreme Court based its decisions on the Civil Rights Act of 1871 and reversed an earlier ruling in *Monroe v. Pape* in 1961, which had virtually exempted municipal governments from the Act.[171] Finally, in 1986, in *Pembaur v. the City of Cincinnati*, the Supreme Court held that municipalities were liable for violating constitutional rights on the basis of a single decision by an employee, even though the decision might have been contrary to official policy.[172] In 1988, however, it backtracked somewhat from this decision by making it more difficult for victims of alleged unconstitutional actions by local officials to win damages.[173]

Beginning in 1984, state and local governments turned to Congress and state legislatures for relief. They urged Congress to adopt the following measures:

1. Tighten up the rules of liability under Section 1983 of the Civil Rights Act to limit their applicability solely to constitutional issues.

2. Eliminate the costly doctrine of "joint and several liability" under which a jurisdiction found to be 5 percent at fault could be held liable for 100 percent of the damages.

3. Establish a federal indemnification program in environmental control and pollution control to avoid suits against state and local governments.

4. Establish national minimum standards for insurance policies governing policy cancellations; filing of rates with state governments; availability of loss data; insurance rates based on experience; and federal reinsurance to guarantee availability of insurance.

5. Limit federal intervention in state laws. State governments should be free to cap attorneys' fees, limit awards, and establish their own standards for product liability and other liability. These policies would hold for state courts. Federal policies should govern federal courts.[174]

On their part, state governments were considering changes to limit liability for damages solely to the percent of wrongdoing attributable to state and local governments; cap previously unlimited damage awards; bar punitive damage awards; restrict legal fees; define activities for which states are liable and set liability ceilings; initiate risk management programs; initiate state liability insurance coverage (in effect in eight states); and sponsor municipal insurance pools (in effect in twenty-three states). In 1988, eight states joined forces in an antitrust suit against thirty-one insurance companies and other insurance groups. They charged the industry with a boycott of certain types of general liability insurance, conspiracy to eliminate coverage for environmental damages, and collusion to raise premiums.[175]

Rather than settling controversies, the court decisions on tort liability have opened the floodgates to thousands of cases with a serious budgetary impact. In the impasse that resulted, only a political solution appeared to be feasible, but that required a consensus on the part of contending interest groups. By 1988 none was in sight—only marginal adjustments by state and local governments.

SHOULD THE "JUDICIAL POWER OF THE PURSE" BE CURBED?

Whether chief executives and legislatures like it or not, they now share budgetmaking powers with the courts. Only in the last few years have researchers begun to document the impact of judicial decisions on budgets. And, indeed, it has been dramatic, running into billions of dollars.[176] The broad sweep of court decrees has also resulted in major policy changes in governmental programs and projects.

As critics of judicial activism see it, the courts are usurping the policymaking and budgeting prerogatives of chief executives and legislatures. They concede that courts traditionally have protected individual rights, and, of necessity, have interpreted constitutions, statutes, regulations and executive orders. To that extent they engage in policymaking. The issue, however, is not whether they make policy, but whether they should supplant the policy choices of elected officials by becoming a super-legislature.[177] Not content with responding to grievances, the courts, in the view of the critics, have moved into problem solving, thus encroaching on the powers of executives and legislatures.[178] It is one thing to protect procedural safeguards such as due process. It is another to force new substantive policy requirements on governments.[179] The effect of decisions by an "imperial judiciary" has been to erode budgeting as a tool of popular control and to curb the authority and discretion of administrators.[180]

Another line of attack on judicial zeal turns on the piecemeal nature of judicial decisions. Unlike elected officials, courts set no overall fiscal and programmatic priorities. They decide issues only on an ad hoc basis, depending on the plaintiffs who get to them first. Courts do not initiate policy. They act solely on the basis of complaints. Typically, well-organized groups who are dissatisfied with legislative and administrative decisions try to gain in the courts what they lose in the political process.[181] By taking a case-by-case approach, the courts of necessity limit their options, ignore the interrelationships of programs and budgets and fail to appreciate the complexity of the issues they adjudicate. Focusing on individual cases, the courts are indifferent to the overall effect of their decisions on taxpayers and budgets.[182] As a result, the critics argue, the courts, in what is a zerosum game, have forced redistributive budget policies on state and local governments. Compelled by judicial decrees to increase expenditures for some programs, governments have reduced them for others.[183]

By their training and experience as lawyers, judges are generalists and not specialists. They are therefore, it is charged, ill-equipped to deal with the complex social problems before them. For data and interpretation of the problems, they rely on the litigants. They give a good deal of weight to theoretical knowledge and the tentative findings of social scientists which, at best, are educated guesses subject to change.[184] Yet, the uncertain state of knowledge does not deter the courts from setting standards and policies in a variety of fields. Politically insulated, they take little risk in imposing their policy preferences on governments.

No longer is a court decision a one-time event. The courts maintain jurisdiction over cases until the problems are solved to their satisfaction. To assure compliance with their decrees, they have established their own bureaucracies: masters, monitors, referees, ombudsmen and human rights committees.[185] In extreme situations, they supervise programs directly. This type of direct intervention, the critics charge, is beyond the capacity of the courts.[186]

Despite the many naysayers who deplore judicial intervention in the operation of schools, prisons, mental hospitals and institutions for the mentally retarded, the courts have no lack of defenders. Supporters see them as the only means of protecting the constitutional rights of individuals. Only intolerable conditions and urgent needs bring plaintiffs to the courts. The court neither encourage nor initiate such litigation. Frequently, the question before the courts is not "who should do it," but whether anything should be done at all.[187] When the courts act, they exercise their authority reluctantly because no other remedies exist.

Courts generally intervene on three grounds: the failure of officials to comply with the constitutions and laws; the reluctance of elected officials to act on unpopular measures; and the need to interpret broad and ambiguous statutory measures.[188] Judge Frank M. Johnson, Jr., whose decisions had led to unprecedented reforms in prisons, mental hospitals and schools for the mentally retarded blames the defaults of elected officials for judicial activism:

> On far too many occasions the intransigent and unremitting opposition of state officials who have neglected or refused to correct unconstitutional or unlawful state policies and practices has necessitated federal intervention to enforce the law.[189]

When legislatures fail to act on controversial policies, the courts, in the view of their defenders, stand ready in the American constitutional system to fill the breach. Unwillingly, but necessarily, they become mediators and buffers between conflicting interests.[190] Lacking a consensus on policy, legislatures at times take refuge in general and fuzzy statutory language in order to pass legislation. Inevitably, the courts are called upon to interpret the arcane terminology.[191]

Those who support judicial intervention have little patience with the argument that the courts act on the basis of inadequate and tentative data. First, they emphasize that, in many cases, both parties concur with the same set of facts. Second, they applaud the adversary process as a means of bringing out all the critical information and subjecting it to close examination.

Even in the most complex areas, expert witnesses can be used. And the courts have shown a good deal of zeal, flexibility and impartiality in ferreting out all the essential data.[192]

Finally, the activists argue that courts are as much creatures of elected officials as they are of constitutions. Disgruntled legislators and executives can narrow the jurisdiction of courts. Presidents and governors can and do approve judges sympathetic to their ideological bent. If legislatures are unhappy about judicial interpretations of statutes, they can change the legislation. Alternatively, they could attempt to avoid ambiguity in statutory language in the first place.[193] The worst possible course of action is to challenge the legitimacy of the courts' role. This could result in a serious undermining of the protection of individual rights.[194]

In the light of the strong views held by the proponents and opponents of judicial activism, what are the prospects of limiting the "judicial power of the purse"? Neither conservative nor liberal courts demonstrate any discernible self-restraint in this regard when constitutional issues are at stake. During the late 1930s, the Roosevelt administration attempted unsuccessfully to curb the Supreme Court. In the 1960s and 1970s, the rulings of the Warren Court (with Earl Warren as chief justice) drew the ire of conservative critics. Yet, a relatively conservative court, the Burger Court (headed by Warren Burger in the 1970s and 1980s), showed no signs of restraining the far-reaching decisions of the lower courts.[195] In fact, its decisions, as in the Garcia Case (applying the Fair Labor Standards Act to state and local governments), show as much disregard for the impact of court decrees on budgets as any other rulings.

Many of the decisions with major fiscal implications, including consent decrees, were rulings of lower federal courts. At any point, state and local governments could have appealed them to the Supreme Court. That they refrained from doing so suggests that the court orders created a climate for change which elected officials were reluctant to resist. In fact, nearly all of the major court decisions, even those that went against the plaintiffs, served as catalysts for major shifts in budgets, programs and policy. The mere threat of court action also had this effect. Both actual and potential litigation brought a sense of urgency to legislative deliberations, and apparently executives and legislatures act most decisively only in an atmosphere of real or perceived crisis. Undoubtedly, these developments will continue as disadvantaged and advocacy groups turn to the courts for relief denied to them in the political arena.

Federal and state governments are inviting more, rather than less, judicial intervention by rewriting constitutions and statutes to set tax and expenditure limits and mandate balanced budgets. What they fail to achieve by political consensus they hope to gain by new statutory formulas. This opens the way for still more court rulings as litigants challenge or seek interpretations of the legal provisions. Every sign suggests that the courts will also continue to substitute their views for vague, elusive and ambiguous statutory language. To keep them at arm's length, legislatures and executives would have to take an unequivocal stand on controversial issues in authorizing statutes and appropriation acts. This may be asking too much of the political process in this country. Any policy vacuum left by elected officials will be filled by the courts.

In the foreseeable future, then, courts will continue to participate in budget decision-making in the United States. Policymakers and budgeteers at all levels of government will have to reckon with the impact of judicial decrees. This has important implications for the process of policy development, budget formulation and implementation. No planning, no analysis of major programs and projects can take place without an eye to potential litigation. For budgeteers and administrators, skills in fiscal, program, policy and management analysis are not enough. Still another string is needed in their bow-legal analysis.

≡ 3 THE LEVERAGE OF THE BUDGET PROCESS TO IMPROVE GOVERNMENTAL MANAGEMENT

From the earliest days of the executive budget system, especially in the United States, the budget process has been a major means of pressuring departments to improve the management of their programs and projects.[1] As used here, management improvement encompasses the efficiency, economy, effectiveness, productivity, impact and results of governmental activities.[2] The budget process focuses systematically on all of these issues. In fact, no other decision-making system offers as many opportunities to identify administrative failings and to take corrective action. The power of the purse, if exercised, can be a formidable weapon to alter organizational structures, operating systems, programs and policies.

Three major developments fostered the close relationship between budgeting and management improvement to the point that they are opposite sides of the same coin. First, the landmark Budget and Accounting Act of 1921 lodged responsibility for government-wide administrative improvements in the Bureau of the Budget (BOB), the precursor of OMB.[3] Second, the Brownlow Committee Report of 1937, which was instrumental in shaping the Executive Office of the President (EOP), took a strong position that BOB was the logical staff agency for stimulating management improvement.[4] Third, after Congress in 1939 approved the creation of EOP, with BOB one of its major constituent units, President Roosevelt issued Executive Order 8248, which spelled out BOB's responsibilities for management improvement:

> Conduct research in the development of improved plans of administrative management and . . . advise the executive departments and agencies of government with respect to improved administrative organization and practice . . . .

> Aid the President to bring about more efficient and economical conduct of government service . . . .

> Keep the President informed of the progress of activities by agencies of the Government with respect to work proposed, work actually initiated and work completed, together with the relative timing of work between the several agencies of the Government; all to the end that the monies appropriated by Congress may be expended in the most economical manner possible with the least possible overlapping and duplication of effort.[5]

With this charter, BOB institutionalized its management functions in a Division of Administrative Management, headed by Donald C. Stone. So creative and influential were the activities of this Division that they stimulated management improvement among federal agencies, state governments and municipalities. In most cases, management improvement programs were closely intertwined with the budget process.

While other countries were also influenced by the BOB model, they placed less emphasis on the linkage between budgeting and management improvement. Several countries established separate offices of management services or administrative reform that were coequal with the budget agency.

In the five decades that followed the creation of the Administrative Management Division, the role of budget offices in management improvement changed continuously, depending on the management values, styles and priorities of presidents, governors, mayors and budget directors. From the 1940s through the 1950s, the stress was on operational efficiency, with policy development and program evaluation secondary factors. In the 1960s, the implementation of the Great Society programs raised issues as to their effectiveness as well as the capacity of federal, state and local governments to coordinate and conduct intergovernmental activities. As a result, program evaluation and policy coordination dominated the agenda for management improvement.[6] In the wake of the recessions of the 1970s and early 1980s, revenue shortfalls and deficits, the emphasis in management improvement once again shifted to efficiency, cost reduction, productivity, automation, tight financial management and the elimination of "waste." This was coupled with the thrust of the Reagan administration to reduce the size of government and "privatize" selected activities.

As a result of these developments, central budget offices in the federal and state governments and large cities and counties carry on, in varying degree, the following management activities:

1. Promote management improvement programs in operating agencies.
2. Monitor the results of such programs.
3. Conduct surveys of urgent organizational, systems and policy problems.
4. Develop organizational plans and plans of operation.
5. Evaluate the efficiency and effectiveness of programs and projects.
6. Participate in the development of new programs and policies.
7. Develop methods of measuring work and productivity.
8. Participate with the operating agencies in establishing performance standards based on work and productivity measurement.
9. Analyze staff utilization.
10. Foster and monitor the use of computer systems.
11. Further the development of management information systems.
12. Eliminate unnecessary paperwork.
13. Participate in the solution of intergovernmental problems.
14. Reduce the burden of unnecessary regulations affecting private businesses, individuals and other governmental levels (primarily an OMB function).
15. Tighten and reduce the cost of administrative support activities such as the management of space, travel, vehicles, printing and reproduction, procurement and office machines and equipment.
16. Identify governmental activities that should be farmed out to the private sector (privatization).
17. Improve financial management in collaboration with comptrollers' and treasurers' offices (especially accounting systems, cash management and debt management.)

No one budget office can possibly conduct this formidable array of activities by itself. To be effective it must work closely with the operating departments and with other central staff agencies such as offices of comptrollers, accountants, auditors, administrative services and personnel management. Above all, it depends on the management capability of the operating departments, for, in the final analysis, management improvement is the responsibility of each agency. At best, central budget offices can stimulate, goad and even inspire agencies to strengthen their programs, operating systems and organizational structures. They can suggest priorities and orchestrate government-wide efforts to improve management. They can persuade agency heads to establish strong offices of management and program analysis. Ultimately, however, a management improvement program is no better than the combined efforts of individual agencies.

Keeping this framework in mind, this section discusses the role and strategies of central budget offices in effecting management improvements; assesses the results of management improvement programs; analyzes the extent to which management improvement is integrated with the budget process; considers the impact of other agencies on management improvement, especially independent auditors and one-time studies by external groups such as Hoover Commissions; and weighs proposals to entrust management improvement to agencies other than budget offices. It deals separately with the experiences of the federal, state and local governments in the United States and, finally, highlights some relevant approaches taken by other countries.

THE FIFTY-YEAR BATTLE OF THE FEDERAL GOVERNMENT TO IMPROVE MANAGEMENT VIA THE BUDGET PROCESS

Over nearly fifty years, beginning in 1939, each administration in the federal government attempted to strengthen management in accordance with its own needs, political outlook, management orientation and economic and non-economic values. Appreciating the fact that management improvement can't be left to happenstance, presidents have searched for ways to get operating agencies to effect necessary changes systematically. For most presidents, although not all, the focal point for management improvement was BOB/OMB. The following quick canvass outlines the major management themes of each administration and the relationship between the management efforts and the budget process.

≡ The Roosevelt Administration lays the foundation
   for management improvement programs (1939–1945)

Policies to combat the Depression and the conduct of World War II were central to all the activities of the Roosevelt administration and of course the newly established Division of Administrative Management. During the war, the management group won its spurs by participating in the establishment of new war agencies and solving problems of coordination among them. It conducted organization and systems studies of individual agencies and problems common to all agencies. Later, it fostered improved management through a series of pamphlets and bulletins, still relevant, on management surveys, work measurement, production planning and control and the like. It encouraged the development and strengthening of organization and management units in the federal agencies and worked closely with them in management surveys. The Division participated in major budgetary decisions, although the responsibility for recommendations lay with the budget examining units.[7]

Despite the successes of the Division (or possibly because of them), schisms developed between it and the budget examination units. In later administrations, the relationship between budget examiners and specialized units such as management units and program evaluation units turned out to be a chronic problem. If these units were isolated from the budget process, they would have little impact on the operating agencies. If they participated in budget decisionmaking, they seemingly usurped the prerogatives of budget examiners.[8] Only strong and gifted budget directors could harmonize the efforts of the various specialists in the central budget office.

≡ President Truman launches the first systematic and sustained program of management improvement (1949–1951)

For President Truman, like President Roosevelt, management improvement via the budget process was an article of faith. In 1949, he launched the first systematic management improvement program by establishing an Advisory Committee on Management Improvement and directing the heads of all agencies to make periodic and systematic appraisals of their operations. He called upon BOB to review the agency plans, to assist them in improving their operations and to report to him on the progress and results achieved.[9]

In 1950, the Bureau of the Budget issued a precedent-making directive to all agencies—Circular No. A-8, "Agency Responsibilities under the President's Management Improvement Program." The circular called upon the agencies to establish a formal management improvement program by identifying major problem areas in organization, operations, policies and procedures; mounting projects to correct these problems; and reporting annually to BOB on the projects underway and the results accomplished. To make the management improvement program relevant for the budget process, agencies were asked to incorporate the management improvement reports in their regular budget submissions. The management group in BOB worked closely with the agencies in identifying opportunities for improvement and cost reduction, participating in some projects, interchanging information on workable management techniques and analyzing the management improvement reports. Through the management improvement program, it appeared to be possible for a small cadre of management specialists in BOB to spread its expertise throughout the entire bureaucracy.

The program had the strong support of the first Hoover Commission

on Government Organization (1947–1949). The Commission was especially
helpful in urging Congress to approve the Budget and Accounting Procedures Act of 1950, which provided the following statutory base for a continuing management improvement program:

> The President, through the Director of the Bureau of the Budget, is
> authorized and directed to evaluate and develop improved plans for the
> organization, coordination and management of the executive branch of
> the government with a view to efficient and economical service.[11]

≡ The Eisenhower Administration downgrades the role of a central management unit (1952–1959)

Upon taking office, the Eisenhower administration reviewed its options
in management improvement, which all later administrations also faced:
(1) centralize the responsibilities for management improvement in budget
examination units rather than in specialized units dealing with management issues across-the-board; (2) concentrate on specific ad hoc problems
rather than on management improvement programs in all agencies; and
(3) utilize external bodies for advice on management improvement. On all
three issues, the administration reversed the course of the Truman and
Roosevelt administrations. It dismantled the formal and systematic management improvement program. It decided that the focus on management
problems should be part of the normal process of budgetary review without the intervention of a specialized staff such as the Administrative Management Division.[12] Hence, it established a staff unit on management and
organization in BOB for occasional studies, assistance in program development and participation in a joint financial management improvement
program with GAO and the Treasury. Finally, for advice on reorganization and major systems and policy changes, the President looked to his
Committee on Government Reorganization, composed of Nelson A. Rockefeller, Arthur Flemming and Milton Eisenhower, and to the second Hoover
Commission.[13]

The effect of these changes was to diminish the role of BOB in management improvement, with a marked deterioration, in the view of the second Hoover Commission, of both the managerial and budgeting functions
of BOB. Hence, the Commission recommended a renewed stress on management improvement and an expansion of the management staff.[14] In the
waning days of the Eisenhower administration, in 1959, the Budget Director concluded that more emphasis should be placed on Bureau leadership in
management improvement throughout the executive branch. He was therefore instrumental in appointing an Interagency Advisory Council on Management Improvement to advise the Bureau on management activities.[15]

≡ The Kennedy Administration reemphasizes management improvement despite the president's lack of interest (1960–1963)

Whatever the budget office does, including management improvement, reflects the personal style of the president as well as the interests of the budget director. This was as true of President Kennedy, who assumed office in 1960, as his predecessors. Hess noted Kennedy's disinterest in questions of management, and Sorensen commented that Kennedy "was always more interested in policy than administration."[16] Nevertheless, a budget director with a strong management orientation can turn a president around. During the short-lived Kennedy administration, BOB created a Management Services Branch as a focal point for management improvement, expanded its staff, and also established a central Automatic Data Processing Section to advise agencies and BOB on computer systems and policies. At the same time, it initiated its own version of a systematic management improvement program with two major components: (1) an inventory of management accomplishments and opportunities for future improvements, and (2) a productivity improvement program, which was to prove influential during the next twenty-five years.

In effect, the "inventory" succeeded the management improvement reporting system of the Truman administration. But the aim was the same — to disseminate information about successful management practices and to lay the basis for joint Budget Bureau–agency studies on a priority basis. The annual inventory summarized major improvements that had taken place in twenty-five agencies.[17] What makes the published inventory especially noteworthy is that it was the first significant attempt at the federal level to publicize management improvements in a budget document.

The productivity program was similar to the formal management improvement program of the Truman administration, although it sported a new label: "Improving Manpower Controls and Utilization in the Executive Branch." Launched by President Kennedy in October 1962, the program had the following major components:

1. The submission by each agency to the Bureau of the Budget of an "over-all program for manpower control and utilization."
2. Incorporation of detailed employment plans, based on productivity increases, in the budget requests submitted by the agencies.
3. "A systematic program of manpower inspections and reviews" conducted jointly by the Bureau of the Budget, the Civil Service Commission and the agencies, with BOB assuming leadership of the project. The President directed that the inspections, on a selective basis, should focus on those areas "where the most significant problems and potential savings exist."

4. Keeping the President informed of the findings, recommendations, and actions taken.
5. Research and experimentation, under the leadership of BOB, in methods of measuring over-all agency productivity as a basis for improved manpower control.[18]

≡ The Johnson Administration focuses on cost reduction and intergovernmental problems (1963–1969)

Alarmed by the growing cost of social programs and seemingly intractable problems of coordinating these programs among federal agencies and among federal, state and local governments, the Johnson administration devised its own management improvement program, with BOB once again the spearhead. In October 1965, the President launched a cost reduction program which he termed the "war on waste."[19] While the rhetoric was different, the approach was similar to the methods employed by previous administrations. In his "new comprehensive and formal cost reduction program," the President directed the head of each department and agency to:

☐ . . . assume "direct supervision" of the program;
☐ . . . "establish specific dollar cost reduction goals";
☐ . . . review programs and operations systematically and periodically to determine relative priorities;
☐ . . . "identify roadblocks to cost reduction which may require legislative action or cooperation from other agencies";
☐ . . . "subject every major proposed expenditure to *searching scrutiny* [italics mine] in terms of cost and benefits";
☐ . . . verify reported savings through independent means;
☐ . . . "recommend high-priority uses of savings achieved";
☐ . . . report periodically results achieved to the President through the Bureau of the Budget.[20]

To implement the program, BOB issued in March 1965 the influential government-wide Circular A-44, "Cost Reduction and Management Improvement in Government Operations." Replacing an earlier circular issued by BOB during the Kennedy administration, the revised circular focused on the themes of the Johnson administration. By September 1 of each year, the head of each agency was to report to the President through the Director of BOB on cost reduction goals for the current and following years, together with estimated man-year and dollar savings. This was to be followed by semi-annual reports on progress in achieving targets. BOB stressed its availability to advise agencies on their management improvement and cost reduction programs and to serve as a clearinghouse to exchange management techniques. Where an agency lacked the resources to undertake management studies, BOB stood ready to provide funds for consultants. BOB also announced "a systematic program of agency management and manpower reviews of areas with the most significant problems and greatest potential savings." These reviews would be conducted jointly with the Civil Service Commission and the agency concerned.[21]

While the President boasted about the results of the cost reduction program in terms of savings and a variety of management improvements, increasing doubts arose about the capacity of BOB to deal with complex interagency and intergovernmental problems. As a defensive move, the Budget Director appointed a task force on Intergovernmental Program Coordination, chaired by Stephen K. Bailey, Dean of the Maxwell School of Syracuse University. Among its many recommendations, the Bailey task force proposed that BOB should either expand its management staff or establish a new office for intergovernmental coordination. Congress denied funds to increase the staff and at the same time criticized BOB for its poor handling of problems of intergovernmental management. Some members of Congress suggested that responsibility for improved management should be shifted to a new agency in the Executive Office of the President.[22]

Concerned about such outside threats and uncertain about its own changing role, BOB undertook a "self-study" in 1967 to determine what it "needed to do to serve the President better in the context of today's problems." This resulted in a reorganization which, among other steps, abolished the Office of Management and Organization (then the focal point of management improvement) and replaced it with an Office of Executive Management, with the mission of focusing on interagency and intergovernmental management problems.[23]

As BOB leaped from one ad hoc management problem to another, interest in a sustained and systematic management improvement program dwindled. Furthermore, with great fanfare, President Johnson had also launched the Planning, Programming and Budget System (PPBS) in July 1965. The administration saw in the new decision-making system a means of evaluating and developing programs and improving management.[24] The previous Truman, Kennedy and early Johnson emphasis on management improvement became of secondary importance, and the institutional responsibility of BOB for management leadership eroded.

☰ The Nixon Administration highlights management by reorganizing BOB into The Office of Management and Budget (OMB) (1970–1975)

Determined to improve the management of the executive branch, President Nixon proposed on March 12, 1970, a reorganization plan which would replace BOB with an Office of Management and Budget. By emphasizing "management," the new title would symbolize the administration's

determination to "create a climate more conductive to managerial effectiveness."[25] At the same time, the President recommended the creation
of a Domestic Council in the White House that would concentrate on policy
development. In a tidy dichotomy, the Domestic Council would focus on
the what and OMB on the how and the how well, thus separating policy
from program management. In practice, the attempt to separate policy from
administration turned out to be a confusing and sterile exercise, for policy
management *is* policy.[26]

Despite opposition by a determined minority that did not support a
change in BOB's structure and functions, Congress went along with the
reorganization plan, effective July 1970. Under the leadership of George
P. Shultz, President Nixon's first budget director (1970–1972), the linkage between budgeting and management was strengthened. To underscore
the resurgence of management in the hierarchy of OMB, Shultz appointed
an associate director for management with two offices under his wing, an
Organization and Management Systems Division and a Program Coordination Division, each headed by an assistant director. Shultz also stepped up
activities that had been permitted to wane in the last years of the Johnson
administration: the requirement in Revised Circular A-44, "Management
Improvement," for an annual management report from the operating agencies covering past accomplishments and plans for later years; an annual
management review by OMB to identify necessary improvements; assessment of the progress of management improvement projects; and special
attention to cost reduction, ADP, productivity, financial management and
federal reporting requirements. At the fall budget review sessions with the
agencies, OMB brought up the major management issues to get department
heads to commit themselves to appropriate action.[27]

Shultz's successor, Roy Ash (1973–1975), was equally management-
minded, but he minimized the systematic "A-44" approach in favor of management by objectives (MBO). Through MBO techniques he hoped to force
the agencies to consider management and budgetary problems simultane-
ously instead of fragmenting them through the departmental hierarchy.[28]
To implement this new process, OMB created thirty new positions of management associates to work side-by-side with budget examiners in identifying departmental objectives and monitoring their implementation. At the
departmental level, agency heads typically allocated the responsibility for
MBO-cum-budgeting to a strengthened office of administration and management headed by an assistant secretary.[29]

In the end, the Nixon administration fared no better than its predecessors in using the budget process as a tool to improve management, but
for different reasons. No sooner was MBO under way with its round of
reports, studies and "management review" meetings than it was swamped
by Watergate, energy problems and other crises of the administration. The
management associates, and, for that matter, all of OMB, were diverted to
"troubleshooting" on behalf of the administration. Demoralized, politicized

and manipulated for partisan purposes, OMB lost its credibility. The management improvement program fizzled, and in the closing days of the Nixon administration the "M" in OMB hardly merited a capital letter.[30]

☰ The short-lived Ford Administration tries a more selective approach to management improvement (1975–1976)

During the short-lived Ford administration that followed the demise of the Nixon Administration, a panel of the National Academy of the Public Administration advised the President that the "deterioration of the management role of OMB" was one of his most serious problems. It reported that "the existing lack of an effective staff arm to the President for stimulating management improvement in the agencies and for developing further means of meeting problems common to groups of agencies is one of the most serious issues needing quick resolution by the President."[31]

As a former senior member of the House of Repesentatives and veteran of the Appropriations Committee, President Ford appreciated the clout of the budget process in effecting presidential objectives and improving management. He therefore launched in July 1976 through OMB a selective approach to management problems which he termed Presidential Management Intitiatives (PMI). It turned out to be the shortest "major presidential management reform in recent memory" when it was terminated seven months later by the new Carter administration.[32] PMI deserves, however, more than a minor footnote to budget history. Instead of attacking all management problems across the board, it concentrated at the outset on twenty-four major issues or "initiatives" in twenty agencies. OMB prepared issue papers and developed a tracking system to provide program reports to the president. The thrust of PMI was ambitious. It was to be a mechanism for setting agency priorities, implementing decisions and evaluating the efficiency and effectiveness of results. Among the issues were organizational restructuring, program evaluation, efficiency evaluation, the reduction of unnecessary paperwork and regulations, contracting with private firms for selected activities, productivity improvement and the control of overhead costs (ADP, cash management, printing and reproduction telecommunications). So as not to make PMI an academic exercise, it was integrated with the annual preparation of the budget.[33]

☰ The Carter Administration upgrades management improvement in the budget process and highlights program evaluation (1977–1980)

Although the Carter administration rejected PMI, it upgraded management improvement activities in OMB in a manner somewhat reminiscent of the Truman administration and, in several respects, went beyond the Truman period in the broad sweep of its program. It allocated the responsibility for management improvement to an executive associate director for organization and management who enjoyed co-equal status with an executive associate director responsible for budget examination. It gave the new management office a broad portfolio of responsibilities: agency reorganization; improvement of management processes in the Executive Office of the President; systems improvements; reform of regulatory administration; strengthening financial management; enhancing agency management capability; and program evaluation.[34] The Carter administration had resurrected familiar themes, but played them differently.

What was unique in the systematic management improvement program of the administration was its stress on program evaluation. While every administration had employed various mechanisms to evaluate programs, and program evaluation was central to Johnson's PPBS, no other administration had entrenched it as part of the on-going process of management improvement. OMB did this by rescinding previous circulars on management improvement (Circular A-44 on management improvement and Circular A-113 on PMI and management reviews) and issuing in March 1979 a new directive, Circular A-117, that combined, for the first time, requirements for management analysis and program evaluation.[35]

Circular A-117 still emphasized management improvement and cost reduction. In addition, it directed agencies to develop a program evaluation system that would assist management in identifying program objectives; provide explicit statements of intended outputs; formulate "realistic" performance measures; and relate the results of evaluation to the budget process. Unlike previous circulars, which had called upon agency heads to report their accomplishments and plans for improvement, the new requirements were relatively simple. Agencies merely had to summarize the resources devoted to management improvement and program evaluation. OMB saw its role as spotting significant potential management and program improvements and taking all necessary steps to accomplish them. It intended to monitor continuously agency management improvement and evaluation activities. It planned to conduct or sponsor a limited number of management improvement projects of "presidential interest" on its own and disseminate information about successful government-wide management improvements. It also planned to promote the development and use of valid performance measures.[36]

At first blush, the integration of management analysis and program evaluation in a broad management improvement program may appear to be a narrow technical issue. Yet this step aroused veteran practitioners and academicians who objected to the new directive. For example, President Dwight A. Ink of the American Society for Public Administration and Alan Dean, chairman of the National Academy of Public Administration, advised OMB of several major reservations. They noted that Circular A-44 had long been associated with management improvement and that this emphasis should be continued since "major changes are easier to implement if bridges are built back to familiar and accepted objectives." They therefore proposed the following:

> While closely related, there are many differences between the processes involved in installing more effective ways of managing an agency and those associated with assessing the benefits and shortcomings of substantive programs. We suggest that OMB may wish to develop a different circular governing program evaluation and focus the proposed issuance on management review and improvements, as did Circular A-44.[37]

This exchange was no trivial debate over bureaucratic perquisites and professional turf. In effect, it raised the question as to the best ways of structuring the budget process to deal with the efficiency and effectiveness of programs and projects. Ink and Dean would handle issues of efficiency and effectiveness separately as two different analytical paths. Yet, the management of a program cannot be divorced from its effectiveness; nor can any program be any better than its execution. Both management analysis and program evaluation are inseparable parts of the total management framework, although they may require different professional and technical skills. In its directive, OMB wisely wedded the two approaches.

Pleased with its handiwork, the Carter administration went further than its predecessors in summarizing management improvements in one of the budget documents, *Special Analyses*. It cited as its major accomplishments civil service reform; reduction of the regulatory burden on the private sector; significant organizational changes under the leadership of OMB; the use of ZBB (zero-based budgeting) for resource allocation, program evaluation and management improvement; reduction of paperwork; simplification of the federal grant system; the creation of the Office of Inspector General in most large departments to investigate and prevent fraud and waste; improvements in cash management, accounting systems and audits; program changes and terminations; more intensive use of computers and telecommunications; and systems changes that resulted in economies.[38] Allowing for inflated claims typical of budget documents, the scope of activities still reflected a revitalized management thrust in OMB.

≡ The Reagan Administration mounts an attack on inefficiency, waste and fraud as part of Reform '88 (1981–88)

As the new Reagan administration assumed office in 1981, a special panel of the National Academy of Public Administration (NAPA) took a bleak view of OMB's managerial capability despite the programs of the Carter administration:

> During recent years, especially in the decade of the 70s, the manage-
> ment function in OMB has been persistently downgraded to the point
> where the present staff capability is inadequate in relation to need. In
> earlier periods of OMB and the predecessor Bureau of the Budget the
> management function enjoyed far greater stature in the agency operat-
> ing on a par with the budget side. Unfortunately, the overriding dom-
> ination of the budget function as the driving mechanism in Presiden-
> tial decisionmaking has tended to displace the management function.
> Politicization and fragmentation of OMB staff have also contributed to
> this deterioration.

> Now the cleavage between the budget and management sides of OMB
> has become so great that they seem to be two different worlds. A "we"
> and "they" relationship has evolved since the early 1970s. *The potential
> for mutual reinforcement between the two functions remains largely
> unrealized* (Italics mine). Indeed, if budgeting is perceived as one of the
> instruments of management, the need for meshing the two functions in
> a harmonious relationship becomes fully apparent.[39]

To strengthen OMB as the "management arm of the President" and to "increase its capability to deal with the growing concerns about the economy, efficiency and effectiveness with which federal programs are carried out," NAPA urged the administration to concentrate on the following nine priority areas:

1. Intergovernmental management.
2. Organization policy and planning, especially directed at interagency and intergovernmental problems.
3. Administrative planning to make certain that program changes take into account organizational and managerial needs.
4. Assistance to agencies to improve management systems and procedures.
5. Procurement policies and standards.
6. Information and regulatory affairs.
7. Financial management improvement.
8. Program evaluation "to be based on a small core of professional specialists able to complement the work of the General Accounting Office in this area."
9. Interagency relations and coordinating mechanisms.[40]

Familiar themes! The Reagan administration, however, had its own agenda for management improvement, which included not only some of the issues raised by NAPA, but several others more in tune with the ideology and values of the administration. Terming its management improvement program Reform '88 in the hope that it would be implemented by the last year of President Reagan's second term, the program focused on waste, fraud, cost reduction, inefficiency, financial control, program cutbacks, reductions in overhead costs, further easing of regulations affecting businesses and "privatization" of appropriate governmental activities.[41] Permeating the entire program was the ideological outlook of the Reagan administration, with three major emphases: eliminate activities which should not be performed by government at all; return to the private sector those functions that could be performed more efficiently and economically outside of government; and delegate more responsibilities to state and local governments.[42]

Once again, OMB became the lead agency for management improvement and assumed in this area, a status it had not since the Roosevelt and Truman administrations. The driving force behind policy was generally the budget, and a management improvement program aimed at program cuts and savings became an important instrument of deficit reduction. The Reagan administration regarded its approach to management improvement as different from its predecessors in at least four respects: (1) it was comprehensive and continuous rather than narrow, piecemeal and sporadic; (2) it focused on management systems and processes, not just on organizational structures; (3) it was inextricably tied in with budget preparation, unlike the abortive attempts in the past to link management and budget processes; and (4) it was designed to produce savings and cut deficits.[43]

To highlight the importance attached to Reagan-style management improvement, the administration designated a deputy director in OMB to conduct the program and expanded and strengthened the management staff. A cabinet council on management and administration, chaired by one of the senior members of the White House staff, provided policy guidance, a sense of priorities and oversight. To enlist the participation of the operating agencies, the White House and OMB created two interagency groups: (1) a Presidential Task Force on Management Reform, composed of assistant secretaries of agencies and chaired by the deputy director of OMB for management, and (2) a Council on Integrity and Efficiency, also chaired by the deputy director and composed of seventeen statutory Inspectors General, the Director of the Office of Personnel Management, the Executive Assistant Director of the Federal Bureau of Investigation and an Assistant Attorney General. In addition, in 1982 the President appointed J. Peter Grace, a prominent businessman, to head the President's Private Sector Survey on Cost Control (PPSSCC), the first farflung external study of governmental management since the second Hoover Commission in 1955.[44] Seemingly, the means were on hand to orchestrate a concerted attack on management failings.

More so than most of its predecessors, the administration highlighted management themes in the annual budget documents and, for the first time, pursuant to the Deficit Reduction Act of 1984, issued a precedent making annual report on management improvement, *Management of the United States Government*. In 1988–89, the administration anticipated savings from management improvements of about $13 billion, including the sale of loan assets to the private sector, privatization, user fees and numerous systems and organizational and policy changes.[45]

To intensify pressure on the agencies, OMB also required annual management plans and conducted annual management reviews based on the plans and the results of previous projects. Underscoring the importance the administration attached to these activities, OMB, in July 1987, appointed the first Chief Financial Officer for the federal government, with responsibility for financial management and information systems, productivity measurement and improvement, credit and asset management, cash management and internal controls against fraud and abuse.[46]

THE RESULTS OF INSTITUTIONALIZING MANAGEMENT IMPROVEMENT PROGRAMS IN THE CENTRAL BUDGET OFFICE OVER A FIFTY-YEAR PERIOD

How successful were the management improvement programs in producing more efficient, economical and effective programs and projects? To what extent has it been possible to employ the budget process to effect management improvements? Those who followed the shifting fortunes of management improvement programs over a fifty-year span gave them mixed reviews, mainly negative. Their critique falls into ten categories:

1. *Betrayal of the "golden" days of the 1940s and 1950s.* The "old timers" mourned the lack of a central focus on management in budgeting that had characterized the Roosevelt and Truman administrations. In pronouncements and studies, mainly sponsored by NAPA (the National Academy of Public Administration), they attributed the downgrading of managerial issues to "politicization" and a lack of understanding on the part of the budget directors and the White House staff of the leverage of the budget process to improve management. These critics, however, never lost their faith in the process.[47] Once presidents learned to use OMB as their managerial arm, the good old days would return.

2. *The gains of management improvement programs are minimal.* Bernstein gave short shrift to the results of management improvement programs:

The history of management improvement in the federal government is a story of inflated rhetoric, shifting emphasis from one fashionable managerial skill to another, and a relatively low level of managerial achievement.[48]

Even more telling was a GAO review of management improvement efforts during the 1970s. GAO concluded:

The several results of these reforms were sufficiently discouraging as to lead various experts to suggest that the problem of sustaining broad management improvement needs urgent attention . . . . Given the poor track record of centrally directed management reform initiatives, GAO believes more of the responsibility should be placed on individual agencies for improving their managerial capacities.[49]

Despite the revitalization of management improvement programs in the 1980s, Levine faulted the Reagan administration for a negative outlook on government; success in only limited areas; and policies that led federal managers "to thrash about in an environment made more complex by the very strategies the President thinks will simplify government."[50]

3. *Budget directors and their deputies come and go, and so do management improvement programs.* Critics argue that management improvement programs have not failed because of lack of effort, but because of the turnover of budget directors and their assistants responsible for directing management efforts. With presidential blessings, over a dozen budget directors had launched such programs, only to leave after their projects had barely sunk fragile roots.[51]

4. *Budget examination drives out management analysis and program evaluation.* In OMB and the operating agencies, specialized units typically headed management improvement programs. They had, however, little effect on budgetary decisions, which were the domain of budget examination units. The cleavages between these units continued despite abortive attempts to integrate them.[51]

5. *The budget process is inhospitable to management improvement.* So complex and detailed has budgeting become, and so driven is it by inexorable timetables, that it cannot accommodate a careful consideration of management issues.[53]

6. *Operating agencies lack incentives to implement management improvements.* Unless agencies clearly benefit from proposed management improvements they will resist them even while giving lip service to the changes. If the change enhances OMB control over the agency, it becomes especially objectionable.[54]

7. *Management improvement programs can succeed only if they are directed by a special office in the White House.* Picking up the theme that management improvement programs get mired in the swamps of the budget process, several presidential advisers have urged the creation in the White House of a special office that would concentrate solely on management. For example, President Eisenhower's Advisory Committee on Government Organization (PACGO), headed by Nelson A. Rockefeller, favored the establishment of an Office of Administration in the Executive Office of the President that would deal with management problems in the executive branch. Under this proposal, the Budget Director would report to the Director of Administration. When the Budget Bureau successfully resisted this change as a downgrading of the budget office, PACGO came up with a "second best" proposal: an Assistant to the President for Management with coordinating and not operating responsibilities.[55] (When Rockefeller became Governor of New York in 1955, he gave his Secretary, rather than the budget office, broad powers to coordinate the organization and management of state government.)

In 1966, a task force appointed by President Johnson concluded that BOB did not function well as a management staff and recommended that a new Office of Program Coordination be established in the Executive Office of the President. The President "buried the report."[56] An even sterner critic was Senator Abraham Ribicoff, Chairman of a Senate subcommittee on the organization and management of the executive branch. In 1968, Ribicoff castigated BOB for many of the administrative failures of the Great Society and recommended that the President "seek authority to establish an Office of Management and Coordination in the Executive Office."[57]

Prior to the creation of OMB, President Nixon favored a recommendation by his advisers that an Office of Executive Management (OEM) replace BOB as the President's chief management arm. OEM would not be just a change in title, but "a fundamental departure and innovation . . . (and) embody a concept of management that goes well beyond the present emphasis on budget. . . . A substantially different orientation to the President's managerial job will emerge." [58] Nevertheless, in the face of congressional opposition, Nixon settled for OMB.

In 1983, The Grace Commission supported the creation of an Office of Federal Management (OFM) in the Executive Office of the President. Arguing that executive management was hopelessly splintered among the central staff agencies and was of secondary importance in OMB, the Commission advised the President that OFM could be the focal point for government-wide management activities.[59] Former senior officials of OMB, the National Academy of Public Administration and the Chairman of the Senate Government Operations Committee generally concurred with this recommendation. In 1986 the Committee considered a bill which would create two offices: an Office of Federal Budget (the erstwhile OMB); and an Office of Federal Management, which would assume the management functions of OMB.[60] Although Reagan was an enthusiastic admirer of the work of the Grace Commission, he continued to rely on OMB for management improvement.

8. *OMB is no longer the sole resource for management improvement programs.* Unlike the 1940s and 1950s, it is argued that OMB is no longer the sole resource for centrally directed management improvement efforts. By the 1970s, GAO had overshadowed it in program evaluations and in the early 1980s had begun broad management studies of agencies, including the role of OMB and other central staff agencies in fostering improved management.[61] For FY 1984, GAO claimed savings of $5.2 billion as a result of its efforts.[62] Congressional staff agencies and committees staffs were also aggressively conducting management and program studies.

Largely at the instigation of OMB and GAO, the operating agencies had over the years built up staff units responsible for management audits and program evaluation. To strengthen further internal financial and management control, Congress in 1978 had approved the Inspector General Act (PL 95-452), which initially established the offices of inspectors general in twelve agencies and later in eighteen (seventeen statutory). Their primary mission was to ferret out inefficiency, waste, fraud and abuse in the activities of their agencies.[63] As general guidelines they followed GAO's standards for internal auditing ("Internal Auditing in Federal Agencies") and OMB's policies and procedures that emphasized an evaluation of the economy, efficiency and effectiveness of programs in the course of internal audits (OMB Circular A-123).

During the Reagan administration, the activities of the IGs were buttressed by the passage of the Federal Managers Financial Integrity Act of 1982 (PL 97-255) and, as noted, the creation of the President's Council on Integrity and Efficiency. The former intensified internal controls over expenditures, revenues and assets in agencies and the latter harmonized the efforts of the IGs with those of central staff agencies.[64] For the first half of FY 1985, the Council reported the recovery or better use of some $8 billion.[65]

9. *For resolution of major management problems depend on Hoover and Grace Commissions.* Notwithstanding OMB, the federal gov-

ernment at times creates one-time special commissions to probe into the efficiency and effectiveness of all activities and to develop a blueprint for management improvements affecting the entire government. Such was the case in 1947–49 and 1953–55, when the President and Congress established and financed the Hoover Commission (U.S. Commission on Organization of the Executive Branch of the Government), and in 1983–84, when President Reagan appointed the Grace Commission (the President's Private Sector Survey on Cost Control—PPSSCC) entirely supported by the private sector.[66]

The two Hoover Commissions came up with hundreds of recommendations, and the Grace Commission with 2,160 unduplicated recommendations. The first Hoover Commission was reasonably successful in getting the government to implement many of its recommendations on organization, financial management and operating systems. The second Hoover Commission was more ideological in attacking "big government" and various governmental policies and hence achieved relatively minor gains.[67] The Grace Commission aimed even higher. Attempting to reduce the burgeoning deficit, it proposed numerous changes in organizational structures, operating systems, revenue collections, personnel management and substantive policies that would save, according to the Commission, $424 billion over a three-year period. Without analyzing the merits of the recommendations, CBO and OMB jointly estimated the savings at $98 billion if implementation of the changes began in October 1984.[68] No small figure! According to CBO and OMB, only relatively minor savings would result from eliminating waste and inefficiency. The bulk of the savings required changes in law and public policy.[69] On its own, GAO also reviewed the proposals and found some merit in about 242 of them, dealing mainly with management issues.[70]

In 1988, OMB reported that the President had accepted 1,788, or about 83 percent, of the Commission's recommendations, with the other recommendations either deferred or approved for further study. Congress concurred with 1,604, or 90 percent, of the recommendations accepted by the President. The budget incorporated the savings supported by Congress and the President. However, no estimates of the savings were included in the budget.[71]

10. *Management improvement lacks a theoretical framework for effective results.* On a more abstruse level, some academicians attribute the alleged failures of management improvement programs to the lack of a theoretical framework. To the extent that any theory guides

such programs, it is an outmoded belief in the values of scientific management which supposedly have had their day. Without a sense of direction, attempts at administrative reforms flounder, lack objectivity, suffer from poor data and fail to anticipate future developments. They cannot cope with complex programs and overloaded administrative systems.[72] Presumably, some new conceptual insights will guide government out of the administrative wilderness.

Despite this formidable critique of management improvement programs and the role of OMB as the chief architect of such efforts, Presidents and budget directors persist in ignoring it. Under different labels and with varying emphases, they have resurrected systematic management improvement programs. Contrary to the recommendations of trusted advisers, Presidents have continued to make OMB responsible for the central direction of management activities. Is this perversity, blind optimism, a stubborn refusal to face up to the facts? Or could the critics be wrong?

Part of the dilemma results from the expectations of the critics. Management improvements don't occur by fiat or in dramatic and easily documented happenings. They result from thousands of actions, large and small, over time to improve policies, operating systems and organizational structures. None of these changes take place once and for all. No perfect "end state" exists. The pace of change is uneven, cyclical and even contradictory.[73] As conditions alter and new problems arise, further adjustments and new solutions are needed. Hence, management improvement must necessarily be an unceasing and dynamic process. For these reasons, a central staff agency, close to the President, must exercise continuing pressure on the operating departments. With a government-wide outlook, such an agency can deal with management problems to which departments assign low priority or are reluctant to handle.

To be sure, it doesn't follow that the orchestration of management improvements should be a responsibility of the central budget office, especially one enmeshed in presidential politics. Nevertheless, most Presidents have opted for this position. Without management and program analysis, budgeting becomes a superficial exercise. How can a budget office allocate resources unless it knows whether the agencies are using the resources efficiently, economically and effectively? To implement recommendations for management improvement, few pressures are as potent as the power of the purse. Otherwise, tomes of proposed management changes generated by a separate agency without budget responsibilities will merely gather dust. Furthermore, such an agency would be no more immune to overriding political necessities than a budget office.

THE LEGACY OF MANAGEMENT IMPROVEMENT PROGRAMS

Apart from general considerations, the ultimate test of the management improvement programs is the empirical one. What specific benefits resulted from these efforts over a fifty-year period? What legacy was left? What is the outlook for the future? To attempt to answer these questions, this section considers the following major components of federal management improvement programs: restructuring agencies and operating systems; productivity improvement; program evaluation; the stress on automatic data processing; paperwork reduction; privatizing governmental activities; and cutting administrative costs.

≡ Restructuring agencies and strengthening operating systems

Since the 1940s, a major focus of management improvement programs has been organizing new agencies, restructuring existing ones, designing and redesigning programs, and devising more efficient and effective operating systems. OMB has had a hand in all of these developments. To appreciate fully OMB's role, it would be necessary to review the changes on a case by case basis. The battle to improve governmental structures and delivery systems is a never-ending one, as the National Academy of Public Administration reminded us in 1983 when it cited systems which "are becoming obsolete or falling into disrepair faster than we currently know how to fix them."[74] As conditions and policies change, every administration finds it necessary to realign the field structures of agencies, alter programs and reorganize departments. Predictably, succeeding administrations regard the results as unsatisfactory, and so the "fixing" process resumes under the aegis of OMB.[75]

≡ Measuring and improving productivity

An integral part of management improvement programs has been the measurement of productivity of the workforce, the largest single component of operating budgets. Through continuing measurements, the aim is to make governmental activities more efficient, economical and effective. Productivity improvement is a broad umbrella that covers a variety of analyses, such as:

☐ *Work measurement*. This is a count of the units of work performed and the staff hours or costs required to produce each unit. Typically, it is expressed as the unit cost or the unit time to, say, process a claim for unemployment insurance or maintain a mile of road.[76]

□ *Broad measures of productivity.* To analyze productivity in the private sector, the U.S. Bureau of Labor Statistics measures the resources (inputs) utilized to produce final outputs, e.g., a ton of steel. While inputs includes labor, capital, energy and materials, labor inputs (staff hours or staff years) are primarily used. They are a necessity in all types of production and are more readily measurable.[77] The federal government follows a similar approach for most activities in the operating agencies. In emphasizing the *final output*, productivity measurement differs from work measurement. The latter covers all the intermediate operations leading up to the final output. For example, among the final outputs of the U.S. Treasury are checks and bonds. To produce them, the Treasury resorts to at least ten different operations. Work measurement covers each of these activities. Productivity measurement, however, focuses solely on the final product and the staff hours consumed.

□ *Miscellaneous productivity measures.* These include the establishment of targets for different activities and determining the extent to which agencies meet these targets; the analysis of productive and non-productive hours; and the measurement of the utilization and downtime of equipment.[78]

The federal government has implemented at various times these three components of productivity improvement. In the late 1940s, BOB/OMB fostered work measurement through seminal publications, training programs, and requirements that work measurement systems be used to justify staffing needs in budget requests. After this initial enthusiasm, OMB's interest in work measurement flagged. In 1978, GAO reported that two-fifths of the departments lacked work measurement systems in whole or part to determine staffing needs. Among them were the Environmental Protection Agency (26 percent coverage), the Army Corps of Engineers (none) and the National Aeronautics and Space Administration (none).[78] Two years later, GAO found that workforce planning based on work measurement in the federal government was still negligible and that agencies lacked an adequate basis for justifying staffing requirements.[79]

GAO attributed these problems, among other things, to limited leadership by the Office of Management and Budget, "slow progress in developing work and productivity measurement systems," and a variety of personnel constraints (personnel ceilings, average grade controls and hiring and promotion freezes) that gave departments little incentive to install work measurement systems.[80] After all, why develop a rational system for justifying staffing needs when it is ignored in budget allocations? Furthermore, many agency heads frequently regarded work measurement as a boring "nuts and bolts" detail, better left to the technicians. Hence, they gave it little support. Numerous problems of implementation arose. Work measurement may be conceptually simple, but painfully difficult to install in the far reaches of the federal bureaucracy. In addition, some administrators argue that not all federal activities are susceptible to work measurement. Yet, the best estimate is that about two-thirds of federal positions can be covered by standard techniques of work measurement.[81] For the others, proxy indicators can be developed even in "creative," "judgmental," and "service oriented" functions.

In the mid-1950s, OMB attempted to breathe new life into work measurement by intensifying the use of unit costs for some 700 major functions.[82]

Beginning in 1964, OMB followed the BLS (Bureau of Labor Statistics) model in measuring productivity. First, as noted, it measured the final output of operations, not the results of the intermediate steps à la work measurement. Second, it depended on the construction of indexes of productivity to measure the percent change in efficiency from year to year, beginning with a base year. Like work measurement, the concept is relatively simple. For example:

in the base year, both resource inputs and production outputs are given as indexes of 100. The base year productivity, defined as a ratio of output divided by input, is:

$$\frac{\text{Output}}{\text{Input}} = \frac{100}{100} \times 100 = 100 \text{ percent}$$

If, in the second year, the output increases 8 percent and the input increases 5 percent, the productivity ratio reflects an increase in productive efficiency of almost 3 percent, as follows:

$$\frac{\text{Output}}{\text{Input}} = \frac{108}{105} \times 100 = 102.9,$$

an increase of 2.9 percent over the first year.[83]

The development of productivity measures along these lines did not begin in earnest until 1970. In that year, largely at the prodding of Senator William Proxmire of Wisconsin, OMB joined with the Civil Service Commission (now the Office of Personnel Management), the General Accounting Office and seventeen operating agencies in inaugurating a productivity measurement and improvement program. Later, the General Services Administration and BLS participated in the project. OMB had overall responsibility for the program, but the analyses were conducted in behalf of the central staff agencies by the staff of Joint Financial Management Improvement Program.[84]

The early results looked promising. In 1973, the productivity measurement system covered some 200 major subdivisions of forty-six agencies, included 850 final outputs and encompassed the activities of 61 percent of all federal civilian employees. The Joint Financial Management Improvement Program (JFMIP) reported that from 1967 to 1973, productivity had increased at an annual rate of 1.8 percent and that productivity gains resulted in cumulative savings of $2 billion in labor costs.[85] These were average figures. Some agencies turned out to be markedly inefficient. Others experienced sharp increases in productivity. Encouraged by these changes, OMB integrated productivity measurements with the budget process and required agencies to submit productivity improvement data in justification of their budget requests (OMB Circular A-11).

JFMIP continued to report steady gains in productivity that up to 1981 averaged about 1.5 percent annually.[86] Seemingly, productivity improvement programs were soldily entrenched in the federal structure. Some misgivings, however, dogged the productivity measurement program from the start. So broad were the measures that they merely showed overall trends in input-output ratios. By themselves they could not be used to pinpoint specific problems of productivity. Only a work measurement system could do that. Furthermore, the indexes did not reflect the quality or effectiveness of activities. To assess such factors, it would be necessary to combine ratios of efficiency with other performance measures on the effectiveness and impact of programs.[87]

Other problems were more serious. Depending on the interests and whims of budget directors and the White House, OMB waffled in its support of productivity measurement, just as it had with regard to other management improvements. During the first term of the Reagan administration (1981–1984), it "essentailly abandoned the Federal Productivity Measurement Program." It expected, but did not require, agencies to improve their performance measures in justifying their budget requests.[88] In 1983, OMB also rescinded Circular A-117, of the Carter administration, that required an annual agency report on evaluation including measures of productivity, efficiency and effectiveness.

As Reform '88 took off, however, the Reagan administration reversed course in the use of productivity measures. In fact, it made productivity improvement an integral part of the administration's management improvement program.[89] Claiming that previous programs lacked top support and had little impact on expenditures, OMB initiated a "reinvigorated" approach with these elements: the development of the President's productivity improvement program; the preparation in each agency of a five-year productivity improvement plan; the intensified development of performance standards, unit costs, annual productivity goals in each agency and the growing use of measures of quality; an incentive system that would allow agencies to benefit from productivity gains; a planned increase of 20 percent in productivity in targeted functions by 1992; the establishment of a Productivity Clearing House to disseminate management improvements among agencies; and an annual report to Congress on productivity improvements as part of the budget document. The focus of the entire effort was on cost reduction.[90] In its second term, the Reagan administration reemphasized the three major components of productivity improvement and applied them to 680 functions and about two million employees. By mid-1988, however, the results were inconclusive.[91]

The Reagan OMB thus resurrected some workable ideas on productivity that had been afloat since the 1940s, but packaged them differently. Future administrations will also undoubteldy continue to put old wine in new bottles. The label hardly matters. What counts is top support, no let-up in pressure on agencies to improve productivity, and the use of productivity measures in budgeting. All else is rhetoric.

≡ Program evaluation is a sometimes shaky keystone
of management improvement in the federal government

In budgeting, the linkage between program evaluation and budget formulation is now accepted conventional wisdom. Much of the budgetary literature attributes this emphasis to the advent of PPBS (Planning, Programming, Budgetary Systems) in the 1960s. Actually, however, program development and evaluation as integral parts of the budget process go back to the New Deal, World War II and the post-war period. Without snappy and fashionable acronyms, BOB, as part of the overall management improvement program, developed and improved several major programs. In fact, the golden age of program evaluation/management improvement were the Roosevelt and Truman administrations, when program and performance budgeting had barely gained a foothold, and PPBS, ZBB and MBO had not yet emerged as revealed truths of the moment.

With the coming of the Great Society, the sharp rise in the cost of domestic programs, and the quantum jump in federal grants to state and local governments, the evaluation boom began in earnest in OMB, the operating agencies and Congress. And the mainspring of every proposed budgetary reform was program evaluation. As a result, program evaluation today is institutionalized and entrenched as never before in the federal government. Congress has taken it to its bosom. At least forty major legislative acts mandate evaluation, and some even specify the methodology.[92]

≡ Some workable definitions of program evaluation

As the following definition suggests, program evaluation should lead to more effective programs and more informed resource allocations:

> Program evaluation is the systematic collection of information about program requirements, activities, outputs and outcomes for the purposes of management and service delivery improvement. By tying the evaluation results to budgeting and planning, executives and managers are able to identify opportunities for program improvements and to establish priorities for resource allocation.[93]

A growing, abstruse and sophisticated literature on program evaluation spins some fine distinctions between program evaluation, program analysis and policy analysis. For many practitioners and academicians, program evaluation is an after-the-event exercise. It is, therefore, essentially retrospective, since it focuses on the results of past actions. On the other hand, program or policy analysis is supposed to be "anticipatory." It is a "search for new policy directions as the government attempts to cope with problems for which there are not easy solutions."[94] Such semantical shadings, however, can be overdrawn.[95] Program evaluation is as much a valid guide to the future as policy and program analysis. In fact, how can new policies be developed without a close look at the results of past programs? As GAO reminds us:

> Drawing sharp distinctions between evaluation and analysis is less useful than focusing on two basic questions which decision-makers and their staffs face: (1) what actually has happened as a result of past or current policies and programs and what have we learned, and, (2) what should be done in the future and what are our options?[96]

Program evaluation is part of a continuum, part of a decision-making loop. On the basis of an assessment of needs and a consideration of several alternatives, a decision is made to launch a new program or policy. Once the program is operational, the results are appraised. The evaluation can lead to additional program changes. While the evaluation is proceeding, a new analysis of needs may take place. Other alternatives, which were not considered originally, may be developed. These, too, can shape the program. Any on-going program is therefore a product of a continuing appraisal of program results and societal needs (modified by political judgments). The accompanying diagram (Figure 3-1) captures some of the interrelated factors central to program evaluation.

Looked at another way, program evaluation tests a whole set of assumptions built into the budget process. In budgeting, we assume we will achieve

Figure 3·1
Example of the concurrent processes in the continuum (for a new need and a new program)

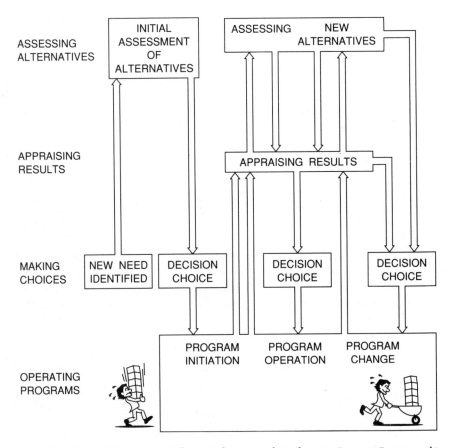

Source: U.S. General Accounting Office, *Evaluation and Analysis to Support Decisionmaking* (Washington, D.C., 1976), p. 8

specified outputs or services in a given program if we invest in that program the required funds, staff, equipment and materials and engage in specified administrative and technical processes. If we produce the intended outputs, for example, prescribed units of housing, then, presumably, we satisfy our annual program objectives, which in this case might mean housing a certain number of low-income families. If we meet our annual objectives, then we advance toward our long-range goal of providing adequate housing for low-income groups in various parts of the country. Program evaluation tests every part of this formulation. Have the objectives been met? To what extent is this attributable to the program, or external forces unrelated to the program? Is the program cost-effective in terms of producing adequate results at acceptable costs? Is the objective valid and realistic, or does it fall short of meeting program needs? What alternatives appear to be preferable to the present program? These are but a few of the difficult questions that surface in any rigorous program evaluation and, in theory, should affect budget decisions.

Budgeting is the only comprehensive decisionmaking process for comparing the results and costs of programs and projects with their intended purposes.[97] For this reason, program evaluation is central in budgeting, and the capacity of operating agencies to undertake program evaluations is a chronic concern in management improvement programs.

The evaluation process employs a body of techniques and methodologies drawn from the various disciplines in the social sciences, but primarily economics. Among the tools are cost-benefit analysis, cost effectiveness analysis, operations research, impact analysis, demonstration projects, feasibility studies, systems analysis and a variety of statistical techniques. Some call for sophisticated conceptualizing and computer modeling. Others require relatively simple and unsophisticated analytical exercises. All are aimed at "rational" decisionmaking, which will produce optimal results. The underlying hope is that out of the crucible of rational analysis, political values, and bureaucratic behavior will emerge the preferred policy, program or project that will be funded.

The political dimensions of program evaluation are pervasive. Political values hem in so-called rational evaluation at every point and cannot be separated from it. The very policies, programs and projects which are being evaluated spring from political decisions. Any evaluations intended to influence decisions on program and funding levels must stand the heat of the political process where factors extraneous to the evaluations may carry far more weight than the evaluations themselves. By its very nature, evaluation is political, for, unless it is an impotent exercise, it challenges the status quo and goes to the heart of the most political of all questions: "Who gets what, how, when and where?"[98]

☰ Program evaluation and the budget process

The central budget office has at least four strings to its bow in program evaluation:

1. *Program development.* Over the years, the OMB/BOB has played a major role in developing and shaping new programs. At the request of the White House, it has either initiated proposals, drawing on its vast institutional memory of the past performance of programs, or reacted to program ideas submitted by others. In both roles, it is "unparalleled for offering an analytic and reasonably impartial perspective on Executive Branch programs."[99] No other central staff

agency is in a better position to develop the budgetary implications of options for the President and in synchronizing program development and budgeting.

2. *Clearing proposed legislation with OMB.* Through its function of "legislative clearance," OMB evaluates the program and policy implications of proposed legislation and executive orders originating in the executive branch. The focus in the review is on the compatability of the proposed bills with the President's policies and programs; the justification for new or changed programs; current and future costs; possible advantages and weaknesses; administrative feasibility; and realistic options.

In 1975, the program evaluation staff in OMB proposed that the legislative clearance functions be broadened to include the "evaluability" of new programs. Under this approach, legislation proposed by agencies would not be approved unless it included a clear statement of objectives for each program, an evaluation plan and criteria for evaluation.[100]

The budget office also serves as checkpoint for proposed legislation initiated by the White House staff and outside advisers as part of the President's annual legislative program. At times, OMB's comprehensive and objective analysis incurs the displeasure of zealots on the President's staff.

3. *Program monitoring is an indispensable ingredient of evaluation.* Invaluable though special program evaluations may be, they represent action after the event. Only then is it possible to identify failures and successes, and problems of implementation. Such corrective action as is taken becomes a case of locking the barn after the horse is stolen. It is therefore essential for operating agencies and the central budget office to have an early warning system that signals actual and emerging programmatic and budgeting problems before they become acute. In short, some mechanism of program monitoring should be part of the overall evaluation scheme. The responsibility for developing such a system rests primarily with the operating agency. In fact, it is difficult to see how any agency can manage its affairs without continuous monitoring of programs and projects as an integral part of the administrative process. With a program monitoring system in place, both the agency and OMB benefit. As a byproduct of the system, OMB can get necessary data without imposing special reporting requirements on the agency.

Program monitoring systems linked to budgeting abound in varying degree in the federal agencies in Washington and in their far-flung offices and facilities. One of the most influential was the Operational Planning System (OPS), developed by the Department of Health, Education and Welfare (HEW) in 1969, now the Department of Health and Human Services (DHHS). Essentially a system of management by objectives (MBO), OPS was an attempt to develop program priorities; provide policy direction to the HEW bureaucracy; establish some 700 objectives for the constituent units of HEW; relate budget requirements to the fulfillment of objectives; monitor the results and costs of key activities through monthly reports and bimonthly conferences; and alter policies, activities and funding levels in the light of the evaluation of the results.[101]

So impressed was the Nixon Administration by the seeming success of OPS that in April 1973 it initiated MBO, Nixon-style, throughout the government.[102] The new system looked like a practical means of institutionalizing the Administration's control over policy, money and manpower. MBO had virtually all the appurtenances of OPS in HEW. It covered two sets of objectives—those of special interest to the President, and those of immediate concern to the departments and agencies. As in HEW, MBO called for specific, doable, and feasible objectives; a short time-frame, not usually more than one year; measurability of results and progress in terms of time-phased milestones; resource allocations based on operational plans; tracking and evaluation; and, where necessary, reassessment and replanning of objectives.[103]

After some equivocation, OMB decided to link MBO with the budget process for the 1975–76 fiscal year. In June 1974, OMB instructed departments to include in their budget requests statements of their chief departmental objectives and "specifically to discuss them in the context of the agency written justification material." It further called upon them to indicate the "end results that will be produced," applicable performance measures, and, preliminarily, the milestones that would point the way to the fulfillment of objectives.[104]

That a special request should be made for data so central to budget decisionmaking reflects either the level to which federal budgeting had plunged in 1974 or represents redundancy in budgetary instructions. In the end, MBO made no special splash, and had little effect on policy choices and budget allocations.[105] Nevertheless, potentially it still remains a potent mechanism for assessing and improving programs.

4. *OMB attempts to strengthen program evaluation through "Evaluation Management."* Beginning in the 1970s, OMB promoted formal and systematic program evaluations with a four-prong approach: (a) providing additional resources to operating agencies and requiring the development of detailed agency plans for evaluation; (b) strengthening OMB's internal capability to evaluate across-the-board programs affecting more than one agency; (c) relating

evaluations to budget decisions; and (d) acting on evaluations conducted by GAO, other congressional staff agencies, and committee
staffs. OMB termed the renewed emphasis on the continuing assessment of programs "evaluation management." It arose from the lack
of an adequate handle on the performance of programs; disenchant-
ment with the Great Society; the conservative bias of administrations bent on appraising the costs and results of existing programs
rather than launching new ventures; the onset of austerity in budgeting; and a sensitivity on the part of OMB that in program evaluation it played second fiddle to GAO.[106]

For all its efforts, OMB was relegated to a secondary role in program
evaluation as GAO increasingly conducted studies on the effectiveness and
efficiency of departmental operations. Two legislative acts expanded the
powers of GAO to undertake comprehensive program audits: (1) the Legislative Reorganization Act of 1970, which directed GAO "to review and
analyze the results of government programs and activities carried on under
existing law including the making of cost benefit studies"; and (2) the Congressional Budget Act of 1974, which required GAO "to develop and recommend to the Congress methods for review and evaluation of government
programs carried on under existing law."[107]

≡ Evaluating the evaluations in terms of their impact
   on the effectiveness and efficiency of programs
   and on resource allocations

Despite the obvious need for program evaluation in budgeting and
program management, it has hardly been a shining success, even though
notable exceptions exist in various agencies. To be relevant, program evaluations should enhance the efficiency, effectiveness and impact of programs.
They should influence the allocation of resources. They should be timely
and realistic. Methodologically, they should be sound, reliable and defensi-
ble, and the data should be solid. By these criteria, program evaluation has
turned out to be a fragile prop for budgetary and program development.
Several factors account for this troubling state of affairs despite the sizable
investments in program evaluation: the indifferent quality of many program
evaluations; wavering support in OMB; lack of agency incentives to improve
program evaluations; ambiguous statutory statements of program objectives;
and failure to use the results of evaluation.[108]

Paradoxically, however, evaluations have continued to flourish rather
than diminish. More than ever, the evaluation process is institutionalized
in OMB, the operating departments and congressional staff agencies (e.g.,
GAO) and committees. For all the conceptual, methodological, political and
institutional problems associated with evaluation in the federal government,

decision-makers find that continuing assessments of programs are necessary in making budget choices. Ultimately, interrelated political, fiscal and economic considerations will determine the fate and funding levels of programs and projects. To the extent that evaluations provide comprehensive and reliable data and develop options, they can at times make a difference for the better in the budget process. This would be no small achievement.

≡ Automatic Data Processing (ADP) and telecommunications are vital elements of management improvement programs

OMB has had a key role in the automation of governmental operations from the 1940s and 1950s, when punchcard equipment was extensively used, to the 1980s, when the federal government in FY 1988 relied on some 20,000 powerful main-frame computers at an annual cost of over $17 billion for its major functions.[109] Because of the profound impact of automatic data processing (ADP) on systems and costs, information technology has been a vital element of management improvement programs. OMB's concerns have been wide ranging: the acquisition, management and use of ADP equipment; the productivity and costs of ADP applications; the need to upgrade equipment and software; the use of telecommunications to transmit data; the adequacy of feasibility studies and of planning for the installation of computer systems; the development of computerized information management systems; sharing of equipment and data among agencies to cut costs; the capacity of agencies to manage their ADP resources; consolidation of related small systems; adequacy of competition among manufacturers of computers; and breakdowns in computer systems.[110]

The stakes are high in management improvement, since the federal government is the largest single user of computer systems in the world.[111] No other government, or for that matter private firm, has computer applications that came close to those of the Social Security Administration, with 200 million accounts and 35 million recipients of monthly checks, or the Internal Revenue Service, with 130 million accounts.[112]

A key element in OMB's control over major computer systems is an updated five-year ADP plan which each agency is required to prepare annually for major systems and include in its budget submission. On the basis of individual agency plans, OMB prepares government-wide five-year ADP and telecommunications plans.[113] In its review of proposed ADP and related telecommunications equipment, OMB focuses on the relevance of the proposed systems to agency needs and goals; the quality of the cost-benefit analysis; the agency's "track record" with similar investments; management planning for systems changes; the state of the art of the proposed technology; available options; and procurement policies.[114] Despite the central controls and reviews, major systems breakdowns occur, and GAO continues to unearth evidence of mismanagement.[115]

≡ Reducing the paperwork burdens of the private sector
   and governments

Since the early 1970s, various administrations have attempted to reduce
the amount of "paperwork" imposed on the private sector and state and
local governments by federal statutes and regulations. (For example, in
1977, the processing and filing of federal forms cost an estimated $100
billion.) In an anti-paperwork crusade, Congress created the Commission
on Federal Paperwork in 1974 (PL 93-536) "to minimize the information
reporting burden" and in 1980 approved the Paperwork Reduction Act (PL
96-511) to reduce information processing costs for both the private and
public sectors.[116] In this effort, OMB was the lead agency. It created an
Office of Information and Regulatory Affairs (OIRA) to work on federal
forms, information processing and "regulatory reform."[117] By 1983, OMB
claimed that it had cut paperwork requirements by some 29 percent, with
more cuts yet to come.

A less sanguine GAO acknowledged some of the improvements, but
found that OMB had made less progress in several critical areas. It claimed
that OIRA gave more priority to eliminating and simplifying regulations
affecting the private sector than to guiding agencies on paperwork reduction
and information processing.[118]

≡ "Privatizing" governmental activities

"Privatization" of governmental activities is not new, although it became
a fashionable term with ideological overtones in the mid-1980s. Since the
late 1950s, in both liberal and conservative administrations, OMB, pursuant
to Circular A-76, "Performance of Commercial Activities", has required
agencies to analyze their operations and to determine which activities could
be conducted more economically and efficiently by the private sector.[119]
Among the alternatives to governmental delivery of services are selling
assets such as railroads, the rural telephone bank, uranium enrichment
facilities, the federal prison industries, and oil reserves to the private sector;
divesiture of activities in favor of the private sector; use of vouchers, such as
food stamps and rent or education vouchers; subsidies to non-profit agencies
for health progams; and performance contracts with the private sector for
a variety of services.[145] Nearly every option is controversial in varying
degrees, with less heat generated by performance contracts, subsidies and
food stamps.

OMB has used A-76 as an instrument to encourage efficiency in departmental operations. In comparing costs of public and private operations,
agencies are required to take all costs into account, including fringe benefits.
By 1985, the latter had become an appreciable factor, amounting to 34.4
percent. For every dollar in payroll costs, the government had to spend an

additional 34.4 cents for retirement, health insurance and other benefits.[146] On the basis of comparisons covering all costs, it may turn out that private vendors are more economical in furnishing various services. Agencies then have the choice of "contracting out" or cutting their costs by improved operations.

In the belief that competition enhances productivity, OMB, in 1983, introduced performance standards as another criterion for comparing governmental and private activities. If departmental operations are cheaper and more productive than comparable commercial operations, then the activities should remain "in-house." Otherwise, they should be contracted out.[122] The implementation of Circular A-76 provoked opposition in Congress, which exempted several agencies, including the Veterans Administration, from the efficiency studies and cost reviews required by the Circular.[123]

≡ Cutting administrative costs

Administrative costs are not dramatic and rarely stir the imagination of agency heads. But a significant portion of a department's budget can be consumed by such mundane items as printing, reproduction, telephone service, travel, office space and payroll and personnel systems. With varying degrees of success, OMB, as part of its management improvement program, has attempted to cut these costs. For example, in FY 1986 the President set as a target a 10 percent reduction in administrative costs, with an estimated savings of $594 million.[124]

≡ Some reflections on the seven major components of management improvement programs

A review of the seven major components of federal management improvement programs suggests that the results were uneven. In large part, this is attributable to the lack of continuity in these programs as administrations come and go. In time, each administration, in its own way, discovers the seven magic keys to the administrative kingdom. Until it does, the budget office, though battered and politicized at times, provides some stability in management improvement.

MANAGEMENT IMPROVEMENT PROGRAMS IN STATE GOVERNMENT

In virtually every respect, state governments in the United States parallel the experience of the federal government in conducting management improvement programs as an integral part of the budget process. Beginning in the late 1940s and early 1950s, several state budget officers established management analysis units modeled after BOB. Among the early leaders were the Organization and Cost Control Division of the California Department of Finance; the Administrative Management Unit of the New York State Division of the Budget; and the Organization and Management Bureau of the Connecticut Division of the Budget.

By the 1970s, nearly all state governments had central management analysis units.[125] The organizational patterns vary. In most cases, the central budget office carries the main responsibility for stimulating management improvement among the agencies. In some states, such as Wisconsin, Minnesota, Ohio and California, an umbrella organization, either a department of administration or a department of finance, centralizes all or nearly all government-wide staff services, including budgeting and management analysis. Among other variations are a special unit in the Governor's office in New York, the Office of Management and Productivity, and the Office of the Inspector General in Florida, which works closely with the budget office. In many states, major departments have also established management analysis units, frequently at the urging of the budget office.

After the recession of 1982–83, cuts in federal grants and ceilings on taxes and expenditures, state governments emphasized even more strongly the need for management capability. As a result, the management improvement activities in most states include comprehensive management surveys; organizational and systems studies; program analysis and evaluation; productivity improvement; performance measurement; the development of computer systems, including management information systems; and improvements in financial management.[126] All of these activities are closely linked with the budget process.[127] Nearly all projects designed to improve management are ad hoc in nature and are triggered by crises, shortcomings in services and budgetary cutbacks. Few state governments have engaged in comprehensive, systematic government-wide management improvement programs. Among these few are New York, Wisconsin and Minnesota. Their experience is revealing.

≡ Attempts at systematic management improvement programs

From 1955 to the early 1970s, during the Harriman and Rockefeller administrations, New York conducted ambitious management improvement programs under the aegis of the Division of the Budget.[128] Initially, agencies sent to the budget office annual reports on administrative improvements, together with estimates as to savings and other benefits.[129] Some of the more outstanding examples of improvements were summarized in an appendix to the budget message. In this way, the budget office began the process of urging agencies to deal with their most critical management problems, monitoring the results of their efforts, and participating in some of the larger studies.

Soon the annual reporting system turned out to be cumbersome and was succeeded by a simpler approach, which merely required agencies to prepare one form for each proposed project and one for each completed project. Rarely did any agency submit more than twelve forms. The forms served as a basis for discussions between the agencies and the budget office (including the budget examination and management groups) with regard to determining, in priority order, the state's most urgent management needs; developing a schedule of management improvement projects; putting together project teams; following up results of projects; and ascertaining their impact on the budget.[130] The program reached its high point in 1963–64, when over 150 management improvement projects were launched, with some notable results.[131] Thereafter, the program waned for several reasons: a preoccupation with PPBS, which diverted limited resources from management improvement programs for about five years; the emphasis on crisis management during the administration of Governor Hugh A. Carey (1975–1982) because of financial problems in New York City and the state; and the difficulty of maintaining gubernatorial interest in an undramatic program.

The Wisconsin management improvement program had a relatively short life. Called PIP (Productivity Improvement Program), it was launched by Governor Patrick J. Lucey in 1972 at a time when agencies were preparing their budget requests for the 1973–75 biennium. PIP mandated a cut of 2.5 percent in the 1972–73 base budget and a cumulative biennial savings of 7.5 percent. The budget office worked closely with the operating agencies in initiating improvement projects that would produce the necessary savings.[157] Exceeding the target, the program resulted in a savings of 7.8 percent, or $33.2 million, for the biennium. Of this amount, agencies were authorized to invest $3.6 million for future gains in productivity.[158] For the 1973–75 biennium, the target was a 1 percent annual saving.[132] After Governor Lucey left office, PIP faded away to mixed reviews because of several shortcomings and was succeeded by ad hoc management studies under the supervision of the budget office.[133]

Crude and imperfect as it may have been, it met its limited goals because it had behind it the support and enthusiasm of top management. Without such support, even the most comprehensive and conceptually-sound system becomes an exercise in futility. What flawed the program was its "crash" nature and its transitory links with the political fortunes of the governor.

With an obligatory acronym, STEP (Strive Toward Excellence in Performance), Minnesota initiated a management improvement program in 1985 under the direction of the Commissioner of Administration. A steering

committee with representatives of labor, management and the general public selected thirty-five major projects out of some 3,000 proposals that had
been submitted. Unlike the Wisconsin program, STEP didn't focus on dollar
savings as such, but on improvement in the productivity and effectiveness
of services.[134]

≡ Management improvement by grand design

State governments have also attempted to stimulate management
improvement by establishing little Hoover Commissions, as in California,
Delaware, Illinois, New Jersey, Oregon, Vermont, Washington, Wisconsin,
New York and Ohio. During a one- to two-year period in which most of the
Commissions are in existence, they attempt to revamp state government by
grand design and lay out proposed major changes in organizational structures and operating systems. Within this framework, they look to budget
offices and the agencies to carry on. In some instances, private firms finance
the work of the commissions and/or contribute the services of consultants.
This is no place to generalize on the results of the numerous studies by
commissions which can only be assessed on a state by state basis. In virtually every state with one-time study groups, however, the management and
budget process has been bolstered.[135]

≡ Other approaches to management improvement

Apart from systematic management improvement programs and
restructuring state government by grand design, most of the management
efforts have focused on ad hoc projects, productivity improvement, program
evaluation and automation of activities:

1. *Ad hoc projects.* One merely has to look at the quarterly bulletins
   and the *Newsletter* of the National Association of Budget Officers to
   appreciate the wide sweep of management improvement projects.
   They cover virtually every nook and cranny of state governments and
   range from quick "troubleshooting" to comprehensive management
   surveys of individual agencies. The studies led to major changes in
   policy, organization and operating structures and systems.[136]

2. *Productivity improvement.* No less than in the federal government, productivity improvement among the states is an uncertain art. Few states have comprehensive productivity improvement
   programs. On the other hand, some encouraging developments have
   occurred. Toward the end of the 1970s, twenty-one state governments had introduced productivity improvement and measurement

systems tied in with cost control.[137] At least two-thirds of the states included some data, albeit sparse, on performance measures, including productivity, in the budget document and in other related publications. In many states, the central budget office was the prime mover in developing and using productivity measurements and the "best enforcement muscle" for improved management.[138] Among the states with relatively comprehensive programs were Washington, Florida and Wisconsin. Yet, in every state the results were mixed—some good, some mediocre.[139]

3. *Program evaluation and state budgeting.* Program evaluation in state budget offices and in the operating agencies has mushroomed in a concerted effort to cut costs and improve management.[140] Between 1975 and 1979, sixty-three evaluation units in thirty-nine states had prepared 805 major reports on evaluations, a five-fold increase over the 1970–1974 period.[141] During that period, two-thirds of the states had modified the budget process to examine the efficiency and effectiveness of programs more closely. Several central budget offices have created special program evaluation units to assist the decision-makers in the hard choices of cutting, changing, expanding or continuing programs. Among the states with such units are Florida, California and New Jersey.[142]

Program evaluation includes periodic evaluation of programs and projects, as in Illinois, Wisconsin, New Jersey and California; performance monitoring, as in Texas and New York; the development of program and policy guidelines, as in Florida, Michigan and Pennsylvania; performance audits, as are practiced in most states; and incorporation of data on program evaluation in budget requests.[143] The results of the evaluation efforts have yet to be measured definitively. In some cases, they have had an obvious effect on budgetary decisions. In other instances, the influence has been indirect or negligible. Under the best of circumstances, financial stress proved to be the overriding imperative, with evaluation accorded second priority.[144]

4. *The growing use of ADP.* Virtually all state governments have made notable progress in the use of ADP for major governmental functions, including budgeting. Many of their applications are innovative and creative and on occasion serve as a model for the federal government. The same problems, however, that affect the federal government also dog the states: the lack of a long range plan; lack of top management understanding of or commitment to ADP; the shortage of qualified personnel; stop and go financing; and the difficulties of establishing a common data base that can serve a number of agencies.[145] In many states, the central budget office or the

department of administration has a major role in developing and approving ADP systems. Special ADP units exist in these offices, or they are combined with management and analysis units.

A QUICK LOOK AT MANAGEMENT IMPROVEMENT PROGRAMS IN LOCAL GOVERNMENTS

Given the diversity of local governments in the United States, it is difficult to generalize about linkages between budgeting and management improvement. At one extreme, some municipalities maintain sustained programs of management improvement. At the other extreme, local political systems thwart any attempts at management improvement.[146] In between, one can find reasonable ground for optimism, as municipalities are increasingly using such management tools as management analysis, program evaluation, productivity improvement, performance measurement and ADP.[147] Nearly all local governments integrate such management improvements as exist with the budget process, which remains the only mechanism for central policy choice and review.

A quick canvass of the state of the art of management improvements among municipalities follows, with some examples of current trends:

1. *Management analysis.* Through management surveys and performance audits, special units, usually attached to the budget office, analyze major organizational and procedural problems.[189] Among local governments with reasonably effective programs are Baltimore, Dallas, Los Angeles County, Washington, Phoenix and Portland.[148]

2. *Productivity improvement.* Under the rubric of productivity improvement, municipalities have initiated a variety of management improvements: productivity and work measurement; realignment of methods and procedures; organizational change; increased use of automation; and organizational development. Of more than 300 local governments that responded to a GAO questionnaire in 1978, 46.4 percent of the counties and 65.9 percent of the cities reported that they had introduced such improvements. In an intensive evaluation of productivity programs in eight local governments in 1975–76, Hayes found poor results in Detroit and Nassau County in New York; an indifferent performance in New York City; and noteworthy accomplishments in Dallas, Milwaukee, Palo Alto, Phoenix and Tacoma.[149]

3. *Program evaluation.* Starting at a distressingly low level in the early 1970s, program evaluation, with its major components of

special studies, performance measures, and management information systems, has made slow and uneven progress among local
governments.[150] A study by the International City Managers Association attributed deficiencies to:

> a lack of well-developed goal and objective setting systems, a lack
> of information systems to support these planning systems, and a
> lack of personal experience in making such evaluation.[151]

Lehan found an encouraging use of measures of performance as
a basis for evaluation in local government budgets throughout the
country, although in many cases no explicit linkage with budgetary allocations is apparent. For example, in the budgets of
Oxnard, California; Lake, Colorado; and Savannah, Georgia, he
found selected measures of performance, including outputs and unit
costs. Savannah goes further and includes "quality standards," such
as meeting EPA standards in well operations; trimming and remov-
ing trees within two weeks of a request; and collecting 88 percent
of current taxes by the due dates.[152]

4. *Development of ADP systems.* Computer systems are in wide use in
   local governments, primarily for routine operations such as billing,
   taxation and accounting. To a lesser extent, several large cities (e.g.,
   Washington, D.C.; Los Angeles; Milwaukee; and others) have developed comprehensive management information systems for budgeting, personnel management, land use and transportation planning.
   The road to the implementation of such systems is a rocky one
   strewn, on occasion, with failures and breakdowns. No system is better than the data that go into it. The information is often skimpy and
   covers only inputs rather than outputs, consumption of resources
   rather than results.[153]

5. *Privatization.* Just as the federal and state governments do, local
   governments rely on private firms for architectural and engineering
   services, public works construction and computer and consultant
   services in highly specialized areas.[154] In addition, many local governments "privatize" a variety of activities, including refuse collection, building maintenance, school bus transportation, catchbasin
   clearing, ambulance services, sewage treatment, snow removal,
   street lighting, maintenance of equipment (e.g., traffic signal lights
   and vehicles), cafeteria operations and street cleaning.[155] A number
   of governments also use private firms for property tax assessments
   and police and fire services.[156]

   The major reasons for contracting out are to cut costs and
   stimulate competition and productivity among local government
   employees.[157]

While comparative data on the costs and performance of private vendors vs. local agencies are sparse, scattered studies indicate that the private collection of refuse is cheaper and more effective. This is also true of some functions in various cities.[158] The road to privatization, however, is beset with several obstacles: poor feasibility studies; inadequate cost analysis; skimpy evaluation; poor criteria; lack of comprehensive specifications; and indifferent monitoring of performance.[159] Other problems are the need to promote competition among vendors; safeguards against price rigging; and union resistance.

THE LINKAGE OF MANAGEMENT IMPROVEMENT AND BUDGETING IN OTHER COUNTRIES (SOME NOTES)

Only in a minority of countries outside the United States is the budget office or the ministry of finance responsible for fostering management improvement as part of the budget process. This is the case, for example, in Britain, France, Japan, Mexico, the Philippines and Thailand. In other countries, management services are variously lodged in the office of the prime minister, as in Malaysia; the office of president, as in Senegal; a ministry of administrative reform, as in Indonesia and Egypt; a central government-wide agency for management improvement, as in Norway, Argentina and Iraq; a ministry of supply and services, as in Canada; a ministry of manpower planning, as in Tanzania; and institutes of public administration, as in Turkey. Even where the central management improvement function is not the prerogative of the budget office, the management techniques in some countries have been used to strengthen budgetary control.[160]

Among noteworthy attempts under way to strengthen management analysis and program evaluation are the following:

≡ Management analysis

In fostering management analysis, many countries followed as a model the prestigious Management Services Division (previously termed the Organization and Methods Division) in the British Treasury. In the quality of its management surveys and management literature, it proved to be an equal of the Division of Administrative Management in the early days of the U.S. BOB. Among influential agencies following the British lead are the Bureau of Management Consultancy (Ministry of Supply and Services) in Canada; the Government Institution of Organization and Management in Norway; and the Advisory Commission on the Development of Management Analysis in the Netherlands.[161] The Soviet Union also emphasizes the importance of organization and management studies.[162]

At various times, nearly every developing country has established an organization and management unit or a similar vehicle for management improvement. In the early 1970s, some seventy-five countries had taken such steps, with minimal results.[163] Some of the problems encountered in mounting management improvement programs include a tenuous relationship with the budget process; concentration on fairly minor issues; and lack of top support by the government. In addition, developing countries contend with shortages of trained staffs.[164] Among the few exceptions to this dreary state of affairs is the central agency for management improvement in Malaysia—MAMPU (Administrative Modernization and Manpower Planning Unit). Located in the Prime Minister's Department for maximum political leverage, MAMPU provides management consultancy services to federal and state governments, with special emphasis on strengthening the administrative capacity to implement national economic plans.

≡ Program evaluation and auditing

The emphasis on evaluation in budgeting systems in the United States has had wide repercussions throughout the world. So pervasive has been the American influence that it is difficult to find planning and budgeting systems anywhere that do not reflect some formal attempts, however crude and minor, to analyze the efficiency and effectiveness of programs and projects and to relate program results to resource allocations. Nearly all governments stress the need to develop performance indicators and to analyze selectively major issues in program management.

Various countries have adopted different approaches. For example, in Britain, the government has fostered evaluation in several ways. Under the umbrella of its annual projection of expenditures and revenues for a three-year period through PESC (Public Expenditure Survey Committee), the Treasury and the operating departments attempt to identify issues that require further analysis. Through its Management Accounting Unit, the Treasury has encouraged agencies to expand the use of analytical techniques, such as cost benefit analysis in budgeting. Finally, since 1970, the Treasury, the cabinet staff and the departments have joined in selecting annually a small number of major programs for detailed analysis and the development of appropriate alternatives.[166]

In developing countries, program evaluations frequently take place within the framework of multiyear development plans. Through the planning process, these countries attempt to identify administrative obstacles to development and to develop corrective measures on a phased basis.[167] One of the problems is the weak linkage between program evaluation and the budget process.

A major resource for program audits is the office of independent auditor-general or comptroller general (à la GAO in Washington) in both developed and developing countries. (In France, West Germany, Austria, Italy and several other countries, a judicial body, a court of accounts, serves as the independent auditor.)[168] Among the more notable and influential offices engaged in audits of the effectiveness and efficiency of programs and projects are the National Audit Board of Sweden; the Court of Accounts of Germany; the Auditors General in Malaysia, Thailand and India; and the Comptroller General in Canada. Program audits by these offices have an obvious impact on budget decisions.[169]

□ □ □

Everywhere in the world, attempts to link management improvement with the budget process are inconclusive. Governments give a good deal of lip service to the need to rationalize public expenditures through management analysis and program evaluations. In practice, they frequently downgrade the use of these techniques in decisionmaking. At times, chief executives and legislatures are indifferent to what appear to them to be lackluster management improvement programs. Such programs rarely become the centerpiece of political agenda. Management fads come and go. So urgent, however, is the need to judge the efficiency, effectiveness and results of programs and projects, especially in an era of austerity, that management improvement in one form or another will continue to be an integral part of budgeting.

≡ 4 INTERGOVERNMENTAL BUDGETING

In budgeting, no one level of government stands alone, either on the expenditure or revenue side. State and local governments depend heavily on the national government for grants and subsidies in this and other countries. Such aid often represents the largest single source of revenue for the recipients and a significant part of the grantor's budget. Paralleling the national system, state and provincial governments also subsidize local governments on a massive scale. In all governments, a major budgeting issue is the distribution of revenue from all sources among the different parts of the public sector. For example, of 31.9 percent of national income collected by all governments in the United States in 1986, what proportions should go to the federal, state and local governments, respectively?[1]

The federal and state governments provide financial aid to lower levels of government for a variety of reasons. First, the massive funds constitute an irresistible incentive to achieve national and state priorities and standards of service. Second, they partially overcome disparities in fiscal resources among the various levels of government. Third, they induce subnational governments to participate in national programs. Fourth, they influence governments to provide services that otherwise might not be initiated. Fifth, they make it possible for national and state governments to decentralize activities to lower levels of government by paying for them. Financial assistance is the cement that binds the different tiers of government in the pursuit of common purposes.[2]

The interdependence of the different levels of government also extends to the performance of major functions. Local governments generally conduct more than limited local activities. They also carry on programs and projects mandated or authorized by state and national governments. Similarly a state government performs both state and joint state-national functions. Only a few functions are the sole prerogative of one level of government, such as defense, international affairs and social security at the national level. Typically, in the United States, three levels of government participate in the administration of the major domestic programs: health, education and welfare.

The distribution of functions has direct budgetary implications. If functions are shared, each level of government must pay a share of the costs. If one level of government assumes complete responsibility for a function, it relieves other governmental units of a fiscal burden while increasing its own costs. Few state and local governments have adequate resources to finance shared ventures, let alone conduct their own growing activities. Hence, local governments pressure state and national governments for assistance. And state governments in turn count on the national government for help.

In this cooperative fiscal and administrative system, national governments are the major bankers. They preempt the lion's share of lucrative taxes, such as personal income and business taxes. Hence, they are in a position to finance extensive grant programs designed to achieve national purposes. In addition, state and local governments obviously have their own revenue sources. For example, in 1986 the federal government collected 61.6 percent of all public sector receipts; state governments 23.0 percent; and local governments 15.4 percent.[3] For the greater part of their revenue, state governments depend on such major tax sources as personal income, corporate income and sales taxes. For local governments, property taxes remain a heavy producer of revenue. In addition, some local governments levy income taxes, and many collect sales taxes. To support their activities, all levels of government thus tap similar tax bases and in the process produce a complex system of overlapping taxes.

Ultimately, subnational governments are at the mercy of national economic, fiscal and monetary policy. This can be far more significant than grants and subsidies. Recessions result in revenue shortfalls, expenditure cutbacks in some areas and expenditure increases in others. Conversely, an expansion of the economy raises both revenue and expenditures. Inflation and high interest rates have a direct and obvious impact on state and local budgets. Only the national government, with its massive resources, can attempt to stabilize the economy and come to the rescue of other governmental units. To cushion the effects of economic downturns, it relies on grants to assist state and local governments. Where the grant system is insufficient, it frequently provides additional funds for public works projects to stimulate the economy and increase employment.

The intergovernmental budgetary system thus rests on four pillars: grants; shared functions; reliance on similar tax resources by different levels of government; and national economic, fiscal and monetary policy. This intricate relationship raises some major policy and political issues: What activities should government conduct? How should governmental functions be distributed among the many governmental units in a country? Who should pay for them? Where will the money come from? To what extent should higher level governments subsidize lower level governments? Which taxes should be the domain of each governmental level? Which tax sources should be shared? How can the national government best assist subnational governments in a faltering economy? What role, if any, should subnational governments have in formulating national economic, fiscal and monetary policy? The stakes are indeed high. Small wonder, then, that these issues generate continuing political controversies in virtually all countries and, in large part, shape budget policy.

This section explores these issues by focusing on the distribution of costs and functions among federal, state and local governments in the United States; the impact of federal grants and other aid on state and local budgets; the impact of state aid on local budgets; the major types of grants and their strengths and weaknesses; the "strings" and conditions attached to the allocation of grants; the major problems raised by grants and other assistance; proposals to reform the intergovernmental budgeting system; and concerns about the erosion of states' powers in a federal system dominated by the national government. By no means are these problems unique to the United States. Hence, this chapter also highlights the relevant experiences of several other countries in intergovernmental financing. Such cross-national comparisons may point up the distinctive features of different governmental systems in allocating funds among subnational governments.

FEDERAL, STATE AND LOCAL GOVERNMENTS SHARE THE COST OF MAJOR GOVERNMENTAL FUNCTIONS IN THE UNITED STATES

Federal, state and local governments share the costs of major governmental functions in the United States. Since the end of World War II, the federal government has been by far the senior partner. The three levels of government spent nearly $1.5 trillion from their own revenues in 1986. Of this amount, the federal government accounted for 69.4 percent of total expenditures, state governments 17.4 percent and local governments 13.2 percent. During a thirty-two-year span, 1954–1986, the federal share of expenditures ranged from 65.3 to 72.0 percent. Until 1964, local governments outspent state governments. Thereafter, state spending steadily exceeded local spending as state governments assumed more functions and expanded aid to local governments. In this analysis of expenditures, federal aid to state and local governments counts as federal expenditures. State grants to local governments count as state expenditures. When such grants are considered as part of the expenditures of the receiving governments, the spending share of each governmental level changes significantly. After intergovernmental transfers, the federal government in 1986 was responsible for 62.4 percent of expenditures and not 69.9 percent. And local spending topped state spending in every year.[4]

Because of inflation and program expansion, expenditures for the entire public sector have risen dramatically, reaching the $1 trillion mark in 1981. What counts, though, is the value of the dollar in real terms. In constant (1972) dollars, governmental expenditures by federal, state and local governments increased, but not as sharply as in current dollars. As Table 4-1 shows, per capita expenditures, after intergovernmental transfers, climbed slowly but steadily in the federal government from 1974 to 1984 but fluctuated among state and local governments. During the recession of 1981–1982, per capita state and local expenditures actually fell.

≡ Sharing the costs of welfare, highways, health and education

In the 1980s, the three levels of government participated extensively in the financing of the most costly functions: welfare, highways, health and

Table 4-1
Per capita governmental expenditures in constant (1972) dollars after intergovernmental transfers, 1974–1985

Year	All governments	Federal government	State government	Local government
1974	$1,872	$1,039	$309	$524
1976	1,996	1,124	322	550
1978	2,034	1,146	330	558
1980	2,139	1,264	336	540
1981	2,186	1,336	331	519
1982	2,263	1,414	332	517
1983	2,312	1,414	336	524
1984	2,379	1,489	348	543
1985[e]	2,491	1,561	. . .	. . .

e–estimated

Source: Advisory Commission on Intergovernmental Relations, *Significant Features of Fiscal Federalism*, 1985–86 Edition (Washington, D.C.: 1985), p. 10.

Table 4-2
Federal, state and local share of direct expenditures for major functions, FY 1985

Function	Percent financed by level of government			Percent of state-local expenditures from own revenue sources	
	(1) Federal	(2) State	(3) Local	(4) State	(5) Local
Public welfare	56.0	36.0	8.0	82.0	18.0
Highways	29.0	45.0	27.0	63.0	37.0
Elementary and secondary education[a]	6.6	49.6	43.7	54.3	45.7
Health and hospitals	7.0	47.0	45.0	51.0[a]	49.0[a]

[a]FY 1984 data

Source: Advisory Commission on Intergovernmental Relations, Significant Features of Fiscal Federalism, 1987 Edition (Washington, D.C.: 1987), Tables 21–27, pp. 30–36.

education. As Table 4-2 shows, by 1984 the federal government was mainly responsible for welfare expenditures, state governments for education and highways and state and local governments for health and hospitals.

The data reflect some major long term trends and changes in the federal-state-local partnership since 1942. Over a forty-one-year span, 1942 to 1983, the federal share of welfare expenditures soared from 31 to 57 percent, then dropped to 55.0 percent in 1984 and 56.0 percent in 1985. Similarly, the state share of solely state-local expenditures for welfare climbed from 61 to 87 percent (82 percent in 1985), leaving local governments very much a junior partner in welfare programs.

In financing highway costs, the federal share more than doubled, from 11 to 29 percent in 1985. Considering state-local expenditures for highways alone, the states still paid over 60 percent of the costs in the 1980s. But their share had declined from a high point of 73 percent in 1942. The financing of health and hospital programs has been primarily a state-local responsibility, with the costs roughly divided between the two governmental levels. In 1942, federal aid for this purpose was negligible. It reached a peak of 11 percent of total expenditures, then ranged from 7 to 8 percent from 1983 to 1985.

In financing elementary and secondary education, local governments carried the heaviest burden for many years. As late as 1970, they still bore over half the costs. Gradually, the local share fell and was exceeded by the state share. With virtually no role to speak of in elementary and secondary education in 1942, the federal government slowly, over the years, provided assistance which reached 9.2 percent of total expenditures in 1980, only to fall to 6.6 percent in 1984.[5]

THE GROWING DEPENDENCE OF STATE AND LOCAL GOVERNMENTS ON FEDERAL GRANTS

From small beginnings, the federal government has supported major programs of state and local governments. Table 4-3 shows trends in federal aid from 1950 to 1987.

From a high of 26.8 percent of state-local expenditures in FY 1978, federal aid tumbled to 18.2 percent in FY 1987. As a percent of federal budget outlays, grants-in-aid declined during the Reagan years from 14.0 percent in FY 1981 to an estimated 10.8 percent in FY 1987. Adjusting for inflation and looked at in terms of constant dollars, the picture is even bleaker. In FY 1980, grants in 1982 constant dollars peaked at $105.9 billion. In FY 1987, they dropped by 15 percent, to $90.2 billion. Furthermore, not all federal grants support the operating programs of state and local governments. Over 56 percent of the grants in FY 1987 represented payments to individuals and families, largely for welfare and health programs.[7]

Table 4-3
Federal grant-in-aid outlays, FY 1950–1987 (in billions)

	Total grants-in aid	Federal grants as a percent of			
		Federal outlays		State and local expenditures	Gross national product
		Total	Domestic programs		
Five year intervals:					
1950	$ 2.3	5.3%	11.6%	10.4%	0.8%
1955	3.2	4.7	17.2	10.1	0.8
1960	7.0	7.6	20.6	14.6	1.4
1965	10.9	9.2	20.3	15.2	1.6
1970	24.1	12.3	25.3	19.2	2.4
1975	49.8	15.0	23.1	22.7	3.3
Annually:					
1980	91.5	15.5	23.3	25.8	3.4
1981	94.8	14.0	21.6	24.6	3.2
1982	88.2	11.8	19.0	21.6	2.8
1983	92.5	11.4	18.6	21.3	2.8
1984	97.6	11.5	19.6	21.1	2.6
1985	105.9	11.2	19.3	21.0	2.7
1986	112.4	11.4	19.8	20.6	2.7
1987	108.4	10.8	18.9	18.2	2.5

Source: *Budget of the United States Government, Fiscal Year 1989, Special Analyses,* "Special Analysis H, Federal Aid to State and Local Governments," p. H21.

Table 4-4

Percentage distribution of federal grant-in-aid outlays by function, FY 1960–1987

	1960	1970	1980	1986	1987
Natural resources and environment	2	2	6	4	4
Agriculture	3	3	1	2	2
Transportation	43	19	14	16	16
Community and regional development	2	7	7	4	4
Education, training, employment and social services	7	27	24	17	17
Health	3	16	17	24	24
Income security	38	24	20	26	28
General purpose fiscal assistance	2	2	9	6	. . .
Other general government	*	1	1	1	5
Total	100	100	100	100	100

*0.5% or less; because of rounding percentages may not total 100.

Source: Budget of the United States Government, Fiscal Year 1988, Special Analysis, "Special Analysis H, Federal Aid to State and Local Governments", p. H20; ——— ,FY 1989

Another important way of understanding federal grants-in-aid is to look at the allocation of grants by major function. For this purpose, Table 4-4 highlights the distribution of such outlays for selected years from 1960 to 1987.

The health function reflects the largest increase, going from only 3 percent in FY 1960 to 24 percent of federal aid in FY 1986. Funding for transportation dropped from 43 percent in 1960 to 16 percent in 1987. Income security also declined, compared with a high of 38 percent in 1960.

THE ANATOMY OF FEDERAL GRANTS AND OTHER AID TO STATE AND LOCAL GOVERNMENTS

Grants are the major form of federal assistance to state and local governments. By no means, however, are they the only aid received by these governments. In several other direct and indirect ways, the federal government eases the pressure on state and local budgets. Especially significant are federal income tax deductions for state and local taxes and interest on bonds issued by state and local governments. While individuals, rather than governments, enjoy such tax exemptions, the governments benefit in two ways. First, state and local taxes become more palatable to high income taxpayers because of the deductibility feature. Second, tax exempt bonds carry lower interest charges than taxable bonds. Of course, the federal

Table 4-5
Forms of federal assistance, various years (in billions)

Federal grants	$108.4 (FY 1987)
Tax exemptions (also termed tax expenditures)	46.9 (FY 1987)
Loans and loan guarantees	2.6 (FY 1987)
Federal expenditures among the states (Grants; salaries and wages; benefit payments; procurement; special programs)	745.6 (FY 1984)

Note: Expenditure data exclude payments for interest, international aid, the operations of selected federal agencies and foreign outlays. These could not or should not be distributed by state.

Source: Budget of the United States Government, FY 1989, "Special Analysis H," pp. H16, 20; U.S. Department of Commerce, Bureau of the Census, *Federal Expenditures by State for Fiscal Year 1984* (Washington, D.C.: 1985).

government is the loser, since it foregoes taxes. The Tax Reform Act of 1986 reduced these tax advantages by eliminating deductions for sales taxes and restricting deductions of interest on municipal bonds used for private rather than public purposes.

A lesser but still meaningful form of federal assistance consists of loans and loan guarantees. This enables state and local governments to obtain credit on favorable terms.[8]

Finally, the federal government affects state and local economies through the sheer magnitude of its expenditures. Where it buys its goods and services, locates its employees and distributes such benefits as social security has a direct impact on the level of economic activity.

Table 4-5 quantifies the four major types of assistance for FY 1987 and other years.

Each type of assistance reinforces the links between the federal, state and local governments in budgeting. An examination of each category of aid follows, centering on the impact of aid on the three governmental levels and on proposals to change the intergovernmental fiscal structure.

≡ The federal grant system

Federal grants come in three forms: categorical grants, block grants and general support grants (misnamed revenue sharing). As the term suggests, categorical grants focus on specific programs and narrowly defined activities. To obtain such grants, state and local governments must comply with a variety of programmatic, fiscal and administrative conditions spelled out in statutes and regulations.

Unlike restrictive categorical grants, block grants support broad functions such as health, education and community development and give state and local governments considerable discretion in allocating funds. Fewer conditions surround the use of block grants. And even fewer restrictions govern the third type of aid, general support grants, including revenue sharing. It can be used for any general governmental activity.

None of the definitions are hard and fast. Some categorical grants, such as education and social services, come in large lump sums and are akin to block grants. Conversely, block grants vary in the restrictions they impose on recipients. To a greater or lesser degree, conditions affect the use of all federal grants, including revenue sharing. They stem from statutes, regulations and court decisions.

As Table 4-6 shows, categorical grants are the chief vehicle of aid, accounting in recent years for 80 percent or more of the oulays for all grants.

Prior to 1966, categorical grants were virtually the only means of federal assistance. In 1966, block grants emerged, and in 1972, general revenue sharing started for both state and local governments (only to be limited to local governments in 1980 and finally eliminated in 1987). As block grants and revenue sharing became more significant, categorical grants as a percent of federal aid declined to the point where in the 1980s they hovered between 79.1 and 90.1 percent.

None of this came about by accident. The present grant structure is the outcome of a continuing political struggle between the President, Congress, state and local governments, special interest groups, liberals and conservatives and federal and state bureaucracies. Shifting alliances of chairmen of congressional committees, interest groups, and governmental bureaucracies have favored categorical grants. They constitute the so-called "iron triangle,"

Table 4-6
Percent of outlays by type of grant, selected years 1972–1987

Year	Total	Categorical grants	Block or broad based grants	General purpose grants Including revenue sharing
1972	100.0	90.1	8.3	1.6
1975	100.0	76.7	9.2	14.1
1980	100.0	79.3	11.3	9.4
1983	100.0	79.1	13.9	7.0
1987	100.0	86.0	12.1	1.9

Source: United States Budget, FY 1989, "Special Analysis H," p. H 23.

or, possibly more aptly, the "golden triangle." Members of Congress found that visible categorical grants focusing on specific programs paid more handsome political rewards than diffused block grants. Their political careers were often tied in closely with programs funded by categorical grants. For special interest groups and bureaucracies at all levels of government, categorical grants protected favorite programs against the incursions of presidents, governors and state legislatures. On the whole, liberals supported categorical grants as a mechanism for achieving specific national objectives in health, education, welfare, housing and transportation.

Conversely, conservatives leaned to block grants and revenue sharing in order to limit the role of the federal government and to give more power to the states.[9] Such forms of aid are therefore in general associated more with Republicans than Democrats.[10] Regardless of party, however, state governors and legislatures were enthusiastic supporters of block grants and revenue sharing. This type of funding gave them the discretion and flexibility to allocate billions of dollars. In contrast, local governments preferred only grants earmarked for them regardless of the form of the grant. They opposed federal grants controlled by state governments.

Mechanisms for distributing grants thus mirror the gains and losses of different groups in American society. To the extent that block grants and revenue sharing take hold, a significant shift in political power occurs. This is the heart of the issue and not just the procedures, technicalities and formulas for doling out federal grants. Since categorical grants are still the most significant form of federal aid, it follows that the political forces favoring such grants continue to be dominant.

≡ Categorical grants still rule the grant structure

Categorical grants are vintage Americana. They first became significant in the early part of the nineteenth century when the federal government sold land and turned over the proceeds to state governments for education. Later, in 1862, the federal government assisted states in establishing land grant colleges. Beginning in 1913, the federal government, flush with revenue from the newly enacted personal income tax, assisted state governments in several programs, including construction of highways, vocational rehabilitation and maternal and child health. It took the Great Depression of the 1930s, however, to initiate a wide variety of categorical grants for welfare, other forms of income maintenance, health, public works, assistance to business, housing and other programs and to lay the basis for a comprehensive structure of federal aid.[11] The next big impetus came in the first five years of the Johnson administration (1963–1967), when over 200 categorical grant programs were enacted, all bearing the imprint of the Great Society. In subsequent administrations, the number of categorical grants increased at a slower rate, never again to achieve the peaks of the 1930s and 1960s.[12]

Starting in 1981, they began to decline because of block grants that consolidated separate categorical grants, elimination of several grants, and some merging of smaller grants into larger categories.

To determine the number of categorical grants is akin to the medieval game of counting the number of angels on the head of a pin. In the 1970s and 1980s, estimates ranged from about 300 to over 500. Even federal agencies differ in their counts. Cutting through the maze of confusion, the Advisory Commission on Intergovernmental Relations identified in 1987 422 categorical grants and 13 block grants.[13]

From a fiscal standpoint, some grants are more significant than others. Of 328 categorical grants available in FY 1985, the federal government spent an estimated $86.7 billion for 196 grants. This represented 81 percent of all outlays for grants. Mere numbers, however, obscure the fact that twenty-five programs accounted for 88 percent of expenditures for categorical grants.[14] The "big ticket" items include Medicaid, which is the largest grant-in-aid program; AFDC (Aid to Families with Dependent Children); highway construction; housing assistance; nutrition assistance; and various education programs.

No matter how large or small the categorical grants are, the funds do not flow automatically to state and local governments. Allocation formulas and other criteria built into the statutes and regulations prescribe which grants go to state governments only; which only to local governments; which to non-profit groups; and which to a combination of all three. Nearly 32 percent of all the grants are based on such legislative formulas. They account, however, for the greater part of expenditures, such as income maintenance programs and Medicaid.[15]

≡ Block grants: A vehicle for more power to state governments and less power to local governments

Long on the agenda of state governors, state legislatures and Republican presidents, block grants in any form did not materialize until 1966. In that year, the Johnson administration successfully urged the passage of the Partnership for Health Act, which consolidated nine categorical and seven project grants (a surprising turn in view of its bias toward categorical grants). Two years later, in 1968, it persuaded Congress to enact the Omnibus Crime Control and Safe Streets Act, which gave state governments unprecedented power to allocate federal funds for law enforcement.[16] Nixon and Reagan were especially enthusiastic proponents of block grants and proposed more consolidation of categorical grants than a suspicious Congress and its pro-category allies were willing to support. Nevertheless, they succeeded in getting several major block grants through Congress.

Besides a conservative bias associated with block grants, several other factors led to their growing use. Over the years, governors, state legislatures and state budget directors had urged simplification of the maze of categorical grants, the elimination of red tape and burdensome paperwork generated by the grant system, and the reduction of administrative costs. Hence, they preferred block grants.

The Reagan administration had another ploy. The block grants it sponsored in 1981–1982 resulted as much from an attempt to cut the federal budget as from any ideological fervor to return power to the states and to contract the size of the federal bureaucracy. Block grants, which were appropriated in lump sums, were far easier to cut than categorical grants, which are separately authorized and appropriated. And, indeed, in consolidating fifty-seven grant programs into nine block grants in 1981, Congress and the President reduced the overall cost by some 15 percent.[17] From 1980 to 1987, state governments had at their disposal $10.3 billion to $13.1 billion in block grants.[18] Considering the fact, however, that the block grants by FY 1987 represented only about 12.1 percent of all grants, they had a relatively modest impact in widening state flexibility in grant administration.

≡ General revenue sharing dwindles as a share of federal aid

With much fanfare and ballyhoo, President Nixon signed the State and Local Fiscal Assistance Act of 1972, informally termed General Revenue Sharing (GRS). He heralded this act as the start of a "new American revolution" that would transfer power back to state and local governments. The act authorized the payment of about $30 billion, with relatively few restrictions over a five-year period (1972–1976), to all fifty states and nearly 39,000 general purpose local units of government.[19]

The new legislation was the culmination of sporadic attempts to share federal revenue with the states. In the first half of the nineteenth century (1837), the federal government, embarrassed by surpluses, distributed them to state governments. This was indeed a rare historical phenomenon. Another hundred years went by before Congress, in the 1950s, considered several bills to substitute general support grants for categorical grants. In effect, the states would experience no net gain. The bills died quickly in committee.[20]

The issue of federal revenue sharing did not surface again in any significant way until 1964, when Walter W. Heller, Chairman of the Council of Economic Advisors, proposed a revenue sharing program to supplement existing grants-in-aid. He favored setting aside a fixed proportion of federal income taxes in a trust fund for annual distribution to state and local governments without the need for annual appropriations by Congress. Revenue sharing appeared to be an idea whose time had come. The federal government anticipated large surpluses. State and local governments were encountering stiffening opposition to tax and expenditures increases. Their tax structures, which relied heavily on sales and property taxes, were for the most part regressive. The state personal income tax was unpopular. Serious disparities in fiscal resources existed between rich and poor state governments and between local governments. Only the tapping of federal income taxes appeared to be a way of helping state and local governments and equalizing resources among them. [21] During the 1964 presidential campaign, the platforms of the Democratic and Republican parties supported revenue sharing. Nevertheless, the newly elected President Johnson turned down the plan, for reasons which are still unclear.[22]

In the 1968 campaign for the presidency, Richard Nixon picked up the theme of revenue sharing once again, and, on the advice of a task force headed by Richard P. Nathan, recommended a version similar to the Heller formula. Supporters of Nixon's proposal had some of the following objectives in mind: further decentralization of power to state and local governments; brakes on growth of the federal government; substitution of revenue sharing for the patchwork quilt of grants; assistance to state and local governments buffeted by budget crises; provision of additional funds to attack urban problems; redistribution and equalization of funds to areas with low fiscal capacity; and increased dependence on the federal personal income tax to finance the public sector.[23]

The legislation that emerged from Congress in 1972, however, was a far cry from revenue sharing.[24] The formula for the allocation of funds bore no relationship whatsoever to the yield of the personal income taxes. It was no more than a five year general support grant to state and local governments subject to renewal by Congress. The framers of the statutory formula made certain that every general purpose government got something. In the main, funds were distributed on the basis of population, the size of the urban population, per capita income, and tax effort, with roughly one-third going to state governments and two-thirds to local governments. Nevertheless, each local government, regardless of the formula, was guaranteed at least 20 percent of the state-wide per capita average of funds distributed to all local governments. And no government could get more than 145 percent of the average.[25] The legislation did little to overcome fiscal disparities among state and local governments.[26]

For all its weaknesses, the legislation still broke new ground. During the fourteen-year life span of revenue sharing, the federal government distributed over $83.5 billion to state and local governments.[27] From 1972 to 1980, it provided an assured annual $6 billion of virtually unrestricted aid (in some years, the total reached $6.8 billion). Unlike categorical or block grants, which were earmarked for specific programs or broad functions, funds for general revenue sharing were supposed to be spent in five high priority areas including public health, recreation, libraries, social services, and financial administration. The legislation included the priority categories as a "sop" to members of Congress who favored continuing legislative control over the use of funds. In practice, the priorities turned out to be a "charade." The grants were fungible. They could be commingled with other funds so that it was difficult to know with any precision the activities for which federal funds were used. Bowing to the inevitable, Congress eliminated any references to priorities in renewing the general support grants in 1976 for another five years.[28]

After nine years of so-called revenue sharing (1972–1980), the Carter administration and Congress effectively excluded state governments from the program. In renewing the legislation in 1980, they authorized an annual expenditure of $4.6 billion for local governments for the next three fiscal years, 1981 through 1983 (later continued), and also approved an annual distribution of $2.3 billion to state governments only if they gave up an equivalent amount of aid from categorical grants. Predictably, no state government opted for the exchange. The Carter administration rejected general support grants for state governments on two grounds: mounting deficits and the relatively good financial condition of the states. Taking a similar tack, the Reagan administration in 1985 unsuccessfully recommended the elimination of general purpose grants in FY 1986 on the grounds that "federal resources can no longer be spared for programs and activities that do not address national spending priorities."[29] However, it prevailed upon Congress to terminate the program in FY 1987.

The results of the general support grants are mixed in terms of their distributional and fiscal effects. Neither the legislation nor its implementation contemplated a redistribution of funds so as to provide significantly more aid for poorer state and local governments, thus equalizing resources among all. The law contributed only minimally to the leveling of interstate differences in fiscal capacity and effort. For fiscally distressed large local governments and central cities, general support grants were helpful, but not especially significant. For small poor local governments, however, the grants were important.[30]

In terms of their budgetary impact, the grants had varying effects on state and local governments. State governments used the funds to avoid program cuts; offset reductions in federal categorical grants; reduce and stabilize taxes; minimize borrowing; and increase the balances in their general funds. Rather than stimulating new spending for operating programs and capital construction, the grants made it possible to hold the line on existing programs. Among local governments, about 40 percent of the grants in 1974 and 1975 was spent for capital projects; about one-fourth for operating outlays; approximately one-fifth to reduce local taxes; and the rest for miscellaneous activities.[31]

≡ Paying the piper and calling the tune

He who pays the piper calls the tune. This might be the theme song of the entire federal grant structure or, for that matter, any system of intergovernmental grants. Like any prudent donor or lender who wants to get value for his money, the federal government attaches conditions, restrictions, mandates and constraints to all grants, with most in effect for categorical grants. For block grants, fewer restrictions are in effect, and for general support grants, as previously noted, only a limited number of constraints exist. It is virtually impossible to find a grant that is unfettered and condition-free. Such grants are almost as scarce as proverbial free lunches.

Regardless of the nature of the grant—categorical, block or general support—recipients must meet some fifty-nine across-the-board, or so-called "cross-cutting," requirements imposed by law, regulation or court decisions.[32] These include compliance with prevailing wage standards; prohibitions against discrimination in hiring on the basis of age, color, sex, religion or national origin; assistance to the physically handicapped; environmental protection; compliance with health, welfare and safety standards; restrictions on the use of funds for debt retirement; requirements for citizen participation; and prohibitions against the use of fund for lobbying.

Beyond these policies that affect all federally-aided programs and projects, other conditions include requirements for matching federal grants with state and local funds; mandates and direct orders; "crossover sanctions," which compel state and local governments in one program area to comply with requirements in another (denying funds for highway construction authorized by one law because of speed limits in excess of fifty-five miles per hour prohibited in another law); partial preemption, whereby the federal government in certain programs (e.g., meat inspection) takes over the program unless state governments meet federal standards; and compliance with complex formulas in legislation authorizing grants. These conditions impose heavy costs on state and local governments, which, in theory, are free to turn down participation in federal programs. Such is the lure of federal funds, however, that these governments complain bitterly all the way to the bank to collect over $100 billion in grants.[33]

≡ Matching federal grants with state and local funds

Common to many categorical and block grants are matching, or cost-sharing, and maintenance of effort requirements. These affect state and local budgets directly and stimulate increased spending. For each $2.08 spent by the federal government in grants in 1984, state and local governments had to provide $1 in matching funds.[34] In 1987, state-local matching was required by 53.6 percent of all programs funded by categorical grants. As part of the deficit reduction program the federal matching share was capped except for Medicaid and AFDC (Aid to Families with Dependent Children).[35] In some programs, however, the matching requirements are so low that they represent an irresistible lure to state and local governments. For example, the federal-state match is 90-10 percent for the interstate highway system and 80-20 percent for bridge replacement and rehabilitation grants.[36]

Several federal policies serve to cushion the fiscal pressure on state and local governments. In several programs, federal funds (for example, some block grants) can be used for the match. In other programs, federal agencies accept "in kind" contributions (the value of services, equipment and goods committed to a program) instead of cash as a match.[37] Despite such cushions, the matching requirement has significantly stimulated state and local expenditures.[38] From the standpoint of Congress, cost sharing increases service levels and gives recipients an incentive to use resources efficiently.[39]

As a precondition for grants, the federal government, in many programs, also requires "maintenance of effort" by state and local governments. This guards against the possibility that governments will substitute federal grants for their own funds. It is also a means of assuring continuation of pre-grant levels of service and expenditures. The significance of this condition is evident from the fact that in the 1980 fiscal year thirty-nine grant programs, accounting for nearly three-fourths of all federal aid, required some form of maintenance of effort.[40] At times, state and local governments have displayed considerable ingenuity in getting around these constraints through fanciful interpretations of maintenance of effort and high estimates of the value of their "in kind" contributions.[41]

≡ Over a thousand conditions govern categorical grants

Although significant from a budgetary standpoint, requirements for matching and maintenance of effort are but two of more than 1,000 mandates or conditions imposed on recipients of categorical grants. In a study of five states and ten local governments in those states in 1981, Lovell and Tobin found that the federal government, through regulations, had imposed 1,260 mandates on those governments, of which 1,307, or about 96 percent, were conditions of aid and 223 were direct orders applicable to specific situations. Nearly 84 percent of the mandates were procedural in nature and dealt with "how to" provisions such as requirements for planning, evaluation, reporting, budgeting, staffing, auditing and record-keeping. Approximately 16 percent were substantive and focused on programmatic issues, such as program objectives, design, quality and quantity.[42]

That conditions and mandates raise the costs of state and local governments is evident in several preliminary studies. It is difficult, however, to identify the full costs with any degree of precision and to evaluate the corresponding benefits. In the ten local jurisdictions studied by Lovell and Tobin, local governments paid completely or partially for federal as well as state mandates out of their own source revenue.[43] The analysis did not cover the impact of mandates on the costs of state governments. An Urban Institute study in 1978 found that the cost of complying with five major mandates ranged from $6 per capita in Burlington, Vermont, to $51.03 in Newark, New Jersey. The costs of all six mandates comprised "a considerable share of all federal funds received by the communities."[44]

≡ Mandates governing block grants

Several major conditions govern the allocation of funds from block grants. The conditions, however, are not uniform for all block grants, and some block grants are more hemmed in by restrictions than others. Among the conditions are some matching of funds; limits on federal reimbursement for administrative costs; some earmarking of funds for specific activities; some provisions with regard to maintenace of effort; provisions for "pass-through" of funds from state governments to local governments and non-profit organizations; criteria for performance evaluation; reporting requirements; and the role of citizen participation.[46] In general, the requirements are barebone and minimal, with the development of priorities and mechanisms for accountability left to state governments.

≡ Preemption of functions: Who performs them? Who pays for them?

By law and judicial interpretation, the federal government, under the supremacy and commerce clauses of the Constitution, can preempt functions performed by state and local governments in whole or in part. Since 1965, federal legislation has superseded state law in over fifty programmatic areas, including occupational health and safety, environmental protection, product safety, radiation control, civil rights, regulation of cable TV and regulation of tandem trucks on interstate highways—and the end is not in sight. In some fields, federal control is total (e.g., grain standards). In others (so-called partial preemption), it is optional. This is true of several major programs, including meat and poultry inspection, factory inspection, drug abuse control and air and water quality. States that meet or exceed federal standards can carry on these programs if they wish. Conversely, they can let the federal government administer them.

Federal regulation of major programs through total or partial preemption raises two major issues. First, like mandates, it represents extensive federal intervention in the affairs of state and local governments and, as such, is opposed by many officials who regard it as an additional proof of a crumbling federal system. Second, and more significant from the standpoint of budgeting, federal preemption of major activities results in considerable savings for state governments. Consequently, many states have opted for federal administration of erstwhile state activities.[47]

≡ Budgeting amidst a thicket of grants formulas and mandates

Considering the impact of grants, mandates and preemptions on state and local budgets, no meaningful budgeting can take place without a full understanding of the intricacies of the grant formulas, laws, regulations and court decisions spelling out conditions for receiving grants. Of all the conditions, the grant formulas are the most complex and are a statistician's delight. Representing, as noted, about 32 percent of the categorical grants, they account for most federal aid.[48] For example, in FY 1984 the federal government allocated about $85 billion, or 87 percent of all grants in aid to state and local government, through intricate formulas.[49] Incorporated in the formulas are key social and economic factors, including the needs of state and local governments.

Each factor is complex and controversial. How does one measure needs? At best, policymakers, in the absence of precise analytical tools, resort to rough indicators, such as per capita personal income; the gross state product; population trends; fiscal capacity; demographic trends; the percent of individuals at the poverty level; the unemployment rate; the percent of the population in metropolitan areas; enrollments in elementary and secondary schools as a percent of the population; the overall crime rate; the number of individuals who are 65 or older; the infant mortality rate; the percent of minority groups; and the percent of single parent families. Some programs embody many of these factors in a needs index, with each factor given an appropriate weight. All such indices are open to challenge on the basis of the factors employed and the weights accorded to them.[50]

Fiscal capacity and effort are major elements in the construction of grant formulas. They are measures of the potential capability of a government to raise revenue and the extent to which it makes use of such capacity. Some governments are obviously in a better position to finance their activities than others, thus highlighting the disparities in fiscal capacity among governments. To what extent should this be taken into account in designing grant-in-aid formulas? How does one measure fiscal capacity and tax effort? This is not a mere technical issue, for the allocation of billions of dollars of grants depends on such measures.[51]

No matter how complex, every formula symbolizes the values and preferences of society. Some formulas attempt to give governmental jurisdictions with the greatest needs and the most meager resources the largest share of available grants. Others attempt to correct glaring imbalances of resources between rich and poor governments through "equalization" or redistribution of resources. For the most part, however, equalization is not a major factor in the federal grant structure. What state and local governments get depends more on political bargaining than on abtruse statistical formulations and abstract criteria of equity. Regardless of their fiscal capacity, all state and local governments, and the legislators who represent their interests, want to be sure that they are getting their "fair share."

Political jockeying with grant formulas takes place on a year-round basis. In the legislative mills, formulas often go through innumerable changes until a political compromise is struck. In contrast to the zero-sum game, which produces a loser for every winner, in the game of grantsmanship every government gets something, and rarely does any government get less than it got the year before unless, in a general budget cut, all governments get less. Should formulas change, a "hold harmless" clause guarantees that few governments, if any, will suffer a loss in grants. The cumulative effect of these policies is to give more to those who have and to give more, but not enough, to hard-pressed state and local governments.[52]

Because of the large stakes, grantsmanship has become critical in state and local budgeting. To make sure they get their "fair share" (and perhaps more) of formula, project and block grants, state and local governments need the most current information on changes in existing grants and proposals for new grants. Where necessary, they lobby for appropriate revisions through governors, mayors, legislative leaders, congressmen and public interest groups. Nearly all state governments and several large cities maintain "ambassadors" in Washington to look after their interests.[53] In addition, several interest groups represent various levels of government, primarily the United States Conference of Mayors, the National League of Cities, the National Association of Counties, the National Association of Towns and Townships, the National Governors' Association, the Council of State Governments and the National Association of State Budget Officers.[54]

☰ The simmering revolt against the grant structure, mandates and other forms of federal regulation of state and local governments

Since the early 1970s, state and local governments, public interest groups, numerous scholars and some federal agencies have inveighed against the proliferation and fragmentation of grants; the difficulty of focusing accountability for results, with revenue raised by one government and expenditures incurred by another; federal intrusiveness in large and small ways in the affairs of state and local governments; and lack of equity in the present grant structure. Approaching at times a simmering revolt, the attack has focused on interrelated political, managerial and fiscal problems.

☰ Is federalism withering because of the grant structure?

Of all the policy issues raised, the most fundamental one has been the political impact of federal grants and regulations on the federal system. The effect, as some observers see it, is to erode the nature and character of American federalism. From an authentic federal system, the nation, they claim, has evolved into a decentralized national system, with state and local governments mere appendages of a strong central government.[55]

Sympathetic to the views of state governments, the Advisory Commission on Intergovernmental Relations (ACIR) has argued that grants at times result in a transfer of decisionmaking from the state to the national level and a substitution of federal for state priorities. Some categorical grants, in particular, undermine the authority of elected state officials by bypassing them altogether on the way to local governments and private organizations. In some grant programs, federal officials deal directly with the state bureaucracy instead of the political leadership. This, too, impedes the capacity of chief executives and legislative leaders to oversee and manage state affairs.[56]

No clear guides, it is argued, exist on the need for federal participation in major programs. No explicit criteria govern the allocation of functions among different levels of government. In some programs, such as SSI (Supplemental Security Income) and food stamps, the federal government pays the entire cost. In others, such as AFDC (Aid to Families with Dependent Children) and Medicaid, it requires costly participation by state and local governments. Federal authority now extends to functions previously reserved to the states. In addition, federal grants stimulate state and local governments to undertake new activities. Unless an overriding national purpose exists, it is questionable (so it is argued) whether the federal government should intervene in various programs. Unwarranted federal intrusion limits the budgetary options of state and local governments and results in high costs and a misallocation of resources.[57]

Under the domination of both federal and state governments, local governments complain about their withering autonomy. As they see it, they carry the burden and costs of federal and state mandates. Through its policies, the federal government intensifies state control over local governments. In passing grants for local governments through the states, it adds another layer of control. In approving block grants, it gives the states more discretion and flexibility in allocating funds. When the states distribute part of the block grants to local governments, they add so many conditions that effectively the block grants become categorical grants. In general, national grants encourage states to force local compliance with federal and state policies and practices.[58]

☰ Charges of mismanagement of the federal grant system

From a managerial perspective, the criticism is equally severe and is of direct concern to budget offices with responsibility for oversight of the management of programs and projects. Critics cite the proliferation and fragmentation of grants; the avalanche of paperwork; the innumerable delays; and especially the thousands of regulations and guidelines that complicate service delivery and raise costs. They claim that grants have the effect of multiplying the number of intergovernmental transactions, intensifying conflict among the three levels of government, confusing lines of responsibility and weakening accountability.[59] In a report mandated by Congress, OMB in 1980 concurred with many of these charges and castigated the grants system because of the "increasing inflexibility of fiscal and administrative requirements . . . and the hundreds of categorical grants with different matching requirements, timing difficulties, application procedures, duplication of programs, and other administrative problems."[60]

≡ Fiscal problems created by the grant structure

From a fiscal standpoint, observers also find some critical problems in the grants system. While they agree that federal aid constitutes major sources of state and local revenue, they claim that grants have encouraged state and local expenditures and taxes and the growth of a large bureaucracy. Dependent on national financial assistance, state and local governments can not easily give it up. Their budgets, therefore, continue to grow.[61] This might be tolerable, were they assured of steady federal funding. As matters stand now, however, grants are the targets of budget cuts, and state and local officials are rarely certain as to the amounts that will be allocated for programs and projects from year to year. For them, revenue sharing with funding guaranteed for a multiyear period is a model and preferable by far to stop-and-go financing.[62]

≡ A more positive view of intergovernmental budgetary and administrative relationships

In contrast to this bleak outlook, other specialists find that the pillars of federalism are hardly collapsing, despite sundry political, management and fiscal problems. Politically, they argue that federalism is very much alive but, through the grant system, has evolved into different forms of partnership. What worked in the horse-and-buggy days is not relevant today. National problems call for national solutions. And the grant system provides the financial incentives to state and local governments to achieve national goals, standards and service levels in a farflung federal system.[63] Of course, this introduces complexity into the system in view of the interdependence of the three governmental levels. But we have learned to live with such complexity. For example, education is a local function. Yet, local officials must meet state standards and federal constitutional guarantees.[64] The grants-in-aid are the lubricant for the entire process. The frequent charges that grants foster centralized government and jeopardize states' rights are, in the view of proponents of the present grant structure, often just a smokescreen for attempts to gut domestic programs such as welfare and increase defense expenditures.[65]

Without minimizing managerial problems in administering the grants system in general and categorical grants in particular, several researchers have found the criticisms overblown and highly exaggerated. Rather than a proliferation of grants, the number of categorical grants has actually decreased through consolidation, elimination and the development of block grants. Relatively few grants account for most expenditures. The spectre of federal intervention in large and small details of operations is a myth. In fact, the reverse may be true, with federal agencies often unaware of the efficiency and effectiveness of state and local performance. Available evidence suggests that federal enforcement of its own requirements is poor and variable and that state and local governments have a wide range of choices in complying with federal conditions. Each choice has different fiscal implications and varies from jurisdiction to jurisdiction. Rarely is the issue the simplistic one of compliance or non-compliance.[66]

An inordinate emphasis on procedural requirements, red tape and paperwork obscures the contributions of categorical grants in ameliorating social and economic problems since the 1930s. In a variety of fields, the single purpose grants designed for a specific clientele have fostered national norms and stimulated the growth of state and local programs. In any assessment of the grants, one should focus on the results of these programs and consider what might have occurred in their absence.

≡ Successful and unsuccessful attempts to improve the intergovernmental grant system

To correct some of these real or perceived problems, every President since the Roosevelt administration in the 1930s has tried to leave an imprint on the grant system. A rundown of major developments over fifty years suggests that reforms of intergovernmental funding are still high on the national agenda:

☐ *President Roosevelt and the New Deal (1933–1941)*. The Roosevelt administration laid the basis for the intergovernmental grants system and direct aid from the federal government to local governments.[67]

☐ *The Two Hoover Commissions (1947–1949 and 1953–1955)*. To simplify intergovernmental financing, the Commissions recommended block grants and revenue sharing. While they were unsuccessful, they foreshadowed future developments.[68]

☐ *The Eisenhower Administration (1953–1960)*. The administration appointed a Commission on Intergovernmental Relations in 1953 (the Kestnbaum Commission) to recommend an exchange of functions and taxes among the three governmental levels. After two years of labor, the Commission produced significant recommendations, which were ignored. Undaunted, the President established a joint Federal-State Action Committee (1957–1960) composed of federal and state officials to rationalize the intergovernmental system. Finally, the President recommended the creation of the Advisory Commission on Intergovernmental Relations (ACIR) to monitor, research and propose solutions for intergovernmental problems.[69]

☐ *The Johnson Administration and the Era of "Creative Federalism" (1963–1968).* An integral part of the Great Society programs, "creative federalism" (a Johnson label) resulted in an explosion of categorical grants and an extensive participation of the federal government in erstwhile state and local functions.[70]

☐ *The Nixon Administration Launches the "New Federalism" (1969– 1974).* President Nixon laid out an ambitious scheme for a federal takeover of welfare payments, consolidation of hundreds of categorical grants into block grants, shifts of programs to state and local governments, and bona fide revenue sharing. Frustrated in most of his efforts, he still achieved several block grants and so-called general revenue sharing.[71]

☐ *The Ford and Carter Administrations Tinker with the Intergovernmental System (1975–1980).* Apart from some management changes and proposals to create block grants, both administrations had little impact on the intergovernmental system.

☐ *The Reagan Administration's New "New Federalism" (1981–1985).* Under the banner of "new federalism" a la Nixon, the Reagan administration led three onslaughts against the intergovernmental system:

1. *The 1981 cuts.* In an effort to dismantle the Great Society programs, the Reagan administration initiated $34.5 billion in cuts, many of them affecting categorical grant programs for individuals and state and local governments.[72] The effect was to reduce federal grants by 14 percent from FY 1981 to FY 1982, the first decline in federal aid in twenty-five years.[73] A major study of the effect of the cuts in fourteen states and some of their cities indicated that the working poor bore the brunt in such programs as AFDC, food stamps and Medicaid. State and local governments were not affected to the same degree and, in time, managed to replace some of the lost federal funds with their own money and, in later years, with increased congressional appropriations.[74] Other significant changes in 1981 were the emergence of additional block grants and a loosening of some of the direct fiscal links between the federal and local governments. The state governments became the chief intermediary between the two other levels of government.

2. *The "Big Swap" of 1982.* In the abortive "big swap" of 1982, President Reagan attempted to turn back to the states forty-three major programs, including AFDC, food stamps, federal education programs, urban development and highway and mass transportation. To fund these programs, the federal government would relinquish to the states revenue from federal taxes on gasoline, liquor, cigarettes, luxury goods and windfall profits from domestic oil production.[75] By 1988, the revenue transfers would end, and it would be up to the states to continue the taxes or eliminate programs. Opposed by the National Governors' Association, the Reagan program faded fast. The governors had their own agenda: complete federal assumption of responsibility for income maintenance programs, including Medicaid, AFDC and child nutrition, which cost state and local governments $21.8 billion in FY 1981–82. In return for this trade the governors would be willing to take over completely federal programs in education, law enforcement, community development, transportation, employment and training.[76]

3. *Further nibbling at the grant structure.* By 1985 it was clear that the Reagan administration had not let up in its intention to shift programs and fiscal burdens to state and local governments. In his FY 1986 budget, the President proposed the elimination of revenue sharing, the termination of aspects of the urban development program and other programs and heavy cuts in funds for mass transportation. Since 1984, the administration had cited growing surpluses among state and local governments in contrast to the massive deficits of the federal government.[77]

≡ Some useful management improvements simplify the grant system

Despite political failure to realign the grant system by grand design, some useful management improvements have taken place, largely because of pressure by state and local governments. Among them are advance notification to state governments of applications for federal grants; joint funding of common programs by two or more federal agencies; a single audit, instead of multiple audits by several federal agencies; streamlining of federal regulations affecting state and local governments; improved cash management; uniform procurement policies; and standardized reporting requirements.[78]

ANOTHER FORM OF FEDERAL AID:
EFFECT OF FEDERAL EXPENDITURES
ON STATE AND LOCAL GOVERNMENTS

Federal grants-in-aid are direct and visible and have a clear impact on state and local governments. Less obvious but significant is the effect of federal spending, tax, credit and economic policies on subnational governments.[79]

≡ Federal spending affects state and local budgets directly and indirectly

Where and how the federal government spends its money in the fifty states affects state and local budgets directly and indirectly. For example, in FY 1984 the federal government spent about $725 billion in the states and territories for salaries and wages, payments to individuals (e.g., social security and retirement), procurement, grants-in-aid and sundry special programs.[80] Among the states, the per capita expenditures ranged from $2,210 in North Carolina to $4,319 in Maryland, and outside of the contiguous forty-eight states, to $4,642 in Alaska. The average for the nation was $3,022. [81] States are interested in two key measures: (1) federal per capita expenditures in their state and region compared with expenditures in other states and regions, and (2) the per capita ratio of spending in relation to the per capita revenue sent by the states to the federal government. A state receiving $1 in federal expenditures for every tax dollar it channelled to the federal government would break even. It would benefit if the ratio was $1.50, indicating that the federal government spent $1.50 for every $1 in taxes it received from the state. Conversely, it would regard itself as a loser if it had a ratio of under $1. In that event, the federal government would have spent less than it received from the state.[82]

Among the lowest ratios in 1982–1984 were those in Michigan, Texas, Wyoming, Illinois and New Jesey. Among states with the highest ratios (federal expenditures exceeded tax payments) were New Mexico, Mississippi, Virginia, Missouri and Hawaii. In every case, per capita personal income and per capita federal expenditures determined the ratios. Some expenditures are controllable by the federal government (e.g., procurement, contract awards and the location of facilities). Others are not, such as the residences of recipients of social security.[83]

From 1976 to 1984, the differences among the states in federal revenue-expenditure ratios widened. Alarmed by that they regarded as a massive shift of wealth from their states to the Sun Belt and the far west, the governors of northeastern and midwestern states began to compete aggressively for federal outlays. Sixteen states set up a Northeast-Midwest Economic Advancement Coalition in 1976 to pressure the federal government to shift more domestic and defense spending their way. Also, in 1976, a Council of Northeastern governors (composed of seven governors) pressed their claim for "fair shares." Congressmen from New England established a caucus to further the economic aims of their region, and, as a defensive measure, ninety members of the House from seventeen southern and southwestern states organized the Sun Belt Council. The latter was in addition to the preexisting Southern Growth Policies Board. The scramble for federal outlays targeted at specific regions and states intensified.[84]

For the contestants, it is almost an article of faith that federal expenditures stimulate economic development. Hence, they clamor for at least "equalization" of federal expenditures among the states. Much of this analysis is simplistic, as Pack effectively demonstrates. Even if the federal government distributed federal expenditures on an equal per capita basis to all states, this policy would do little to equalize expenditure-revenue ratios. She points out that "substantial disparities would still remain, because differences in per capita incomes among the states would generate differences in per capita revenue payments."[85]

While federal funds influence regional economic growth, especially in the West and South, most studies of long-term regional economic development suggest that the dominant forces are population movements and changes in transportation and communication facilities.[86] In any event, formidable methodological and analytical problems exist in measuring the effect of flows of federal funds in any particular region. Even if these problems could be solved, it is doubtful that Congress would agree on acceptable criteria to reallocate expenditures. Nor, as noted above, would reallocations by themselves wipe out disparities in expenditure-revenue ratios among the states.[87] In the end, national policies will not be shaped by such formulas, but by a political consensus on national goals, "fair shares" and ways of equalizing resources among the states.

≡ The impact of federal tax policy on state and local budgets

In many direct and indirect ways, federal tax policies influence state and local budgets. Among the chief issues in recent years have been the deductibility of state and local taxes and interest on state and local bonds from federal taxable income; proposals to establish a federal value added tax (VAT); and the effects of the Economic Recovery Tax Act (ERTA) of 1981 and the even more sweeping Tax Reform Act of 1986.

≡ Exempting state and local taxes and bonds interest
from federal taxation

The exemption of state and local taxes and interest on bonds from federal taxation has a long history. Since the federal income tax was established
in 1913, state and local taxes (personal income, real estate, personal property
and general sales taxes) have been deductible from federal taxable income.[88]
Similarly, interest on bonds issued by state and local governments has been
tax exempt under the doctrine of "reciprocal immunity" which bars the federal government from taxing state and local governments and vice versa. By
no means, however, do legal scholars agree on the applicability of the doctrine in the absence of a definitive ruling by the Supreme Court. Practically,
though, it still holds within limits, although both the Court and Congress
are chipping away at tax exempt bonds.[89]

In the tax reform of 1986 (and in previous years), both exemptions
came under attack. While the argument for their elimination hinged on
"closing tax loopholes" and simplification, the possibility of gaining about
$41.7 billion in lost revenue in a time of high deficits must have been
irresistible.[90] State and local governments successfully persuaded the House
Ways and Means Committee and the Senate Finance Committee to retain
the deductibility provisions for income and property taxes in the revision of
the tax code in 1986. They failed, however, to win congressional approval
for the continued deductibility of sales taxes.

Without eliminating tax exempt bonds altogether, Congress, in four
major pieces of legislation, severely restricted their use:

1. Two acts—the Mortgage Subsidy Bond Act of 1980 and the Deficit
    Reduction Act of 1984 (DEFRA)—controlled the amount of tax
    exempt mortgage subsidy bonds issued by the states for owner-
    occupied housing.

2. The Tax Equity and Fiscal Responsibility Act (TEFRA) of 1982
    and DEFRA eliminated tax exemption for small issue industrial
    development bonds after 1986 (later changed to December 1989
    for manufacturing facilities). DEFRA also capped the amount of
    industrial revenue bonds for "private purposes" and student loan
    bonds in each state. The maximum amount was $150 per capita or
    $200 million per year, whichever is greater. Under prior law, no
    limitations existed.[91]

3. The Tax Reform Act of 1986 went further and combined mort-
    gage revenue bonds, industrial development bonds and student loan
    bonds under a new unified volume cap of $75 per capita, or $250
    million, for each state through 1987. Thereafter, the amount would

be the greater of $50 per capita, or $150 million.[92] The act also created a new classification of municipal bonds: public purpose and private purpose bonds. Public purpose bonds continued to enjoy tax exemption. Private purpose bonds, covering pollution control, sports and other facilities, lost the tax exemption. The interest of other types of bonds, such as housing bonds, was subject to taxation under certain conditions.[92]

The effect of the legislation on the demand for state and local bonds is uncertain. A major feature of the 1986 tax legislation was the reduction of marginal income tax rates for individuals and corporations. Hence, investors may have less of an incentive to buy tax exempt bonds to shelter their income against taxes. This may force up interest rates and thus increase state and local budgets. On the other hand, the legislation eliminated so many tax shelters that tax exempt bonds may continue to be an attractive investment as the "only game in town."[94]

≡ Other effects on state and local budgets of the Economic Recovery Act (ERTA) of 1981 and the Tax Reform Act of 1986

The effects of ERTA

The largest tax reduction in U.S. history, ERTA cut federal personal income and corporate taxes sharply. Nearly all the changes had an impact on state and local taxes.[95] One major feature was the reduction of the marginal tax rate for personal income taxes from 70 percent to 50 percent. This encouraged wealthy individuals to look for alternative investments to tax exempt bonds. The tax legislation also permitted individuals to defer taxes on part of their income by investing up to $2,000 annually in IRAs (individual retirement accounts) and in all-savers bank certificates. Even individuals in moderate circumstances now had a choice of investing in these instruments or buying shares in mutual funds devoted to tax exempt bonds. Because of competitive investments, the borrowing cost of municipal bonds increased.[96]

Federal cuts of personal income taxes had other unexpected effects. In the interest of uniformity, most states had conformed their personal income tax structure to that of the federal government in various ways. Six states "piggybacked" on federal income tax returns, with the state tax representing a specified percent of the federal income tax. With cuts in the federal income tax, these states faced a potential loss of many millions of dollars in FY 1981–82 and in later years.

Another device used by seven states was to base their taxable income on federal definitions, but to use their own tax rates. Somewhat related to this was the practice in twenty-two states of basing taxes on adjusted gross income as defined by the federal government, but applying to it their own exemptions, deductions and tax rates. All of these states expected significant drops in revenue in 1981 and 1982 because of changes in the federal tax code. Only eight staes which define their own taxable income deductions, exemptions and tax rates without reference to the federal government were unaffected by the federal tax cuts. In 1982, most states began to "uncouple" their tax systems from that of the federal government to reduce revenue losses.[97]

Even more severe has been the effect of changes in the federal corporation tax on state and local governments. Corporation taxes are a major item in the states' revenue structure, accounting overall for nearly 10 percent of all their revenue. Of forty-five states which had a corporation income tax in 1981, thirty-five followed to the letter the definition of federal taxable income as their tax base. With heavy cuts in federal corporation income taxes because of generous depreciation allowances for plant and equipment, the conforming states experienced a loss of over $2 billion in FY 1981–82 and anticipated still heavier losses in subsequent years. In 1982, the states confronted the unhappy dilemma of "uncoupling" and thus increasing corporate taxes or absorbing the loss.[98]

The effect of the Tax Reform Act of 1986

The Tax Reform Act of 1986 had a reverse effect and led to politically embarrassing large tax "windfalls" totaling about $6 billion for many state and local governments. Most states still piggybacked on the federal tax system and used federal definitions for capital gains, taxable income and various deductions. The elimination of many tax shelters in the federal tax legislation meant that income, hitherto sheltered, would be taxed. Because of state conformity with the federal tax system, additional personal and corporate income suddenly became subject to state and local taxation. Unless the windfall was cut, taxes in 1987 were expected to increase in over half the states.[99] By October 1987, thirty-one states had returned $4.6 billion, or 81 percent of the windfall, to taxpayers, with low income groups favored. Whether other states would take a similar course of action became a potent political issue.[100]

Another unexpected effect resulted from the elimination of sales taxes as a deductible item in computing federal taxes beginning on January 1, 1987. As a result, consumers rushed to buy "big ticket" items in the latter part of 1986. For example, in December 1986, retail sales rose 4.6 percent, and state and local governments experienced a sudden jump in sales tax receipts. The demand for consumer goods temporarily satisfied, retail sales began to drop in the early part of 1987. State and local governments faced the unhappy prospect of potential revenue shortfalls in sales tax collections in FY 1987.[101]

≡ The impact of federal economic, fiscal and monetary policy
    on state and local governments

Overshadowing even federal grants, expenditures and specific tax changes
is the impact of federal economic, fiscal and monetary policy on state and
local budgets. In a depression or recession, state and local governments are
relatively impotent. In the late 1970s and early 1980s, they were dogged by
stagnant economies, high unemployment, inflation, high interest rates and
foreign competition that threatened the so-called "smokestack" industries.
The effect on their budgets was immediate and painful: unprecedented revenue shortfalls (an estimated $20 billion in 1982 and 1983). As the economy
picked up, their financial condition improved by the mid-1980s.[102]
   Without the resources and power of the federal government, state and
local governments can do little to stabilize their own economies, which are
inextricably bound with the national economy. If anything, their cumulative
actions have the effect of worsening a recession. Rather than reduce taxes to
stimulate demand, they increase them. Rather than raise expenditures, also
for stimulative purposes, they cut them back whenever possible.[103] In the
post-1979 period, state and local budgets showed no real growth (adjusted
for inflation) in marked contrast to the leap in federal spending. Shannon
attributes the slowdown in state-local spending to the three R's: *Revolt* of
the taxpayers; *Reduction* in federal aid in real terms; and *Recession* with no
federal bailouts.[104]
   Only the federal government can come to the rescue by controlling
interest rates, stimulating employment, combatting inflation, cutting taxes
and spending its way out of a recession (so-called countercyclical spending).
High interest rates and inflation were especially sore points for state and
local governments because of their impact on operating and capital budgets.
Historically, interest rates reached a new high in the late 1970s and early
1980s when the autonomous Federal Reserve Board implemented a tight
money policy. Only in this way, in its view, could inflation be controlled,
despite the resulting fallout in high unemployment and business failures
generated by high interest rates. The effect on the tax exempt bond market
was dramatic. In 1965, the average interest rate for tax exempt bonds was
3.34 percent; in 1970, over 7 percent; and in 1982, over 12 percent.[105] Each
additional percent of interest represents an incremental cost of $629 million
for state and local governments. As a result, their borrowing declined.[106]
   The economic picture brightened for state and local governments by
1985 when the inflation rate dropped to about 4 percent and the interest
on tax exempt bonds hovered around 9 percent. By 1987, the interest rate
fell under 8 percent. The unemployment rate dropped to under 6 percent.
   Prior to 1981, the federal government tended to favor the use of special countercyclical grants to state and local governments to stabilize the
economy. In fact, the Public Works Employment Act of 1976 required the

Congressional Budget Office to study means of stabilizing the national economy by countercyclical use of federal grants to state and local governments. The assumption was that grants should increase in a recession to stimulate demand and, conversely, drop in a thriving economy. On five different occasions, the federal government intervened to assist state and local economies, the last time in 1978.[107]

SOME OBSERVATIONS ON THE STATE OF FEDERAL-STATE-LOCAL FISCAL RELATIONS IN THE UNITED STATES

As Shannon put it, the old affluent federalism has disappeared, and a new austere federalism has emerged. From 1953 to 1978, federal aid was the fastest growing source of revenue in state and local budgets. Beginning in 1979, the reverse was true. In real terms, federal aid dropped and will continue to drop as a result of the fiscal squeeze in Washington. With an increasing share of the federal budget allocated to defense, social security, Medicare and interest on the national debt, federal aid will have a relatively low priority. Haunting any fiscal decisions in the spectre of the federal deficit. State and local governments will be lucky to hang on to what they have. What has emerged (again citing Shannon) is a fend-for-yourself system.[108] But the resilient grant structure, though battered, still stands. So does the commitment to shared funding of major programs.

Shannon found two contrasting signals: "The old federalism message was 'You states and localities should be doing more and Washington is here to help you.' The new federalism message is 'Don't do more and don't expect any more help from Washington.' "[109]

State governments found some mixed blessings in the new policies. For the most part, the federal government severed its direct links to local governments and relied on the state governments as intermediaries for federal aid. The use of block grants accentuated this trend.

National policies have thus had the effect of strengthening state governments as senior partners in the state-local fiscal system. At the same time, the capability of state governments has improved so markedly in the last twenty-five years that a virtually "unnoticed revolution" has occurred. In the intergovernmental system, the states are increasingly the middlemen—the intergovernmental bankers, policymakers, regulators, administrators and monitors. As middlemen, though, they are caught in a local-federal vise. The two other partners now look to them to take the lead in expanding and financing public services.[110] Increasingly, this is what state governments are doing.

STATE-LOCAL BUDGETARY AND ADMINISTRATIVE RELATIONSHIPS

Just as local governments in the United States depend on federal grants, so do they rely heavily on state aid for major functions such as education, welfare, transportation, health and housing. In fact, state aid is their largest single source of revenue. With such grants go a variety of conditions and mandates, under which local governments continue to chafe. In addition, they increasingly look to the states to assume the responsibility for such costly functions as welfare. They also count on the states to give them new taxing powers in order to balance their budgets. And, in the wake of tax-payer revolts, they are subject to state controls over revenues, expenditures and debt. In some states, even their budgets must be approved by state governments. These are the main links in the uneasy alliance between state and local governments.

☰ Forms of state aid to local governments

State aid to local governments exceeds federal aid by a handsome margin. For example, in 1980–81, local governments received $111.4 billion from the federal and state governments. Of this amount, $71.3 billion, or 64 percent, were state dollars and $40.1 billion, or 36 percent, was composed of federal aid. Federal grants came to local governments via two routes: $22.4 billion channeled directly to them, and $17.7 billion passed through the state governments.[111] These ratios of relative assistance have more or less persisted to the present day.

Table 4-7 shows the amount of state aid in selected years.

In 1982, state payments to local governments represented 35.7 percent of all state government general expenditures. Among the states with the lowest percentages were Hawaii with 1.7 percent, Vermont 13.6, Rhode Island 16.3 and New Hampshire 16.9. At the other end of the scale, the states that allocated a larger proportion of their budgets to state aid were California with 47.4 percent, Minnesota 47.1 and New York 45.8.[112]

At best, however, these figures represent trends and should be used with caution for several reasons. First, if a state assumes the direct operating responsibility for a function, its costs are not included in data on state aid. Thus, Hawaii funds elementary and secondary education, and in many states welfare is solely a state function and not a combined state-local activity. Second, some states reimburse local governments for joint services; this is counted as state aid. Others pay for them directly. This is not state aid. Third, the treatment of taxes varies. If a state collects sales taxes and returns part of them to local governments, this constitutes state aid in some states. If local governments collect the taxes directly, the amounts are not considered state aid. Fourth, problems of methodology and definitions bedevil the

Table 4-7
State aid to local governments, selected years

	1985	1984	1983	1982	1981
Total (billions)	$116.4	$106.7	$99.4	$95.4	$89.0
Percent of total state spending	NA	NA	NA	35.7	36.0
State aid as percent of local general revenue from own sources	55.3	54.3	55.6	59.4	62.7

Note: 1. State aid includes the pass-through of federal funds to local governments. To isolate the "pass-throughs" from direct state aid, it would be necessary to conduct a special study as was done by ACIR for 1980–81. Explanation of NA (not available).

2. In 1987, the Bureau of Census conducted its quinqennial study of state payments to local governments. The data were not available at the time this table was prepared.

Source: U.S. Bureau of the Census, *State Payments to Local Governments, 1982 Census of Governments* (Washington, D.C.: 1984), Table 1, p. 1.

U.S. Bureau of the Census, *Governmental Finances*, various years.

Advisory Commission on Intergovernmental Relations, *Significant Features of Fiscal Federalism*, 1987 Edition (Washington, D.C. 1987), Table 43, p. 57; Table 45, p. 59.

collection and interpretation of data. And fifth, it is difficult to isolate "pure" state aid as such from federal dollars. For these assorted reasons, it is a herculean task to provide an adequate answer to a simple question: "How much aid is provided?"[114]

Keeping in mind the limitations of the data, it is nonetheless useful to show at least roughly the extent to which state and local governments share the cost of major functions from their own revenue sources. In 1985, state governments accounted for 82 percent of state-local general expenditures for welfare from their own revenue sources; 63 percent for highways; 52 percent for local education (1984); and 51 percent for health and hospitals.[114] In welfare, state support ranged from a low of 41 percent in New York state to 90 to 100 percent in thirty-two states (100 percent in three states). State support for highway design, construction and maintenance varied from 35 percent in New York to 90 percent in Kentucky and North Carolina. In education, fluctuations in state support were quite marked, going from a low of 8 percent in New Hampshire to a high of 100 percent in Hawaii. In sharing the cost of health and hospital programs, state governments ranged from 18 percent in Nevada to 99 percent in Delaware and Rhode Island.[115]

Of all state aid, most goes for education, as Table 4-8 shows. Next in order of magnitude is state aid for welfare, general local government support (revenue sharing), highways, health and hospitals and other programs.

Which local units of governments get state aid? As would be expected, school districts receive virtually the lion's share, followed by counties, municipalities, towns and special districts. In the last thirty years, the share

Table 4-8
Percent distribution of state aid by function, 1980–85

	1985	1984	1983	1982	1981	1980
Total	100.0	100.0	100.0	100.0	100.0	100.0
Education	62.7	63.3	62.3	62.6	62.7	63.7
Welfare	10.6	11.2	12.9	12.3	12.1	11.2
General support	10.3	10.1	10.4	10.4	10.5	10.4
Highways	5.0	5.3	5.2	5.3	5.2	5.3
Health and hospitals and all other functions	11.4	10.1	9.5	9.5	9.5	9.4

Source: Advisory Commission on Intergovernmental Relations *Significant Features of Fiscal Federalism* 1987 Edition (Washington, D.C. 1987), Table 45, p. 59.

of school districts has hovered around 50 percent. Actually, school districts don't get all the aid for education, since, in various states, cities or counties are also responsible for education.[116] Table 4-9 shows the percent distribution of state aid to units of local government in selected years from 1957 to 1982.

In addition to grants for major functions, state governments also share their revenues with local governments. Long before the federal government initiated its form of revenue sharing, the states had provided such unrestricted aid to local governments. By 1985, general local government support amounted to $12.3 billion and accounted for 10.3 percent of state aid.[116] Forty-nine states now share their revenue with local governments in one or more programs. Revenue sharing assumes a variety of forms: earmarking a specified percent of the state income tax for local governments; sharing motor fuel, alcohol and tobacco and sales taxes; and reimbursing local gov-

Table 4-9
Percent distribution of state aid to local government units in selected years

Local government unit	1982	1981	1977	1967	1957
Total	100.0	100.0	100.0	100.0	100.0
School districts	49.4	50.7	47.6	50.2	48.1
Counties	23.0	23.2	22.6	24.9	27.6
Municipalities	15.3	15.2	19.3	21.3	20.2
Townships and Towns	1.1	1.2	1.2	3.1	3.7
Special districts	1.2	1.4	1.1	0.5	0.3
Other	10.0	8.3	8.2	N.A.	N.A.

Source: U.S. Bureau of the Census, *State Payments to Local Governments*, 1982, 1977, 1967, 1957.

ernments because of state-authorized property tax exemptions. From the start, revenue sharing was an attempt to equalize resources among local governments, provide relief for reduction of property taxes, compensate local governments for property tax exemptions and assist hard-pressed central cities. The allocation formulas reflect these policies and take into account population density, tax capacity, tax effort, the poverty level and the tax structure.[117]

≡ Who does what affects the amount of state aid

The allocation of functions between state and local governments directly influences the size of local budgets. Many state governments, as noted, provide some major services directly, rather than supporting them at the local level through grants. For example, sixteen states have assumed virtually complete responsibility for the court system.[118] In most states, public welfare is a state function, although the responsibility for specific programs varies. The majority of states pay the state share of the federal-state AFDC program without compelling local governments to share the costs. This is also true of the Medicaid program. On the other hand, in some heavily populated, urbanized states like New York, local governments administer welfare programs and pay part of the overall cost.[119] In education, as noted, Hawaii stands alone in paying the entire cost of elementary and secondary education.

To relieve the fiscal pressure on local governments, this trend is likely to continue. Increasingly, state governments will absorb erstwhile state-local functions in whole or part. Increasingly, local governments will turn to state capitals for the relief denied by the federal government.

≡ Mandates condition state aid to local governments

As a precondition for grants, local governments must comply not only with federal mandates, but with an even greater number of state mandates. Running into the thousands, state mandates affect nearly every phase of local operations and result in heavy local costs. Ordained by constitutions, statutes and regulations, the mandates compel local governments to undertake programs; specify the quantity and quality of programs; govern personnel and financial management; and set limits on revenues, expenditures and debt. In defense of the mandates, state governments cite the need for uniform standards of service, the achievement of statewide social and economic goals, the enforcement of performance standards, and oversight of local personnel and financial practices.[120] To local governments, many mandates represent unnecessary shackles and are a continuing source of friction between them and state governments.[121]

That compliance with mandates is costly is beyond doubt, as has been noted above. To ease the fiscal burden, state governments have taken several steps. First, at least fifteen states reimburse local governments for new mandates, although, in the view of local officials, the payments fall short of the actual costs.[122] In 1984, voters in New Hampshire and New Mexico amended the state constitutions to prohibit any additional mandated local expenditures without state funding of the mandates. Second, forty-one states require fiscal notes to be attached to any legislation on state mandates. In this way, the fiscal effect of any proposed mandates might be evident.[123] Third, several states have institutionalized a continuing review of old and new mandates. For example, in Connecticut, the Joint Fiscal Committee of the legislature determines the extent of reimbursement for mandates. In Massachusetts, a Division of Local Mandates reviews old and new mandates and recommends appropriate changes.[124]

≡ State governments blow hot and cold on flexibility in local budgeting

State governments blow hot and cold with regard to local finance. On the one hand, they authorize local governments to levy sales, income and other taxes. Through various devices, they also ease the burden of local property taxes. On the other hand, they impose constitutional and statutory limits on local taxes, expenditures, debt and, in some states, on budgets.

Property taxes still remain the largest single component of own source local revenue. Since 1957, however, they have declined steadily as a proportion of local taxes, while local sales and income taxes have risen. As the following table shows, all local governments depended on property taxes for 86.7 percent of local revenues in 1957. By 1985, the figure had dropped to 74.2 percent.

Table 4-10
Percent distribution of local revenue by major source

	1957	1985
Total own-source local revenue	100.0	100.0
Property taxes	86.7	74.2
Sales taxes	7.2	15.6
Income taxes	1.3	5.9
Other taxes	4.8	4.3

Source: U.S. Advisory Commission on Intergovernmental Relations, *Significant Feature of Fiscal Federalism* 1987 Edition (Washington, D.C.: 1987), Table 32.3, p. 44.

The overall figures mask the variations among local units of government in their dependence on different types of taxes. Cities relied on property taxes for slightly more than one-half of their revenue in 1984. Counties and special districts counted on property taxes for about three-fourths of their revenue. For school districts and townships (towns in New England), the property tax was still the overwhelmingly dominant source of revenue (well over 90 percent).

By the early 1980s, most states permitted some local governments to levy sales or income taxes in order to reduce the reliance on property taxes.[125] As a result of these actions, property taxes in four states accounted for less than 60 percent of local tax revenue. In seventeen states, the proportion ranged from 60 to 80 percent; in ten states, 80 to 90 percent; and in nineteen states, at least 90 percent or more.[126] Apparently the property tax is still very much alive, and the taxpayers are kicking.

More than any other tax, the property tax instigated the taxpayer revolts of the late 1970s. Apart from outright ceilings on property tax increases such as Proposition 13 in California and Proposition 2 1/2 in Massachusetts, some twenty-seven states in the early 1980s adopted several measures of property tax relief. They take the form of tax exemptions, tax credits, and financial assistance to individuals in low-income groups. For the latter groups, so-called "circuit-breaker" programs base the amount of aid on family income. Twenty states reimburse local governments directly for lost revenue from property taxes, and fourteen states channel grants directly to taxpayers, mainly for "circuit-breakers."[127]

Under pressure of tax revolts, state governments not only imposed constitutional and statutory limits on state taxes and expenditures but, as of October 1985, placed the following restrictions on local governments:

Table 4-11
Tax and spending limits on local governments, 1985–86

Restriction	Number of states
Overall property tax rate limit	12
Specific property tax limit	31
Property tax levy limit	21
General revenue limit	6
General expenditure limit	6
Limits on assessment increases	7
Full disclosure requirements (reports, advertisements, public hearings)	13

Source: United States Advisory Commission on Intergovernmental Relations, *Significant Features of Fiscal Federalism* 1985-86 Edition, (Washington, D.C., 1987), Table 9, p. 146.

Nearly all states (with the exception of four) impose debt restrictions on local governments by constitution, statute and local charter. The major constraints are limits on the amount of indebtedness (often expressed as a percentage of the assessed value of property) and requirements for a local referendum. Some states also control interest rates and the maximum number of years bonds can be outstanding. As is true of state government bonds, the restrictions affect mainly general obligation or "full faith and credit" bonds. Ordinarily, they do not affect revenue bonds. Nineteen state governments monitor proposed bond issues, but only nine explicitly approve them. Most states provide technical assistance in packaging and marketing local bonds.[128]

All state actions—grants and restrictions—have a direct and indirect effect on local budgets. Relatively few states, however, oversee and approve local budgets as such. Among them are New Jersey, Kentucky and New York (primarily the budgets of New York City, Buffalo and Yonkers, because of financial emergencies). Many states go no further than prescribing local budgetary formats and collecting and reviewing local budgets.[129]

If a serious financial emergency threatens, the states pull out all stops in controlling local budgets. After all, a default on debt payments by local governments would jeopardize the credit standing of the states. When New York City, Cleveland and some other local governments were at the verge of default in the mid-1970s, state governments intervened in a variety of ways: regulating local budgeting and financial management; providing emergency funds; authorizing new or higher taxes; loaning money or guaranteeing local debt; assuming local functions; placing the local government in virtual receivership; and restructuring the governmental oreganization. In 1983, forty-two states attempted to improve the credit ratings of local governments through guarantees, subsidies and the use of intermediaries for borrowing.[130] Should the fiscal crisis deepen for local governments, they can expect continued state intervention in budgeting in addition to the present array of mandates, restrictions and limits.

≡ What's ahead in the state-local nexus in budgeting

Because of federal budget cuts, local governments will continue to exert pressure on state governments for additional aid. At the same time, they will insist on more autonomy in running local affairs. This may put both levels of government on a collision course. State governments are also under pressure to cut state taxes and expenditures and may not be in a position to offset federal reductions. Given their own fiscal problems, states may prefer to give local governments more tax powers; reduce the number of mandates; stimulate local economic development by endorsing local bond issues; and, selectively, continue to assume complete responsibility for hitherto joint state-local functions. Should a serious recession occur again, however, federal-state-local budgetary relations will change dramatically and unpredictably.

HOW SOME OTHER COUNTRIES HANDLE INTERGOVERNMENTAL BUDGETING

As in the United States, subnational governments (provinces, states and municipalities) in other countries depend heavily on grants from the national government to finance their activities. A sampling of several countries (Western Europe, Japan and India) highlights, however, some major differences in the grant system between these countries and the United States.

Unlike the periodic squabbles and uncertainty in the U.S. with regard to the availability of funds, grants in other countries, while still beset by political controversy, rest on mere secure constitutional and statutory foundations. In several countries, bona fide revenue sharing takes place, with an assured distribution of funds among the various government levels. Supplementing revenue sharing, block grants in some countries are a preferred instrument for transfer payments, with fewer restrictions than in the United States. Special purpose grants that are similar to categorical grants in the U.S. also exist and carry with them the usual conditions. More so than in the U.S., several countries equalize resources among subnational governments, even at the risk of taking funds from the rich and giving them to the poor. In some countries, the several levels of government attempt to act in concert (not always harmoniously) on economic, monetary and fiscal policy, instead of working at cross purposes, as in the U.S.

With the possible exception of West Germany, no one intergovernmental system possesses all these features. Political bargaining over shares of grants in these countries is no less acute than in the U.S. Issues of centralization and decentralization, fiscal autonomy and regional competition divide national and subnational governments. Urban fiscal problems and interregional disparities in fiscal capacity and expenditure needs persist. At every turn, sharp differences exist among the various levels of government with regard to the continuing equity of the existing grant structure, revenue sharing and the allocation of functions.[131] As in the U.S., the resolution of such conflicts takes place in the political arena. What ultimately counts is what is politically acceptable. And this depends on the political strength of states and provinces, the pressures of interest groups, and the fiscal dominance of the national government.

≡ The budgetary impact of the grant system

Bahl has developed the following classification scheme of the components included in grant systems in Western Europe and Japan:

1. *Revenue support for subnational governments.* This category includes shared taxes and forms of revenue sharing.
2. *Grants (categorical and block) as incentives for expenditures to achieve national priorities.* Nearly every country relies on such grants.
3. *Equalization grants to overcome fiscal disparities among subnational governments.* Grant formulas in several countries, including West Germany, Canada and Japan, allocate specific funds for equalization purposes.[132]

Using data from a variety of sources, Bahl has summarized the forms of national aid that crystallized in twelve countries in the late 1970s and early 1980s:

Table 4-12

Percent distribution of central assistance to subnational governments by type of assistance

Country	Year	Shared tax with central government (derivation basis)	General purpose grants		Specific purpose grants
			Total	Equalizing	
Denmark	1977	41.0	17.8[e]	1.7	41.2
Italy	1975	–	50.0	50.0	50.0
Japan	1975	2.3	42.2	42.2	55.4
Canada	1979	–[a]	74.5	19.7	25.5
West Germany	1980	68.2	31.8	8.0[b]	–
Australia	1978	–	56.5[c]	–	43.5
United Kingdom	1979	–	85.0	77.0	15.0
United States	1980	–	9.9	9.9[d]	90.1
Netherlands	1978	–	41.2	–	58.8
Austria	1980	17.8	82.2	–[c]	–
France	1978	–	75.0	–	25.0
Switzerland	1980	13.3[a]	14.9	–	71.8

[a]Provincial (canton) income taxes not included.

[b]Interstate transfer not included.

[c]Includes some loan council borrowing.

[d]General revenue sharing is included here even though it is not entirely allocated on an equalizing basis.

[e]Excluding tax revenue equalization grant.

Source: Roy Bahl, "The Design of Intergovernmental Transfers in Industrialized Countries," *Public Budgeting and Finance*, Vol. 6, No. 4 (Winter 1986), p. 14.

At the beginning of the 1980s, subnational governments in the sample "accounted for over 60 percent of all government spending, raised about one-fourth of tax revenues, and received half of all revenues from intergovernmental transfers."[133]

As the table suggests, in budgeting, state and local governments rely on a varying mix of the three components. In West Germany and Australia, revenue sharing is far more significant than in Canada, Britain and the United States. Unlike the U.S., few fiscal links exist between the national and local governments. For the most part, the central government channels aid to the states or provinces, which, in turn, provide grants to local governments. Taken together, all types of grants loom large in the budgets of local governments. For example, in 1979–80, grants and tax sharing constituted 22 percent of the federal budget in Canada and roughly the same proportion of provincial budgets.[134] For local governments, grants are a fiscal lifeline, representing in various years 50 percent or more of local revenue in Australia, Britain and Canada.[135] In Australia and West Germany, the states count on shared revenues and grants for 60 percent or more of their receipts.[136]

≡ Revenue or tax sharing is a major factor in the grant structure in some countries

Revenue sharing in particular is a major factor in the budgets of several countries in the sample. Through constitutional and statutory arrangements, a specified proportion of personal income, corporate income and consumption taxes goes directly to subnational governments as the summary in Table 4-13 indicates.

Using various statutory formulas, the states in turn share their tax revenue with local governments or use the funds to provide grants. For example, in West Germany, the eight states must by law share income, corporate profits and value added taxes with local governments. In varying years, state allocations from these taxes ranged from 11.1 to 28.5 percent. The states can also opt to share other taxes, of which the major ones are taxes on business, real estate, sales, property and automobiles.[137]

≡ Equalization of resources and services dominates the grant structure in some countries

Nearly all countries in the sample outpace the U.S. in overcoming disparities in financial resources among the states and provinces. Through intricately structured equalization formulas, they attempt to bring poor

Table 4-13
Distribution of tax revenue to facilitate equalization of resources among subnational governments, selected countries and selected years

Country	Percent allocation of taxes
West Germany	Personal income tax: 43% feder-al, 43% state, 14% local; corporate profits tax: 50 % federal, 50% state (with the state allocating funds to the local governments); net value added tax (VAT): distribution based on formula and biennial negotiation, roughly two-thirds federal and one-third states (1980).
Australia	Personal income tax: 39.8% of col-lection of previous year to states and 1.52% to local governments which also get state grants (1980).
Canada	About 40% of personal and corpora-tion income taxes to provinces, 60% to federal government (1980).
India	States get negotiated share of income taxes (roughly 25 percent), export duty and other duties, some excise taxes (about 20 percent), (1970s).

Source: Advisory Commission on Intergovernmental Relations, *Studies In Comparative Federalism: West Germany* (Washington, D.C. 1981); ACIR, *Australia* (1981); ACIR,
Canada (1981); Verda Doss, *Impact of Planning on Central-State Financial Relations
in India* (New Delhi: National, 1978), pp. 188–189.

subnational government up to the level of wealthier governments. In their
formulas, they ignore tax effort for the most part and give a good deal of
weight to fiscal capacity. West Germany leads all the rest in the equity and
fairness of its equalization policies.

Like Robin Hood, West Germany takes surpluses from the rich
states and gives them to the poor states. Every state government is guaranteed revenues that amount to at least 92 percent of the national average per capita taxes. Where governments fall short of this figure, they get
grants from a national equalization fund. The fund receives its income from
the wealthy states. States with revenue amounting to 102 to 110 percent
of the national average contribute 70 percent of the surplus to the equalization fund. State revenues in excess of 110 percent of the average go
entirely to the fund. The value added tax (VAT) is also used to equalize
resources.

One-fourth of VAT revenue allocated to the states is used for equalization, and, if necessary, the federal government yields part of its share of
VAT.[138] So effective is equalization that few marked deviations from the
average per capita state revenue exist among the states. At the local level,
the federal and state governments equalize resources through a combination
of general purpose grants, specific grants and revenue sharing.

≡ The assumption of functions—who does what

A perennial issue in other countries as well as in the U.S. is the distribution of functions among the different levels of government and the
responsibility for funding those functions. In a complex fiscal and functional
mosaic, some functions are shared; some are the exclusive domain of one
governmental level; some are jointly financed by two or more levels of
government; and some are funded by only one tier of government. What
has evolved is not the result of any grand plan. Rather, it is the outcome of
continuing political battles over issues of centralization and decentralization;
disparities in fiscal responses among the different governmental levels; and
cultural, historical and ethnic forces.

As a result of these factors, in West Germany, education, law enforcement, health, housing and welfare are primarily state functions.[139] In
Canada, the provinces are largely responsible for education, health, welfare, civil rights and natural resources. This is also the general pattern in
Australia. In Britain, decentralization of activities has taken place on a modest scale. Local authorities are more or less exclusively responsible for roads,
transport, lighting, law enforcement and planning. Other functions, such
as elementary and secondary education, are national-local responsibilities
with local authorities administering educational programs under national
supervision and with national financial assistance. As of 1988 the entire
grant structure was in a state of flux with the Thatcher Government bent
on changing aid formulas to loosen the grip of the Labor Party on local
authorities.[140]

≡ Institutionalizing grantsmanship in several countries

Several countries have developed institutional arrangements to facilitate
the review, allocation and monitoring of grants and to determine their
impact on the economy. Of all countries, the states in West Germany are
in an especially key position to protect their interests. The second chamber
in the parliament, the Bundesrat, directly represents the states and has
the power to alter, approve or veto any legislation affecting the states.[141]
Beyond these constitutional arrangements, associations of state and local

government officials consult frequently with the federal government on shared taxes and grants.

Canada uses a trilevel consultation machinery to get the perspective of all levels of government on intergovernmental fiscal policy, especially with respect to urban problems. A coordinating body, composed of the Minister of State for Urban Affairs, a representative of the Annual Conference of Ministers of Municipal Affairs in the provinces and the heads of the Canadian Federation of Mayors of Municipalities, meets frequently to thrash out problems of grants, transportation, housing and urban growth.[142] The coordination that really counts takes place at the heated periodic conferences of the federal and state prime ministers. Often these result in agreements to disagree rather than on a consensus on taxes and expenditures.[143]

In Britain, PESC (Public Expenditure Survey Committee), in somewhat limited fashion, coordinates intergovernmental fiscal policy. The three year projection of revenues and expenditures, by function, as developed by PESC and approved by the government in a White Paper, becomes the framework for national and local budgeting. The projections include estimated local authority expenditures by function, regardless of source of funds. With but little consultation with local authorities, ministers in the central government estimate local authority expenditures by function. This weak link in fiscal planning drew the criticism of a government commission on intergovernmental finance, which proposed a central point for coordinating national and local plans and priorities and forecasting expenditures.[144]

Somewhat insulated from the political fray, although obviously influenced by it, highly respected statutory bodies in Australia and India advise the government on the allocation of grants. In Australia, the Commonwealth Grant Commission (with three federal members and three designated by the states) recommends the forms and amount of financial assistance, including equalization grants. Invariably, the government accepts its advice. Three special statutory commissions recommend the distribution of grants in various functional areas. Of these, the most important are the Tertiary Education Commission for post-secondary education and the Schools Commission for elementary and secondary education.[145] In India, a constitutional body, the Finance Commission, periodically advises the government on tax sharing and the allocation of grants. In practice, it has been eclipsed by the Planning Commission, which incorporates in India's five-year development plans necessary funding for states and local governments to implement targets in the plans and influences the preparation of annual budgets.[146]

☰ National-subnational coordination of intergovernmental budget, fiscal and economic policy

More so than in the U.S., several countries attempt to coordinate the fiscal and economic policies of different levels of government. Perhaps the most ambitious approach is the one taken by West Germany to promote economic stabilization. The main components are: (1) government benchmarks or guidelines for tax, expenditure and wage policies developed by an advisory group composed of representatives of business, labor and all levels of government; (2) countercyclical expenditure and borrowing policies proposed by a Business Cycle Council, which includes the federal ministries of finance and economic affairs, a representative of each state, and representatives designated by an association of local governments; and (3) a five year budget plan for all levels of government prepared by the federal government in cooperation with a Fiscal Planning Council, composed of the two federal "economics" ministers (finance and economic affairs), the minister of finance of each state and four representatives of local governments. Parliament has the final say in borrowing by all levels of government and in allocating federal expenditures to depressed regions and economic sectors. In practice, however, the federal and state governments in a recession follow countercyclical policies, while local governments tend to cut back expenditures and raise taxes.[147]

□ □ □

An integral part of budgeting in all countries, the grant system continues to pose major policy, management and fiscal problems. Because of intergovernmental funding, it is difficult to achieve accountability of results and improved management of major functions. Many governments, especially the U.S., have not been able to sort out functions tidily and rationally among the different levels of government. The uncertainty of grants continues to bedevil fiscal planning. As long as grants are dependent on political bargaining, this frustrating state of affairs will persist. The only way to get around it is to insulate grants from the political process through "pure" tax sharing and to freeze them in statutory formulas. But these changes also impose heavy costs. They result in uncontrollable expenditures and inflexible fiscal policies because of the large sums statutorily earmarked for aid.

All things considered, the grant structure will undoubtedly continue to evolve spottily, unevenly and possibly even inequitably in conformity with prior patterns. Hence, more, rather than less, complexity will be introduced in the budget process. To be effective, administrators and budgeteers must somehow learn to cope with such complexity.

═══ NOTES

≡ Section 1

1. Annmarie Walsh, "Foreword" in Xenia W. Duisin, *Government Corporations, Special Districts and Public Authorities: Their Organization and Management: A Selected, Annotated Bibliography* (New York: Institute of Public Administration 1985), p. 5. This covers government corporations in the United States. For references to other countries, see Ira Sharkansky, *Wither the State?* (Chatham, N.J.: Chatham House Publishers, 1979); Mary M. Shirley, *Managing State-Owned Enterprises* (Washington, D.C.: World Bank, 1983); Lloyd D. Musolf, *Mixed Enterprise: A Developmental Perspective* (Lexington, Mass.: Lexington Books, 1972).
2. James T. Bennett and Thomas J. Di Lorenzo, *Underground Government: The Off-Budget Public Sector* (Washington, D.C.: CATO Institute, 1983), p. 9.
3. National Academy of Public Administration, *Report on Government Corporations* (Washington, D.C., 1981), pp. 20–25.
4. Message to Congress, April 10, 1933, Congressional Record—Senate, Vol. 77, Part 2 (73rd Cong., lst Sess., April 4–24, 1933); p. 1423, cited by Jameson W. Doig, "If I See a Murderous Fellow Sharpening a Knife Cleverly . . . The Wilsonian Dichotomy and the Public Authority Tradition," *Public Administration Review*, Vol. 43, No. 4 (July/August 1983), p. 295.
5. Bennett and Di Lorenzo, *Underground Government*, first coined this phrase. The "hidden government" is suggested by Dennis I. Ippolito, *Hidden Spending* (Chapel Hill: University of North Carolina Press, 1984).
6. United States Department of Commerce, Bureau of the Census, *Governmental Organization, 1987 Census of Governments*, Preliminary Report (Washington, D.C., November 1987), p. 3.
7. Walsh in Duisin, *Government Corporations*, p. 6.
8. Bureau of the Census, *1987 Census of Governments*, pp. 1, 3.
9. Walsh, p. 5.
10. Annmarie Hauck Walsh, *The Public's Business* (Cambridge Mass.: Massachusetts Institute of Technology Press, 1978), p. 7.

11. Institute of Public Administration, *State Public Corporations: A Guide for Decision-Making* (New York, 1983), p. 5.

12. The figure for New York State is an estimate made by the New York State Budget Division in March 1985. The data for Pennsylvania are in Bennett and Di Lorenzo, *Underground Government*, p. 7.

13. The higher figure is in United States General Accounting Office, *Congress Should Consider Revising Basic Corporation Control Laws* (Washington, D.C., 1983). The lower figure is in Ronald C. Moe, *Administering Public Functions at the Margin of Government: The Case of Federal Corporations* (Washington, D.C.: Congressional Research Service, 1983). The National Academy of Public Administration (NAPA), *Government Corporations*, covered thirty-five public enterprises in its study.

14. NAPA, *Government Corporations*, p. 8; Walsh, *The Public's Business*, p. 29.

15. NAPA, *Government Corporations*, unpaged appendix.

16. Harold Seidman, "Government-Sponsored Enterprise in the United States," in Bruce L. R. Smith, ed., *The New Political Economy: The Public Use of the Private Sector* (New York: John Wiley & Sons, 1975), pp. 83–108.

17. Shirley, *Managing State-Owned Enterprises*, p. 4.

18. Philip Holland, *The Governance of Quangos* (London: Adam Smith Institute, 1981), cited by Bennett and Di Lorenzo, *Underground Government*, pp. 158–159; John Redwood, *Public Enterprise in Crisis: The Future of Nationalized Industries* (Oxford: Basil Blackwell, 1980), pp. 16–17; Chalmers Johnson, *Japan's Public Policy Companies* (Washington, D.C.: American Enterprise Institute, 1978), cited by Bennett and Di Lorenzo, pp. 163–164; Kiyohiko Yoshitake, *An Introduction to Public Enterprise in Japan* (Beverly Hills: Sage, 1973); Allen Tupper and G. Bruce Doern, eds., *Public Corporations and Public Policy in Canada* (Montreal: The Institute for Research in Public Policy, 1981), pp. 4–6; Jean-Francois Revel, "The Latest French Revolution," *Commentary*, Vol. 73, No. 6 (June 1982), pp. 29–35; *New York Times*, February 15, 1982, p. A1; Steven Solomon, "Europe's Quiet Revolution," *Forbes* (December 14, 1987), p. 52; David Coombes, *State Enterprise* (London: George Allen and Unwin Ltd., 1971), pp. 195–197; *New York Times*, February 11, 1982, p. D1; Alan Riding, "Brazil Acts to Tame State Ownership," *New York Times*, November 25, 1985, p. D8; United Nations, *Development Administration Newsletter*, No. 71 (November 1984–June 1985), p. 12.

19. Council of State Governments, *State Public Authorities* (Lexington, 1970), pp. 13–16.

20. Institute of Public Administration (IPA), *Special Districts and Public Authorities in Public Works Provision*. Report to the National Council on Public Works Improvement (New York City, August 1987), p. 40.

21. Walsh, *The Public's Business*, pp. 27–28, 118.

22. NAPA, *Corporations*, p. 15.

23. Walsh, *Government Corporations*, p. 6.

24. NAPA, *Corporations*, pp. 7, 16; Walsh, *Government Corporations*, p. 29.

25. Tupper and Doern, "Public Corporations," p. 157.

26. *Budget of the U.S. Government, FY 1985*, "Special Analysis F, Federal Credit Programs" in *Special Analyses*, pp. F1, 2.

27. Bennett and Di Lorenzo, p. 4; Doig, "If I See . . . ," pp. 295–302.

28. Letter from New Jersey Department of Treasury, Division of Budget and Accounting, March 31, 1982.

29. NAPA, *Corporations*, p. 14; Bennett and Di Lorenzo, p. 81.

30. Harold Seidman, "Nonprofit Intermediaries: Symptom or Cure?" in Harold Orleans, ed., *Nonprofit Organizations* (New York: Praeger, 1980), pp. 41–43; Harold Seidman, "Government-Sponsored Enterprise," p. 85.

31. OMB, *Budget, FY 1985*, "Special Analysis F," p. 19.

32. Doig, "If I see . . . ," p. 295.

33. John T. Tierney, "Government Corporations and Managing the Public's Business," *Political Science Quarterly*, Vol. 99, No. 1 (Spring 1984), p. 74.

34. Ibid.

35. IPA, *Special Districts*, p. 9.

36. Ibid., p. 8.

37. Bennett and Di Lorenzo, pp. 113, 169.

38. Shirley, *State-Owned Enterprises*, p. 4; United Nations, *Financing of Public Enterprises in Developing Countries* (New York, 1976), p. 6.

39. Richard Pryke, "The Monitoring and Control of Nationalized Industries in Great Britain," in United Nations, *Performance Evaluation of Public Enterprises in Developing Countries: Criteria and Institutions* (New York, 1984), p. 235.

40. Pierre Bauchet, "L'evaluation des performances economiques des enterprises publiques," in United Nations, ibid., pp. 72–77.

41. Ibid., pp. 46, 206–7.

42. Shirley, *State-Owned Enterprises*, p. 4.

43. Moe, *The Case of Federal Corporations*, pp. 65–195.

44. Ibid., pp. 44–45, 52–53; NAPA, *Corporations*, p. 19.

45. Moe, *Case*, p. 54; Congressional Budget Office, *Loan Guarantees* (Washington, D.C., 1979), pp. 19–20.

46. *Budget of the United States Government*, Fiscal Years 1980 to 1985.

47. Moe, *Case*, p. 111.

48. Ibid., p. 109.

49. *Budget of the U.S. Government, FY 1985*, pp. 6–11.

50. Ibid., pp. 6–13.

51. The major loan assets processed in this way are certificates of beneficial ownership (CBO). Several federal agencies, including the Farmers Home Administration, pool individual loans on which payments of principal and interest are due and sell certificates representing a share of ownership in the loan pool. At the same time, they guarantee the repayment of the loans. By selling off loan portfolios to FFB, the agency can make more loans. Through budgetary legerdemain neither the agency's budget nor the unified budget totals includes the CBO transactions. A CBO sale shifts the direct loan to off-budget status. This summary is based on Moe, *Case*, pp. 109–110.

52. Ibid., The Balanced Budget and Emergency Deficit Control Act of 1985, among other measures, provided for the inclusion of FFB transactions in agency budgets. The legislation was fully implemented in FY 1988.

53. Frederick D. Wolf, "Federal Government Credit Activities and How They

Relate to Loan Sales." Statement Before President's Commission on Privatization (Washington, D.C.: United States General Accounting Office, November 10, 1987).

54. *Budget of the United States Government, Fiscal Year 1987, Special Analyses,* "Special Analysis F, Federal Credit Programs," pp. F3, F31.

55. *Budget of the United States Government FY 1989,* "Special Analysis F," p. F94.

56. Ibid., p. F15.

57. "Special Analysis F," FY 1988, p. F9.

58. Ibid., pp. F6,7.

59. Ibid., pp. F22–23.

60. *Budget of the U.S. Government, FY 1985,* "Special Analysis F," p. F22.

61. Ibid., pp. F24–28.

62. *New York Times,* September 22, 1987, p. D1; "Special Analysis F," *FY 1989,* pp. 27–28.

63. Ibid.

64. Joint Financial Management Improvement Program, *Annual Report 1986* (Washington, D.C., 1987), p. 10; Bennett and Di Lorenzo, *Underground Government,* p. 149.

65. "Special analysis F," *FY 1989,* p. F47.

66. "Special Analysis F," *FY 1985,* pp. F31–35.

67. "Special Analysis F," *FY 1989,* p. F45.

68. "Special Analysis F," *FY 1985* pp. F26–27, 69.

69. Ippolito, *Hidden Spending,* pp. 15–16.

70. Ibid., p. 65.

71. Ronald C. Moe, "Government-Sponsored Enterprises," in Congressional Research Service, *The Federal Executive Establishment: Evolution and Trends,* prepared for the Committee on Governmental Affairs, U.S. Senate (Washington, D.C., 1980), pp. 38–58; Walsh, *Government Corporations,* p. 5; Seidman, "Nonprofit Intermediaries," p. 45.

72. NAPA, *Corporations,* p. 9.

73. Ibid., p. 9, "Special Analysis F," *FY 1989,* p. F47.

74. NAPA, *Corporations,* pp. 9–12.

75. Frederick C. Mosher, *The GAO* (Boulder, Colo.: Westview Press, 1974), p. 106.

76. NAPA, *Corporations,* pp. 9–12.

77. Ibid., p. 12.

78. Ibid., p. 14.

79. Ibid., pp. 58–62.

80. Ibid., p. 4.

81. Ibid., pp. 11–14.

82. Ibid., pp. vii-viii, 18.

83. CBO, *Loan Guarantees,* pp. 32–34.

84. Ibid.

85. Ippolito, *Hidden Spending,* pp. 88–90.

86. *Budget of the U.S. Government, FY 1982,* pp. 50–51, 54; *Special Analyses, FY 1987,* "Special Analysis F," p. F6.

87. *Budget of the U.S. Government, Budget Revision, FY 1981,* pp. 17–27.

88. *New York Times*, January 19, 1982, p. D1; Ippolito, *Hidden Spending*, pp. 3–4, 91, 106–121; "Special Analysis F" for *FY 1987* indicates that only "55 percent of credit budget totals for 1985 were capped by Appropriation Act limitations" (see p. F6).

89. Joint Financial Management Improvement Program, *Annual Report 1986*, pp. 11–12; "Special Analysis F," *FY 1989*, p. F7.

90. "Special Analysis F," *FY 1987*, p. F6.

91. *Budget of the U.S. Government, FY 1987*, Tables 14.1, 14.2, 14.3.

92. *Report of the President's Commission on Budget Concepts* (Washington, D.C., 1967), p. 24.

93. President's Commission on Budget Concepts, *Staff Papers and Other Materials* (Washington, D.C., 1967), pp. 189–190.

94. Congressional Budget Office (CBO), *Government-Sponsored Enterprises and Their Implicit Federal Subsidy: The Case of Sallie Mae* (Washington, D.C., 1985), p. 34.

95. Ibid., pp. xi–xiv; OMB, *Management of the United States Government, Fiscal Year 1989* (Washington, D.C., 1988), p. 109.

96. *New York Times*, March 11, 1986, p. D1.

97. *New York Times*, February 4, 1986, p. D1.

98. Shirley Hobbs Scheibla, "Privatizing Debt," *Barron's*, August 3, 1987, p. 30; Frederick D. Wolf," Proposals for Improved Credit Program Budgeting," Statement Before Committee on Budget, U.S. Senate (Washington, D.C., GAO, March 4, 1987).

99. Bennett and Di Lorenzo, *Underground Government*, p. 59.

100. IPA, *Special Districts*, Table 1.1 following p. 32.

101. Tax Foundation, *Facts and Figures on Government Finance* (Washington, D.C., 1979), p. 221, cited by Bennett and Di Lorenzo, pp. 42–43.

102. John E. Petersen, *Financial Planning for State Government* (Washington, D.C.: Council of State Planning Agencies, 1977), p. 31.

103. Tax Foundation, *Monthly Tax Features* (May 1982), cited by Bennett and Di Lorenzo, p. 122.

104. Bennett and Di Lorenzo, pp. 103–106.

105. Petersen, *Financial Planning*, p. 31.

106. Nathan S. Betnun, *Housing Finance Agencies* (New York: Praeger, 1976), pp. 172–3, 155.

107. Walsh, *The Public's Business*, pp. 6–8; see also Diana Henriques, *The Machinery of Greed: The Abuse of Public Authorities and What to Do About It* (Princeton, N.J.: Woodrow Wilson School, Princeton University, 1982).

108. *New York Times*, July 13, 1983, p. B1.

109. Annmarie Walsh and James Leigland, "The Only Planning Game in Town," *Empire State Report* (May 1983), p. 8.

110. Ibid., p. 6.

111. State of New York, *Executive Budget for the Fiscal Year April 1, 1987 to March 31, 1988* (Albany, N.Y., 1987), pp. 521–533.

112. New York State Moreland Act Commission on the Urban Development Corporation and Other State Financing Agencies, *Restoring Credit and Confidence: A Reform Program for New York State and Its Public Authorities* (Albany, N.Y., 1976), pp. 2–5.

113. Ibid., pp. 1–2, 10.
114. New York State, *Executive Budget for the Fiscal Year April 1, 1986 to March 31, 1987* (Albany, N.Y., 1986, pp. 519–531; ———, *Official Statement*, May 19, 1982, pp. 31–37.
115. Ibid., p. 31.
116. IPA, *Special Districts*, pp. 168–169.
117. Bennett and Di Lorenzo, *Underground Government*, p. 37; Walsh, *The Public's Business*, p. 61.
118. Unpublished data from New York State Department of Audit and Control, June 1987.
119. Letter from Office of Financial Management, State of Washington, March 25, 1982.
120. National Council on Public Works Improvement, "Special Districts and Authorities" (Washington, D.C., 1987), unpublished paper.
121. *New York Times*, August 19, 1985, p. D1.
122. Shirley, *State-Owned Enterprises*, p. 4.
123. Ibid., pp. 6–7.
124. Ibid., p. 95, citing data in World Bank files, analyses by a colleague, Peter Short, and data from the United Nations Industrial Development Organization (UNIDO).
125. Ibid., p. 96.
126. Ibid. p. 97, citing studies by Peter Heller and Allen Tait of the World Bank staff.
127. Ibid., p. 97.
128. Basu, "Public Enterprises in India," p. 27.
129. Shirley, *State-Owned Enterprises*, pp. 9–10, 13; United Nations, *Performance Evaluation of Public Enterprises in Developing Countries* (New York, 1984), p. 14.
130. Shirley, *State-Owned Enterprises*, pp. 13, 15–16.
131. A. Premchand, "Control of Non-financial Public Enterprises and Autonomous Agencies" in International Monetary Fund, *Budgeting and Expenditure Control* (Washington, D.C., 1983), p. 138.
132. Shirley, *State-Owned Enterprises*, pp. 17–18.
133. Peter Self, *Econocrats and the Policy Process* (Boulder, Colo.: Westview Press, 1977), p. 186; United Nations, *Performance Evaluation of Public Enterprises*, p. 33.
134. Shirley, *State-Owned Enterprises*, p. 29; Premchand, "Control of Non-financial Public Enterprises," p. 137; Premchand, *Government Budgeting and Expenditure Controls* (Washington, D.C.: International Monetary Fund, 1983), p. 458.
135. Basu, "Public Enterprises in India," pp. 122, 134–136.
136. Coombes, *State Enterprises*, pp. 43, 56–57, 87, 156; John Redwood, *Public Enterprises in Crisis: The Future of Nationalized Industries* (Oxford: Basil Blackwell, 1980), pp. 30, 196; R. Kelf-Cohen, *British Nationalization, 1945–1973* (New York: St. Martin's Press, 1973), p. 119; Richard Pryke, *Public Enterprise in Practice* (New York: St. Martin's Press, 1971), pp. 347–348. The comments are also based on interviews conducted in the British Treasury in August 1987.
137. Barenstein, "Public Enterprises in Mexico," p. 219.

138. Shirley, *State-Owned Enterprises*, pp. 42, 77–78.

139. Ibid., p. 22; Pryke, "Nationalized Industries," pp. 244–268; Peter Jackson and Francis Terry, eds., *Public Domain: The Public Sector Yearbook 1987* (London: Public Finance Foundation, 1987), pp. 111, 115; HM Treasury, "Control Framework for Nationalized Industries in the U.K." (London, 1985): Advisory Group, *Accounting for Economic Costs and Changing Prices. A Report to HM Treasury*, Vols. I and II (London: HMSO, 1986).

140. Shirley, *State-Owned Enterprises*, p. 30; Premchand, *Government Budgeting*, p. 443.

141. Premchand, p. 429.

142. Ibid., pp. 430–437.

143. Shirley, *State-Owned Enterprises*, p. 38. See also United Nations, *Measures for Improving Performance of Public Enterprises in Developing Countries* (New York, 1983); United Nations, *Financing of Public Enterprises in Developing Countries* (New York, 1976); Larry Jones, ed., *Public Enterprises in Less Developed Countries* (Cambridge: Cambridge University Press, 1982); A. H. Hanson, *Public Enterprises and Economic Development* (London: Routledge and Reagan, 1965).

144. Shirley, *State-Owned Enterprises*, p. 29.

145. Premchand, *Government Budgeting*, pp. 431–434; Barenstein, "Public Enterprises in Mexico," p. 209.

146. Shirley, *State-Owned Enterprises*, p. 25; Tupper and Doern, "Public Corporations," p. 33; Coombes, *State Enterprises*, pp. 21–24.

147. Donald Axelrod, "Performance Audit for Development," in United Nations, *Public Auditing Techniques for Performance Improvement* (New York, 1980), pp. 89–91.

148. David Howell, "Trends and Parliamentary Implications," in Bruce L. A. Smith and D. C. Hague, *The Dilemma of Accountability in Modern Government* (New York: St. Martin's Press, 1971), pp. 239–248; Redwood, *Public Enterprises*, pp. 24–25; Kelf-Cohen, *British Nationalization*, pp. 128–132; also based on interviews conducted in the British Treasury in August 1987.

149. Shirley, *State-Owned Enterprises*, p. 30.

150. Ibid., p. 55; Barenstein, "Public Enterprises in Mexico," p. 214; *Wall Street Journal*, February 22, 1986; *New York Times*, March 6, 1986; United Nations, *Development Administration Letter*, p. 12. Much of the information is also based on the writer's review of budgetary systems in Egypt, Thailand, Malaysia, and Sri Lanka between 1979 and 1983.

151. Tupper and Doern, "Public Corporations," p. 43.

152. Shirley, *State-Owned Enterprises*, pp. 60–61.

153. *Financial Times*, March 27, 1987, p. 12; Price Waterhouse, *Privatization: The Facts* (London, 1987); *Forbes*, April 7, 1986, p. 40; J. A. and D. J. Thompson, "Privatization: A Policy in Search of a Rationale," *The Economic Journal*, Vol. 96 (March 1986), pp. 18–32.

154. Steven Greenhouse, "France Embraces 'Popular Capitalism,'" *New York Times*, June 8, 1987, p. D10; *New York Times*, March 21, 1986, p. A1, and March 22, 1986, p. A6; Michael Parrott, "In France Privatization Brings an Embarrassment of Riches," *Barron's*, May 4, 1987.

155. Shirley, *State-Owned Enterprises*, p. 57.

≡ Section 2

1. The title is taken from Gerald E. Frug, "The Judicial Power of the Purse," *University of Pennsylvania Law Review*, Vol. 126, No. 4 (April 1978), pp. 715–793.
2. George E. Hale, "Federal Courts and the State Budgetary Process," *Administration and Society*, Vol. 11, No. 3 (November 1979) p. 358; Linda Harriman and Jeffrey D. Straussman, "Do Judges Determine Budget Decisions? Federal Court Decisions on Prison Reform and State Spending for Corrections," *Public Administration Review*, Vol. 43, No. 4 (July/August 1983), p. 343; "The Wyatt Case: Implementation of a Judicial Decree Ordering Institutional Change," *The Yale Law Journal*, Vol. 84 (May 1975), pp. 1344–1346.
3. Hale, "Federal Courts and the State Budgetary Process," pp. 358, 362.
4. *Benjamin v. Malcolm*, 495 F. Supp. 1357 (S.D.N.Y. 1980), cited by Harriman and Straussman, "Do Judges Determine Budget Decisions?" p. 350. See also *Gates v. Collier*, 390 F. Supp. 482 (N.D. Miss. 1975), aff'd 525 F.2d 965 (5th Cir. 1976) for a vigorous restatement of this position. Cooper argues, however, that in a significant number of cases, courts have been mindful of costs. See Philip J. Cooper, "Conflict or Constructive Tension: The Changing Relationships of Judges and Administrators," *Public Administration Review*, Vol. 45 (November 1985), pp. 644–645.
5. Robert H. Birkby, *The Court and Public Policy* (Washington, D.C.: Congressional Quarterly Press, 1983) p. 10; Donald L. Horowitz, *The Courts and Social Policy* (Washington, D.C.: The Brookings Institution, 1977), pp. 3–4.
6. Advisory Commission on Intergovernmental Relations (ACIR), *Studies in Comparative Federalism: Australia* M-129 (Washington, D.C., 1981), p. 6.
7. Ibid., pp. 28–30.
8. *State of Victoria v. Commonwealth*, 99 CLR575, 611 (1975), cited in Ibid., p. 31.
9. *Regina v. Greater London Council and Another*, Ex Parte London Borough Council (1981).
10. *Pickwell v. London Borough of Camden and Others, Law Report*, April 30, 1982.
11. Horowitz, *The Courts and Social Policy*, pp. 3–4.
12. Birkby, *The Court and Public Policy*, p. 45.
13. 5 U.S. (1 Cranch) 137, cited by Luther M. Swygert, "In Defense of Judicial Activism," *Valparaiso University Law Review*, Vol. 16, No. 3 (Spring 1982), pp. 439, 442.
14. Cited by Hale, "Federal Courts and the State Budgetary Process," p. 359.
15. George C. Greanias and Duane Windsor, "Is Judicial Restraint Possible in an Administrative Society?" *Judicature*, Vol. 64, No. 9 (April 1981), p. 402.
16. Ibid., p. 403; Frug, "The Judicial Power of the Purse," p. 733.,
17. Greanias, p. 401.
18. Frug, "The Judicial Power of the Purse," p. 718.
19. 373 F.2d 451 (D.C. Dist. 1966).
20. This decision was influenced by Morton Birnbaum's seminal article, "The Right to Treatment," *The American Bar Association Journal*, Vol. 46 (May 1960), pp. 449–505. An early critic of Birnbaum's position and of judicial

intervention was Harry L. Miller, "The Right to Treatment: Can the Courts Habilitate and Cure?" *The Public Interest*, Vol. 46 (Winter 1977), pp. 96–118.

21. 334 F. Supp. 1341 (M.D. Ala. N.D. 1971).

22. *Wyatt v. Stickney*, 344 F. Supp. 373 (M.D. Ala. N.D. 1972).

23. "The Wyatt Case," p. 1339.

24. Martin Tolchin, "Intervention by Courts Arouses Deepening Disputes," *New York Times*, April 24, 1977.

25. *Wyatt v. Stickney*, 344 F. Supp. 387 (M.D. Ala. N.D. 1972), modified 503 F. 2d 1354 (5th Cir. 1974); *Wyatt v. Stickney*, 344 F. Supp. 373 (M.D. Ala. N.D. 1972), modified 503 F. 2d 1305 (5th Cir. 1974).

26. *Wyatt v. Aderholt*, 503 F. 2d 1305 (5th Cir. 1974). Aderholt replaced Stickney as commissioner—hence, the change in name.

27. *Patricia Welsch et al. v. Vera Likens et al.*, 550 F. 2d 1122 (8th Cir. 1977).

28. 437 F. Supp. 1209 (E.D. La. 1976).

29. *Halderman v. Pennhurst State School and Hospital*, 446 F. Supp. 1295 (E.D. Pa. 1977), modified 612 F. 2d 84 (3rd Cir. 1977), modified 673 F. 2d 647 (3rd Cir. 1982), rev'd 465 U.S. 89 (1984).

30. *Pennhurst State School and Hospital v. Halderman*, 457 U.S. 1, 20 (1981).

31. 357 F. Supp. 752, 769 (E.D.N.Y. 1973).

32. *New York State Association for Retarded Children Inc. and Patricia Parisi et al. v. Governor Hugh Carey*, 393 F. Supp 715 (E.D.N.Y. 1975), "Final Judgment and Consent Decree." Several later decisions involved the same parties.

33. State of New York, *Executive Budget*, various fiscal years 1975–1976 through 1985–86 (Albany, N.Y.: Division of the Budget).

34. Helen Bloom, "Facing the Fiscal Dilemma," in Valeria Bradley and Gary Clarke, eds., *Paper Victories and Hard Realities: The Implementation of the Legal and Constitutional Rights of the Mentally Disabled* (Washington, D.C.: Health Policy Center of Georgetown University, 1976), pp. 85–91.

35. Michael S. Lottman, "Paper Victories and Hard Realities" in Bradley and Clarke, *Paper Victories*, pp. 94–95; D. J. and S. M. Rothman, *The Willowbrook Wars: A Decade of Struggle for Social Change* (New York: Harper and Row, 1985), cited by John Koh, "The Lawyer's Plot," *New Republic*, (February 4, 1985), p. 28, a review of the Rothman book.

36. Hale, "Federal Courts and the State Budgetary Process," pp. 358–359; Harriman and Straussman, "Do Judges Determine Budget Decisions?" p. 344.

37. 383 F. Supp. 53 (E.D. Texas 1974), rev'd 535 F. 2d 864 (5th Cir. 1976), rev'd 430 U.S. 322 (1977).

38. *N. H. Newman v. State of Alabama*, 503 F. 2d 1320 (5th Cir. 1974), cert. denied 421 U.S. 948 (1975).

39. Cited by Harriman and Straussman, "Do Judges Determine Budget Decisions?" p. 343.

40. *Holt v. Sarver*, 309 F. Supp. 362 (E.D. Ark. 1970), aff'd 442 F. 2d 304 (8th Cir. 1971).

41. *Battle v. Anderson*, 376 F. Supp. 402 (E.D. Okla. 1974), rev'd 594 F. 2d 786 (10th Cir. 1979), 477 F. Supp. 516 (1977), aff'd in part, rem'd in part 564 F.2d 388 (1977), opinion on remand 457 F. Supp. 719 (1978), cited by Harriman and Straussman, p. 351.

42. Frug, "The Judicial Power of the Purse," pp. 716, 772; *Intergovernmental Perspective*, Vol. 8 (Winter 1982), p. 21.

43. *Rhodes v. Chapman*, 49 LW 4677 (June 15, 1983); *Estelle v. Gamble*, 429 U.S. 97 (1976).

44. *Pugh v. Locke*, 406 F. Supp. 318 (M.D. Ala. 1976), aff'd 559 F. 2d 283 (5th Cir. 1977), modified 438 U.S. 781 (1978).

45. Allen L. Ault, "Resource Utilization in Corrections," *Corrections Today*, Vol. 42 (July/August 1970), p. 13, cited by Harriman and Straussman, "Do Judges Determine Budget Decisions?" p. 343.

46. Harriman and Straussman, p. 52.

47. Richard A. L. Gambitta, "Litigation, Judicial Deference and Policy Change," *Law and Policy Quarterly*, Vol. 3, No. 2 (April 1980), pp. 141–2.

48. *Brown v. Board of Education*, 347 U.S. 483 (1954), aff'd and remanded 349 U.S. 294 (1955).

49. John C. Hogan, *The Schools, The Courts and the Public Interest* (Lexington, Mass.: Lexington Books, 1974), p. 26.

50. Robert G. Kaiser, "Garrity Role: Political Issue," *Washington Post*, July 1, 1976, cited by Hale, "Federal Courts and the State Budgetary Process," p. 359.

51. *Milliken v. Bradley*, 433 U.S. 267 (1977).

52. *Hobson et al. v. Hansen et al.*, 327 F. Supp. 844 (D.C. 1971), cited by Horowitz, *The Courts and Social Policy*, pp. 106–170.

53. *State of North Carolina et al. v. Department of Education*, No. 79-217-CIV 5 (E.D. N.C. 1979).

54. For a discussion of the budgetary impact of cases affecting handicapped children, see R. Shep Melnick, "The Politics of Partnership," *Public Administration Review*, Vol. 45 (November 1985), pp. 657–658. Melnick cites in particular *Cherry v. Mathews*, 419 F. Supp. 922 (D.C. Cir. 1976); *Doe v. Anrig*, 692 F. 2d 800 (1st Cir. 1982), overruled *Doe v. Brookline School Committee*, 722 F. 2d 910 (lst Cir. 1983); *Hendrick Hudson Dist. Bd. v. Rowley*, 458 U.S. 176 (1982); see also *Mills v. Board of Education*, 348 F. Supp. 866 (D.C. Cir. 1972); *Pennsylvania Association for Retarded Children v. Pennsylvania*, 343 F. Supp. 279 (E.D. Pa. 1972); *Battle v. Commonwealth of Pennsylvania*, 629 F. 2d 269 (3rd Cir. 1980).

55. *Mindy Linda Panitch v. The State of Wisconsin*, 72-C-461 (E.D. Wis. 1978), cited by Barbara Thompson, "Major Court Decisions Affecting Education Budget Decisions in Wisconsin," (Madison, Wisconsin, Department of Agriculture, March 22, 1982). Department of Administration, March 22, 1982.

56. Data from the Education Commission of the States reported by the *New York Times*, June 24, 1982; Michael W. Kirst, "The New Politics of State Education Finance," *Phi Delta Kappan* (February 1979), pp. 427–436; Hale, "Federal Courts and the State Budgetary Process," p. 361; W. Wilkins and J. Callahan, "Educational Finance," in R. Howard and A. Rosenthal, eds., *Legislative Priorities for Policy Assistance* (New Brunswick, N.J.: Eagleton Institute for Politics, Rutgers University, 1976), pp. 22–24.

57. Lawyers' Committee for Civil Rights under Law, School Finance Project, *Update on State-wide School Finance Cases* (Washington, D.C., April 1980); State of New York, Attorney General, *Reply Brief for Defendants—Appellants*

in Board of Education, Levittown Union Free School District et al. v. Nyquist (Albany, N.Y.: April 30, 1982), Appendices A and B.

58. Robert Briffault, "State-Local Relations and Constitutional Law," *Intergovernmental Perspective*, Vol. 13, No. 3/4 (Summer/Fall 1987), pp. 10–12.

59. 5 Cal. 3d 584, 487 P. 2d 1241, 96 Cal. Repts. 601 (1971), cert. denied 432 U.S. 907 (1977).

60. A. Alan Post and Richard W. Brandsma, "The Legislature's Response to *Serrano v. Priest*," *Pacific Law Journal*, Vol. 4, No. 1 (January 1973), pp. 29–34.

61. *Serrano v. Priest*, 18 Cal. 3d 728, 557 P. 2d 929, 135 Cal. Reptr. 345 (1976), cert. denied 432 U.S. 907 (1977).

62. 411 U.S. 959, 36 L. Ed. 2d 16, (1973), cited by Robert H. Birkby, *The Court and Public Policy* (Washington, D.C.: Congressional Quarterly Press, 1983), p. 200.

63. Gambitta, "Litigation," pp. 153–55.

64. The first two cases were adjudicated in the Superior Court and the Supreme Court in *Robinson v. Cahill*, 119 N.J. Super. 40, 289 A2d 569 (N.J. Super. Ct. Law Div. 1972), modified 62 N.J. 473. The Supreme Court took additional actions in *Robinson III*, 63 N.J. 196 (1973); 306 AD 2d 65 (1973), cert. denied 414 U.S. 976; *Robinson IV*, 67 N.J. 333 (1975); and *Robinson V*, 70 N.J. 155, 358 AD 2d 457 (1976).

65. *Board of Education, Levittown et al. v. Nyquist et al.*, 94, Misc. 2d 466 (1978), aff'd 408 N.Y.S. 2d 606 (1978), modified 83 AD 2d 217, 433 N.Y.S. 2d 843 (1982), modified 57 NY 2d 27, 453 N.Y.S. 2d 643 (1981). An appeal was dismissed by the U.S. Supreme Court in *Levittown et al. v. Nyquist et al.*, 459 U.S. 1139 (1983). See also New York State Division of the Budget, "Levittown: A Reversal with Reservations," *Budget Notes*, June 23, 1982.

66. State of New York, *Executive Budget*, Fiscal Years 1981–82 through 1986–87 (Albany, N.Y.: Division of the Budget).

67. *Jenkins v. Missouri*, No. 77-0420-CV-W-4 (1987).

68. Frug, "The Judicial Power of the Purse," pp. 774–780.

69. 394 U.S. 618 (1969), cited in ibid., p. 779; see also *Dunn v. Rivera*, 404 U.S. 54 (1972).

70. *Memorial Hospital v. Maricopa County*, 413 U.S. 250 (1974).

71. 397 U.S. 397 (1970), cited by Irene Lurie, "Major Changes in the Structure of the AFDC Program Since 1935," *Cornell Law Review*, Vol. 59, No. 5 (June 1974), pp. 843–44.

72. 406 U.S. 535 (1972), cited in ibid., p. 845.

73. 397 U.S. 47 (1970), cited by Frug, "The Judicial Power of the Purse," p. 777.

74. *U.S. Department of Agriculture v. Murray*, 413 U.S. 508 (1977), cited by William O. Jenkins, Jr., "The Judicial Power of the Purse: Court Constraints on Congressional Budgetary Decisions" (Paper presented at annual meeting of Midwest Political Science Association, Chicago, April 24, 1980).

75. *Townsend v. Swank*, 404 U.S. 282 (1971).

76. *Maher v. Roe*, 432 U.S. 464 (1977), and *Beal v. Doe*, 432 U.S. 438 (1977).

77. See Frug, "The Judicial Power of the Purse," p. 780.

78. Jenkins, "The Judicial Power of the Purse," pp. 15–17.

79. Ibid., p. 20.

80. 397 U.S. 254 (1970).

81. Cited by Frug, "The Judical Power of the Purse," pp. 773–774.

82. *Richardson v. Parales*, 402 U.S. 389 (1971).

83. 424 U.S. 319 (1976), cited by Frug, pp. 775–776.

84. Ibid., p. 776.

85. 426 U.S. 833 (1976).

86. In *Kramer v. New Castle Area Transit Authority*, 638 F. 2d 195 (9th Cir.), cert. granted 103 S.Ct. 567. (1982), the Supreme Court held that a local transit authority funded in part by the federal Urban Mass Transportation Act of 1964 was subject to the wage and hour provisions of the Fair Labor Standards Act. In *United Transportation Union v. Long Island Railroad*, 455 U.S. 678 (1982), it ruled that state provisions on strikes by public employees did not apply to public transportation workers.

87. 469 U.S. 528 (1985).

88. S. Kenneth Howard, "A Message From *Garcia*," *Public Administration Review*, Vol. 45 (November 1985), p. 738; *Public Administration Times*, February 19, 1985, p. 1, August 15, 1985, p. 1, and October 1, 1985, p. 1; *Government Computer News*, October 25, 1985, p. 1; Advisory Commission on Intergovernmental Relations, *Reflections on Garcia and Its Implications for Federalism* (Washington, D.C., 1987).

89. *County of Washington v. Gunther*, 452 U.S. 161 (1981).

90. *American Federation of State, County, and Municipal Employees (AFSCME) v. State of Washington*, 578 F. Supp. 846 (W.D. Wash. 1983), rev'd 770 F. 2d 1401 (9th Cir. 1985); Michael Graham, "Comparable Worth: Judicial, Legislative and Administrative Developments" (Paper presented at the National Conference of the American Society for Public Administration, Anaheim, Calif., April 13–16, 1986); *Intergovernmental Perspective*, Vol. II, No. 1 (Winter 1985), p. 23; *Public Administration Times*, September 1, 1985, p. 1.

91. Graham; *Intergovernmental Perspective*, p. 23.

92. *Equal Opportunity Commission v. Wyoming*, 460 US 226 (1983); Cynthia C. Colella, "EEOC v. Wyoming: Whither the NLC Defense? " *Intergovernmental Perspective*, Vol. 9, No. 2 (Spring 1983), pp. 26–27.

93. Louis Fisher, *Court Cases on Impoundment of Funds: A Public Policy Analysis* (Washington, D.C.: Congressional Research Service, 1974), p. 1.

94. Richard A. Lyons, "Nixon's Impoundment of Billions in Federal Money Is a Complicated Issue Abounding in Misconceptions," *New York Times*, June 30, 1983; Dennis I. Ippolito, *Congressional Spending* (Ithaca: Cornell University Press, 1981), p. 152.

95. *The Congressional Digest*, vol. 52, No. 4 (April 7, 1973), pp. 101–112, 118–127.

96. *Train v. City of New York*, 420 U.S. 35 (1975).

97. Fisher, *Court Cases on Impoundment*, pp. 80–90.

98. *Dotson v. Butz*, Civ. No. 73-1210 (D.C. 1973), cited by Jenkins, "Judicial Power of the Purse," pp. 6–8.

99. *City of New York v. Ruckelshaus*, 358 F. Supp. 669 (1973), aff'd F. 2d 1033 (D.C. Cir. 1974), cert. granted (1974), aff'd *Train v. City of New York*, 420 U.S. 35 (1975).

100. *New York Times*, May 7, 1973.

101. *National Association of Counties v. Baker*, 669 F. Supp. 518 (D.D.C. 1987), 842 F. 2d 369, 56 U.S.L.W. 2513 (D.C. Cir. 1988).

102. *School District of La Farge et al. v. Kenneth E. Lindner et al.*, 100 Wis. 2d 111, 301 N.W. 2d 196 (1981).
103. *Mangrabang et al. v. Ariyoshi et al.*, State of Hawaii, Civ. No. 49191 (1980).
104. *Oneida County v. Berle*, 91 Misc. 2d 694 (1977), 390 N.Y.S. 2d 600 (1977), aff'd 66 N.Y. A.D. 2d 985, 411 N.Y.S. 2d 884 (4th Dept. 1978), modified 411 N.Y.S. 407 (1980).
105. Joseph Cooper, "The Legislative Veto in the 1980s," in Lawrence C. Dodd and Bruce I. Oppenheimer, eds., *Congress Reconsidered*, 3rd ed. (Washington, D.C.: Congressional Quarterly Press 1985), p. 368; Louis Fisher, "Judicial Misjudgments about the Lawmaking Process: The Legislative Veto Case," *Public Administration Review*, Vol. 1, No. 45 (November 1985), p. 705.
106. M. S. Cavanagh et al., *Congressional Veto Legislation 97th Congress* (Washington, D.C.: Congressional Research Service, 1982), pp. 1–7, cited by Cooper, p. 367.
107. *INS v. Chadha*, 462 U.S. 919, 952 (1983).
108. *Process Gas Consumers Group v. Consumer Energy Council*, 103 S. Ct. 3556 (1983), 463 U.S. 1216 (1983), and *U.S. Senate v. FTC*, 463 U.S. 1216 (1983), cited by Cooper, p. 361.
109. Cooper, pp. 361, 370.
110. Louis Fisher, "Judicial Misjudgments," p. 706; Louis Fisher, "One Year After *INS v. Chadha:* Congressional and Judicial Developments," typed report (Washington, D.C.: Congressional Research Service, June 23, 1984); Kathleen Sylvester, "After Chadha, A Legal Void," *National Law Journal* (April 23, 1984), pp. 1, 8; James Sundquist, "The Legislative Veto: A Bounced Check," *The Brookings Review* 2 (1983), p. 13, cited by Cooper, pp. 364, 385, 368.
111. Martin Tolchin, "In Spite of the Court the Legislative Veto Lives On," *New York Times*, December 21, 1983, p. B10.
112. Fisher, "Judicial Misjudgments," pp. 706–711.
113. *Dane v. Aetna Casualty and Surety Co.*, 369 Mass. 990, 341 N.E. 2d 254 (1976).
114. *Judge, Governor of the State of Montana v. Legislative Finance Committee*, No. 132001 (Supreme Court, 1975).
115. *TVA v. Hill*, 437 U.S. 153 (1978).
116. Jenkins, "Judicial Power of the Purse."
117. *Sierra Club et al. v. U.S. Army Corps of Engineers et al.*, 771 F. 2d 409 (8th Cir. 1985); *New York Times*, September 12, 1983, pp. A1, B5.
118. *Ely v. Velde*, 451 F. 2d 1130 (4th Cir. 1971).
119. *New York Public Interest Research Group, Inc., v. Carey*, 383 N.Y.S. 2d 197 (1976), aff'd 55 A.D. 2d, 274, 390 N.Y.S. 236 (1976), appeal dismissed 41 N.Y. 2d 1074, 384 N.E. 2d 849, 396 N.Y.S. 2d 185 (1977).
120. George D. Brown, "The Courts and Grant Reform: A Time for Action," *Intergovernmental Perspective*, Vol. 7, No. 4 (Fall 1981), pp. 6–14.
121. Thomas J. Madden, "Future Directions for Federal Assistance Programs: Lessons from Block Grants and Revenue Sharing," *Federal Bar Journal*, Vol. 36 (Summer/Fall 1977), pp. 115–116.
122. 356 F. Supp. 291 (ND Ga 1973).
123. *U.S. v. Chicago*, 549 F. 2d 415–436 (7th Cir. 1977), cert. denied 434 U.S. 875 (1977).
124. *City of Hartford v. Hills*, 408 F. Supp 889 (D. Conn. 1976), rev'd 561 F. 2d

1032 (2nd Cir. 1976), cert. denied 434 U.S. 1034 (1978), cited by Madden, "Future Directions," p. 113.

125. 687 F. 2d 644 (2nd Cir. 1982), cited by *Intergovernmental Perspective*, Vol. 9, No. 2 (Spring 1983), p. 25.

126. *Delaware Valley Citizens Council v. Pennsylvania*, 678 F. 2d 470 (3rd Cir. 1982), cert. denied 103 S. Ct. 298 (1982), cited by *Intergovernmental Perspective*, p. 29.

127. 448 U.S. 448 (1980).

128. 671 F. 2d 702 (2nd Cir. 1982), cert. denied 459 U.S. 857 (1982).

129. 455 F. Supp. 532 (D.N.C. 1977), aff'd 98 S.Ct. 1597 (1978), cited by George D. Brown, "Federal Funds and National Supremacy: The Role of State Legislatures in Federal Grant Programs," *The American University Law Review*, Vol. 28, No. 3 (Spring 1979), p. 305.

130. *Public Administration Times*, March 1985, p. 3 and various issues of *Initiative News Report* published fortnightly in Arlington Virginia by Capital Publications, Inc.

131. *New Jersey Association on Correction v. Lan, Secretary of State of New Jersey*, 403 A. 2d 437 (1979), 80 N.J. 199 (1979).

132. *New York Public Interest Research Group, Inc. et al. v. Hugh L. Carey, Governor*, 42 N.Y. 2d 527, 369 N.E. 2d 1155, 399 N.Y.S. 2d 621 (1977); *New York Times*, November 9, 1977.

133. *Fine v. Firestone*, 448 Fla. 984 (So. 2d 1984); *Public Administration Times*, March 1, 1985.

134. *American Federation of Labor—Congress of Industrial Organization et al. v. Lewis K. Uhler, Secretary of State*, 36 Cal. 3d 687, 686 P. 2d 609, 36 Cal. 3d 687, 206 Cal. Rptr. 89 (1984).

135. *Public Administration Times*, March 1985, p. 3.

136. *State ex rel Warren v. Nussbaum*, 59 Wis. 2d 391, 208 N.W. 2d 780 (1973).

137. *New York State Coalition for Criminal Justice, Inc. et al. v. Thomas Coughlin, III et al.* 103 A.D. 2d 40, 479 N.Y.S. 2d 850, aff'd 64 N.Y. 2d 660, 485 N.Y.S. 2d 247, 474 N.E. 2d 607 (1984).

138. *Flushing National Bank v. Municipal Assistance Corporation*, 84 Misc. 2d 976 (1975), 379 N.Y. 2d 978 (1975), rev'd 40 N.Y. 2d 731, 390 N.Y.S. 22 (1976).

139. For example, see *Public Utility District No. 1 of Lewis County, et al. v. WPPSS and Chemical Bank*, 705 P. 2d (1985); *Chemical Bank v. WPPSS and Public Utility Dist. No. 1 of Benton County, et al.*, 691 P. 2d 524, 102 Wash. 874 (1984), *Chemical Bank v. WPPSS and Columbia Rural Electric Association Inc.*, 666 P. 2d 329 (1983).

140. J. L. Doddy and L. C. Ethridge, "Federalism Before the Courts," *Intergovernmental Perspective*, Vol. 2, No. 2 (Spring 1976), pp. 6–14.

141. For example, see *Austin, et al. v. State of New Hampshire et al.*, 420 U.S. 656 (1975).

142. *Maryland v. Louisiana*, 49 LW 4562 (1981).

143. *Commonwealth Edison v. Montana* 49, LW 4957 (1981), cited by *Intergovernmental Perspective*, Vol. 8, No. 1 (Winter 1982), p. 21.

144. *Armco Inc. v. Hardesty*, 467 U.S. 638 (1984).

145. *Bacchus Imports Ltd. et al. v. H. H. Dias, Director of Taxation of the State of Hawaii*, 464 U.S. 1015 (1983).

146. 554 F. 2d 1094 (D.C. Cir. 1976), cited by David H. Davis, "User Fees for Regulation" (Paper delivered at annual meeting of American Society for Public Administration, Anaheim, Calif., Apr 15, 1986).

147. 415 U.S. 345 (1974), cited by Davis.

148. *Town of Sudbury, et al. v. Commissioner of Corporations and Taxation*, 321 N.E. 2d 641 (1974); *Hallerstein v. Assessor, Town of Islip*, 37 N.Y. 2d 1, 371 N.Y. 2d 388 (1975), modif. 39 N.Y. 2d 920 (1976).

149. For example, see *Tappan Washington Memorial Corp. v. Margetti*, 9 N.J. Super. 212, 75 A. 2d 823 (1950); *Stockton Civic Theater v. Bd. of Supervisors*, 66 (Cal. 2d), 13, 423 P. 2d 810, 56 Cal. Rptr 658 (1967); *Dept. of Revenue ex rel. Luckett v. Isaac W. Bernheim Foundation, Inc.*, 505 S.W. 2d 762 (Ky. 1974); *American Institute of Economic Research v. Assessor*, 324 Mass. 509, 87 N.E. 2d 186 (1949).

150. *Coca-Cola Co. et al. v. Lindley*, Common Pleas, Franklin County Ohio, 81 Civ-11-6214 (1982); *Motorists Development Co. et al. v. Lindley*, 69 Ohio St. 2d 110; *Ames Volkswagen Ltd. v. State Tax Commissioner*, 418 N.Y.S. 2d 324, 47 N.Y. 2d 345 (1979).

151. *South Carolina v. Baker*, 108 S.Ct. 1355, 56 U.S.L.W. 4311 (1988); *Government Finance Officers Association et al. v. Baker*, 680 F. Supp. 1538 (N.D. Ga. 1988); *Public Administration Times*, May 20, 1988, p. 1; Oct. 28, 1987, p. l.

152. *Wein v. Carey*, 41 N.Y. 2d 504, 393 N.Y.S. 2d 959 (1977).

153. *Oneida v. Berle*, 49 N.Y. 2d 515, 427 N.Y.S. 2d 407 (1980).

154. *Bowsher v. Synar*, (No. 85-1377); *U.S. Senate v. Synar*, (No. 85-1378); *O'Neill v. Synar* (No. 85-1379) (1986); *Bowshar v. Synar*, 106 S.Ct. 3181, 92 L.E. 2d 583 (1986); Congressional Budget Office, *Reducing the Deficit* (Washington, D.C., 1986), pp. 9–12.

155. *Alexander v. State of Mississippi*, 441 So. 2d 1329 (1983), cited by Edward J. Clynch, "Mississippi Budgeting at the Crossroads" (Paper delivered at Annual Meeting of ASPA, Anaheim, Cal., April 1986).

156. Among the cases are *Shapp v. Sloan*, 480 Pa. 449, 391 A. 2d 595 (1975), appeal dismissed sub. no. *Thornburgh v. Casey*, 99 S. Ct. 1415 (1979); *MacManus v. Love*, 179 Colo. 218, 499 P. 2d 609 (1972); *Anderson v. Regan*, 437 N.Y. 2d 912 (1981); *Sego v. Kirkpatrick*, 86 N.M. 359, 524 P. 2d 975 (New Mexico, 1974).

157. *Posner v. Rockefeller*, 26 N.Y. 2d 970, 259 N.E. 2d 484, 311 N.Y. 2d 15 (1970).

158. 65 Misc. 2d 954, 320 N.Y.S 2d 836 (1971), rev'd 36 A.D. 2d 387, 320 N.Y.S 2d 957 (3rd Dept 1971), modified 28 N.Y. 2d 439, 322 N.Y.S 2d 687 (1971).

159. *Saxton v. Carey*, aff'd with modification 61 A.D. 2d 645, 403 N.Y.S. 2d 779 (3rd Dept. 1978), aff'd 44 N.Y. 2d 545 (1978), 406 N.Y.S. 2d 732 (1978).

160. 283 MD. 560, 392 A2d 67 (MD 1978).

161. *Kleczka and Shabaz v. Conta et al.*, 264 N.W. 2d 539, 82 W.2d 67 (1978).

162. *Metropolitan Transportation Authority v. Nassau County*, 28 N.Y. 2d 387 (1971), 322 N.Y.S. 2d 228 (1971).

163. Kenneth O. Eikenberry, "Governmental Tort Litigation and the Balance of Power," *Public Administration Review*, Vol. 45 (November 1985), pp. 742–745.

164. Charles R. Wise, "Liability of Federal Officials: An Analysis of Alternatives,

Public Administration Review, Vol. 45 (November 1985), pp. 746–7; *Public Administration Times*, May 20, 1988, p. 16; *Erwin v. Westfall*, 108 St. Ct. 580, 98 L. Ed. 2d 619 (No. 86–714, 1988).

165. Wise, "Liability," p. 750.
166. Eikenberry, "Governmental Tort," p. 742.
167. Yong S. Lee, "Lawsuits Against State and Local Governments," (Paper delivered at annual meeting of the American Society for Public Administration, Anaheim, Calif., April 13–16, 1986. Some of the cases below were cited by Lee.)
168. 436 U.S. 658 (1978).
169. 445 U.S. 622 (1980); 448 U.S. 1 (1980).
170. Wise, "Liability," p. 753.
171. 365 U.S. 167 (1961).
172. 106 S.Ct. Reptr, 1291 (March 15, 1986).
173. *St. Louis v. Praprotnik*, No. 86, 772 (1988); *New York Times*, March 3, 1988, p. A14.
174. *Public Administration Times*, April 15, 1986, p. 3; ———, March 1, p. 1.
175. *Public Administration Times*, November 1, 1985, 1; *New York Times*, March 23, 1988, p. A1.
176. Hale, "Federal Courts and the State Budgetary Process," pp. 362–367; Harriman and Straussman, "Do Judges Determine Budget Decisions?" p. 345.
177. Raoul, Berger, "The Supreme Court As a Legislature: A Dissent," *Cornell Law Review*, Vol. 64 (August 1979), pp. 998–1000; ———, *Government by Judiciary* (Cambridge, Mass.: Harvard University Press, 1977).
178. Horowitz, *The Courts and Social Policy*, pp. 7–11.
179. Nathan Glazer, "Should Judges Administer Social Services?" *The Public Interest*, 5 (Winter 1978), pp. 64–80.
180. Ibid.; Glazer, "Imperial Judiciary," pp. 104–123; Harriman and Straussman, "Do Judges Determine Budget Decisions?" p. 350.
181. R. Shep Melnick, *Regulation and the Courts: The Case of the Clean Air Act* (Washington, D.C.: The Brookings Institution, 1983), pp. 13–18.
182. Glazer, "Social Services," p. 79.
183. Harriman and Straussman, "Do Judges Determine Budget Decisions?" p. 349.
184. Glazer, *Social Services*," pp. 78–79.
185. "The Wyatt Case," pp. 1344–46.
186. Bradley C. Canon, "Defining the Dimension of Judicial Activism," *Judicature*, Vol. 66, No. 6 (December 1982/January 1983), p. 238.
187. Lloyd L. Weinrib, "Judicial Activism," *New York Times*, Feb. 3, 1982, p. A27.
188. Ibid.
189. Frank M. Johnson, Jr., "Observations: The Constitution and the Federal Court Judge," *Texas Law Review*, Vol. 54, No. 5 (June 1976), p. 905.
190. Frank M. Johnson, Jr., "The Role of the Judiciary with Respect to the Other Branches of Government," *Georgia Law Review*, Vol. 11, No. 3 (Spring 1977), pp. 455–473; Gambitta, "Litigation, Judicial Deference," p. 153.
191. Canon, "Defining the Dimensions," pp. 237–247.
192. Abram Chayes, "The Role of the Judge in Public Law Litigation," *Harvard Law Review*, Vol. 89 (May 1976), pp. 1281–1311.
193. Swygert, "In Defense of Judicial Activism," p. 449.

194. Theodore Lowi, *American Government: Incomplete Conquest* (Hinsdale, Ill.: The Dryden Press, 1971), p. 96.
195. Canon, "Defining the Dimensions," pp. 237–238; A. E. Dick Howard, "Judicial Federalism: The States and the Supreme Court" (Paper for the Conference on Federalism at the Institute for Contemporary Studies, Washington D.C., September 8, 1981), cited by *Intergovernmental Perspective*, Vol. 8, No. 1 (Winter 1982), p. 11.

☰ Section 3

1. George P. Shultz and Kenneth Dam, *Policy Making Beyond the Headlines* (New York: W. W. Norton, 1978), p. 421, cited by Donald Haider, "Presidential Management Initiatives: A Ford Legacy to Executive Management Improvement," *Public Administration Review*, Vol. 39, no. 3 (May/June 1979), p. 256.
2. Some rough and ready definitions follow: (1) *efficiency* is the production of more outputs at the same cost or the production of the same outputs at lower cost; (2) *economy* covers savings in operations through efficiency, policy changes and other means; (3) *effectiveness* is the extent to which the objectives of governmental programs are met; (4) *productivity* is the relationship between resources (inputs) and outputs and hence is a measure of efficiency; (5) *impact* is the measure of the effect of programs and projects, good and bad, on social, economic and environmental conditions that led to the implementation of the programs and projects in the first place; and (6) *results* are a broad measure that covers the other five measures.
3. 42 Stat. 20 (1921).
4. U.S. President's Committee on Administrative Management in the Federal Government, *Report of the Committee with Studies of Administrative Management in the Federal Government* (Washington, D.C.: USGPO, 1937), p. 20.
5. Executive Order 8248 was issued on September 9, 1929, cited by Larry Berman, *The Office of Management and Budget and the Presidency, 1921–1979* (Princeton: Princeton University Press, 1979), pp. 13–14.
6. Haider, "Presidential Management Initiatives," pp. 251–52.
7. Based in part on Berman, *Office*, pp. 19–28, and Stephen Hess, *Organizing the Presidency* (Washington, D.C.: The Brookings Institution, 1976), p. 39.
8. Haider, "Presidential Management Initiatives," p. 256.
9. Executive Office of the President (EOP), Bureau of the Budget (BOB), *Management Improvement in the Executive Branch* (Washington, D.C., 1961), p. 1.
10. U.S. Commission on Organization of the Executive Branch of the Government (1947–1949), *A Report to the Congress* (Washington, D.C.: USGPO, 1949).
11. 31 U.S.C. 18, cited by Berman, *Office*, p. 1.
12. Interagency Organization and Methods Conference, "Departmental Management Improvement Reporting System in the Federal Government" (Washington, D.C., November 1958).
13. Hess, *Organizing the Presidency*, p. 76.
14. U.S. Commission on Organization of the Executive Branch of the Government (1953–1955), *Final Report to the Congress* (Washington, D.C.: USGPO, 1955).

15. BOB, *Management Improvement*, p. 2.
16. Hess, *Organizing the Presidency*, p. 90; Theodore Sorensen, *Kennedy* (New York: Bantam Books, 1965), p. 281, cited by Berman, *Office*, p. 69.
17. BOB, *Management Improvement*, pp. 2–52; *Cost Reduction Through Better Management in the Federal Government* (Washington, D.C.: 1963), pp. i–ii.
18. John F. Kennedy, Memorandum to the Heads of Departments and Agencies, "Improving Manpower Control and Utilization in the Executive Branch" (Washington, D.C.: The White House, October 11, 1962).
19. EOP, BOB, *War on Waste* (Washington, D.C., 1964).
20. Ibid., p. 1.
21. EOP, BOB, Circular A-44 (Revised), "Cost Reduction and Management Improvement in Government Operations," March 29, 1965.
22. Berman, *Office*, pp. 81–83.
23. Ibid., p. 101.
24. See Donald Axelrod, *Budgeting for Modern Government* (New York: St. Martin's Press, 1988), ch. 10.
25. Berman, *Office*, p. 107.
26. William D. Carey, "Reorganization Plan No. 2," in Allen Schick, ed., *Perspectives on Budgeting* (Washington, D.C.: American Society for Public Administration, 1981), pp. 145, 148.
27. Berman, *Office*, pp. 112–113; Haider, "Presidential Management Initiatives," p. 249.
28. Haider, p. 248.
29. Lawrence E. Lynn, Jr., *Managing the Public's Business* (New York: Basic Books, 1981), p. 78.
30. Berman, *Office*, p. 125.
31. The National Academy of Public Administration, "The President and Executive Management: Summary of a Symposium" (Washington, D.C., 1976, mimeographed), cited by Berman, p. 115.
32. Haider, "Presidential Management Initiatives," p. 248.
33. Ibid., pp. 250, 251, 255.
34. Berman, *Office*, p. 128, Appendix II, H.
35. EOP, OMB, Circular No. A-117, "Management Improvement and the Use of Evaluation in the Executive Branch" (Washington, D.C., March 23, 1979).
36. Ibid.
37. *Public Administration Times*, November 1979, p. 4.
38. *Budget of the U.S. Government, Fiscal Year 1980–81, Special Analyses*, pp. 339–363.
39. National Academy of Public Administration, "Strengthening OMB's Role in Improving the Management of the Federal Government" (Washington, D.C., February, 1981).
40. Ibid.
41. EOP, OMB, *Management of the United States Government, Fiscal Year 1986* (Washington, D.C., 1985).
42. OMB, *Management of the United States Government, FY 1989*, p. 1.
43. EOP, OMB, *FY 1986*, pp. 2, 4.
44. White House, press release, September 22, 1982; OMB, press release, December 9, 1982; *Washington Post*, August 3, 1983.
45. OMB, *FY 1989*, p. 8.

46. U.S. General Accounting Office, *Compendium of GAO's Views on the Cost Savings Proposals of the Grace Commission*, Report to the Chairman, Senate Committee on Governmental Affairs, *Summary of Findings*, Vol. 1 (Washington, D.C., 1988), p. 10; JFMIP, *News* (Summer 1987).

47. The National Academy of Public Administration, *The President and Executive Management* (Washington, D.C.: NAPA, 1976), cited by Haider, "Presidential Management Initiatives," p. 256.

48. Marver Bernstein, "The Presidency and Management Improvement," *Law and Contemporary Problems*, Vol. 35, No. 3 (1970), p. 58.

49. U.S. General Accounting Office, *Selected Government-wide Management Improvement Efforts—1970 to 1980* (Washington, D.C., 1983), pp. 2–3.

50. Charles H. Levine, "Commentary," *PA Times*, February 5, 1988, p. 2.

51. Haider, "Presidential Management Initiatives," p. 256; GAO, *Compendium*, Vol. II, p. 2.

52. NAPA, "Strengthening OMB's Role."

53. Haider, "Presidential Management Initiatives," pp. 256–257.

54. Ibid., p. 257.

55. Berman, *Office*, pp. 58–64.

56. Ibid., p. 85.

57. U.S. Senate Committee on Government Operations, Subcommittee on Executive Reorganization, *Hearings* (Washington, D.C., 1968), p. 2, cited by Berman, pp. 84–85.

58. Memorandum, Roy Ash to President Nixon, October 17, 1969, cited by Berman, *Office*, p. 107.

59. GAO, *Compendium*, Vol. II, p. 2.

60. Joint Financial Management Improvement Program, *News* (Spring 1986); *Public Administration Times*, December 1, 1983, p. 1. In testifying before the Committee on Governmental Affairs of the U.S. Senate on July 21, 1987, Comptroller General Charles A. Bowsher stated: ". . . former government officials who were instrumental in establishing OMB said . . . that had they to do it over, they would have created a management office separate from the budget office because of the secondary importance OMB has placed on management issues."

61. Roger L. Sperry, "Auditing Evaluation and Management Improvement—The Canadian Experience," *GAO Review* (Spring 1983), p. 26.

62. *Government Computer News*, February 10, 1985.

63. U.S. General Accounting Office, *Improving Interior's Internal Auditing and Investigating Activities* (Washington, D.C., 1979), pp. 2–3; GAO, *Compendium*, Vol. II, p. 44; *Government Computer News*, April 11, 1986, p. 68.

64. GAO, *Compendium*, Vol. II, p. 2.

65. *Government Computer News*, October 25, 1985, p. 5.

66. U.S. Commission on Organization of the Executive Branch of the Government, *Report to Congress* (1947–1949 and 1953–55); President's Private Sector Survey on Cost Control, *Report to the President* (Washington, D.C.: PPSSCC, 1986).

67. Ronald C. Moe, "A New Hoover Commission: A Timely Idea or Misdirected Nostalgia," *Public Administration Review*, Vol. 42, No. 3 (May/June 1982), p. 272.

68. Congressional Budget Office and General Accounting Office, *Analysis of the*

Grace Commission's Major Proposals for Cost Control, A Joint Study (Washington, D.C.: 1984), p. 1.

69. Ibid., p. 2.

70. Ibid., p. 2; see also Charles T. Goodsell, "The Grace Commission; Seeking Efficiency for the Whole People," *Public Administration Review,* Vol. 44, No. 3 (May/June 1984), pp. 197–202.

71. OMB, *FY 1989,* pp. 237–239.

72. Trudi C. Miller, "Overview: The Turning Point," in T. C. Miller, ed., *Public Sector Performance* (Baltimore: The Johns Hopkins University Press, 1984), pp. 2–4.

73. Thomas J. Anton, "Intergovernmental Change in the United States: An Assessment of the Literature," in Miller, *Public Sector,* pp. 16–17.

74. OMB, *FY 1986,* p. 9.

75. For example, see ibid., pp. 53–61.

76. BOB stimulated work measurement by the preparation and dissemination of three influential publications: *Work Measurement: A Case Study in 5 Parts* (1947); *Work Measurement in Performance Budgeting and Management Improvement* (1950); *Progress in Measuring Work* (1962).

77. Joint Financial Management Improvement Program (JFMIP), *Productivity Programs in the Federal Government, Productivity Trends and Current Efforts* (Washington, D.C.: JFMIP, 1976), Appendix F.

78. Harry P. Hatry, "The Status of Productivity Measurement in the Public Sector," *Public Administration Review,* Vol. 38, No. 1 (January/February 1978), pp. 28–29.

79. U.S. General Accounting Office, *OMB Needs to Intensify Its Work Measurement Effort* (Washington, D.C., 1978).

80. U.S. General Accounting Office, *Federal Work Force Planning: Time for Renewed Emphasis* (Washington, D.C., 1980), pp. i–ii.

81. Donald C. Kull, "Productivity Programs in the Federal Government," *Public Administration Review,* Vol. 38, No. 1 (January/February, 1978), p. 6.

82. OMB, *FY 1989,* p. 11.

83. U.S. General Accounting Office, *Government Measures of Private-Public Sector Productivity: Users Recommend Changes* (Washington, D.C., 1980), p. 12.

84. Kull, "Productivity Programs," p. 5.

85. JFMIP, *Report on Federal Productivity,* Vol. 1 (Washington, D.C., 1974), pp. 4–5, 13–14.

86. Kull, "Productivity Programs," pp. 6–7.

87. U.S. General Accounting Office, *Increased Use of Productivity Measurement Can Help Control Government Costs* (Washington, D.C., 1983), pp. 1, 27.

88. GAO, *Increased Use of Productivity,* pp. 6, 23.

89. JFMIP, *News,* Spring 1986.

90. OMB, *FY 1986,* pp. 44, 67–69; ——, *FY 1989,* pp. 52–55.

91. OMB, *FY 1989,* p. 53.

92. Barry Bozeman and Jane Massey, "Investing in Policy Evaluation: Some Guidelines for Skeptical Public Managers," *Public Administration Review,* Vol. 42, No. 3 (June/July 1982), p. 261.

93. GAO, *Compendium,* Vol. II, p. 64.

94. U.S. General Accounting Office, *Evaluation and Analysis to Support Decision-Making* (Washington, D.C., 1976), p. 4.

95. Norman Beckman, Introduction to "A Symposium, Policy Analysis in Government: Alternatives to Muddling Through," *Public Administration Review*, Vol. 37, No. 3 (May/June 1977), p. 222.

96. GAO, *Evaluation*, pp. 6–7.

97. Eleanor Chelimsky, "Using Evaluation in the Budget-Making Process," *Public Budgeting and Finance*, Vol. 2, No. 2 (Summer 1982), pp. 789–80.

98. These comments paraphrase Carol H. Weiss, "Where Politics and Evaluation Meet," *Evaluation*, Vol. 1, No. 3 (1984), pp. 37–45, as summarized by Lee Edwards and Keith E. Marvin, "Setting Evaluation Methods Realistically," *GAO Review*, (Fall 1980), p. 21.

99. Berman, *Office*, p. 129.

100. Susan Salasin and Lawrence Kivens, "Fostering Federal Program Evaluation: A Current OMB Initiative," *Evaluation*, Vol. 2 (February 1975), pp. 40–41.

101. For a pioneering discussion of "evaluability" of programs, see Joseph A. Wholey et al., *Federal Evaluation Policy: Analyzing the Effects of Public Programs* (Washington, D.C.: The Urban Institute, 1971), and Richard Rose, *Managing Presidential Objectives* (New York: The Free Press, 1976), pp. 22–24.

102. For a critical appraisal, see Frank P. Sherwood and William J. Page, Jr., "MBO and Public Management," *Public Administration Review*, Vol. 36, No. 1 (January/February 1976), p. 7.

103. Ibid.

104. Rose, *Presidential Objectives*, pp. 68, 76.

105. Ibid., pp. 139–140.

106. During the Carter administration OMB coined the term "evaluation management." See OMB Circular No. A-117, "Management Improvement and the Use of Evaluation in the Executive Branch," March 23, 1979.

107. Keith E. Marvin, "Trends in Evaluation," *GAO Review* (Winter 1981), p.7; U.S. General Accounting Office, *Evaluating Federal Programs: An Overview for the Congressional User* (Washington, D.C., 1976), p.3.

108. Thomas Cook and Charles L. Grinder, "Motivational Research," *Evaluation Quarterly*, Vol. 2 (February 1978), p. 265, cited by Bozeman and Massey, "Investing in Policy Evaluation," p. 265; GAO, *Compendium*, Vol. II, pp. 6–7; GAO, *Federal Agencies Should Use Good Measures of Performance to Hold Managers Accountable* (Washington, D.C., 1978), p. 78; James T. Lynn, American Society for Public Administration, "Section on Budgeting and Financial Management," Vol. 4, No. 2 (October 1980), p. 1; William A. Niskanen, "Evaluation in OMB," *Evaluation*, Vol. 2 (1975), p. 73.

109. OMB, *FY 1989*, pp. 11–12; *Government Computer News*, June 7, 1985, p. 71.

110. GAO, *Compendium*, Vol. II, pp. 142, 1133, 1138.

111. *Government Computer News*, June 7, 1985, p. 71.

112. *Government Computer News*, May 24, 1985, p. 8.

113. OMB, *FY 1986*, p. 58.

114. *Government Computer News*, April 25, 1986, p. 53.

115. GAO, *Compendium*, Vol. II, p. 142.

116. Based in part on Haider, "Presidential Management Initiatives," p. 252.

117. GAO, *Implementing the Paperwork Reduction Act: Some Progress, But Many Problems Remain* (Washington, D.C., 1983).

118. Ibid., pp. i–vi.
119. Haider, "Presidential Management Initiatives," p. 253; OMB, *Management of the U.S. Government* FY 1986, p. 45.
120. OMB, *FY 1989*, pp. 111–112; Donald Fisk, Herbert Kiesling, and Thomas Muller, *Private Provision of Public Services: An Overview* (Washington, D.C.: The Urban Institute, 1978), p. viii.
121. *Government Computer News*, October 11, 1985, p. 56.
122. OMB, *FY 1986*, pp. 43–44.
123. Ibid., pp. 43, 67.
124. Ibid., p. 16.
125. State and Local Government Research Program, *The Status of Productivity Measurement in State Government: An Initial Examination* (Washington, D.C.: The Urban Institute, 1975), p. 1; *Public Administration Times*, May 1, 1987, p. 1.
126. Stanley J. Botner, "The Use of Budgeting Management Tools by State Government," *Public Administration Review*, Vol. 45, No. 5 (September/October 1985).
127. National Association of State Budget Officers (NASBO), "State Budget Management and Productivity Improvement Projects," Quarterly Bulletin, various issues.
128. New York State Division of the Budget, *The Budget in New York State: A Half Century Perspective* (Albany, N.Y.: DOB, 1981), p. 7.
129. Paul H. Appleby, Memorandum to Heads of All State Departments and Agencies, "Report on Administrative Improvement Program," Albany, N.Y., August 3, 1956.
130. New York State Budget Division, *Budget Examiner's Manual*, July 1, 1970, p. 3.
131. New York State Division of the Budget, internal memoranda on management improvement programs, May 1963.
132. State of Wisconsin, Department of Administration, "Governor's Productivity Improvement Program" (Madison, Wisc., undated, probably 1972).
133. Terry Grogan and Bill Stotesberry, draft of case study on PIP, (Madison, Wisc., 1976).
134. Based on comments by Sandra J. Hale at the annual meeting of the American Society of Public Administration, Anaheim Calif., April 14, 1986.
135. New York State Division of the Budget, *Newsletter*, December 9, 1971.
136. NASBO, *Newsletter* and *Quarterly Bulletin*, various issues.
137. GAO, *State and Local Government Productivity Improvement: What is the Federal Role?* (Washington, D.C., 1978).
138. State and Local Government Research Program, *Productivity Measurement*, pp. v, xix.
139. New York State Senate Task Force on Critical Problems, *Productivity* (Albany, N.Y.: Temporary State Commission on Management and Productivity in the Public Sector, 1975), pp. 69–72; Raymond Ryan, "The Impact of Three Years of Experience and a New Governor on the State of Washington's Productivity Program," *Public Administration Review*, Vol. 38, No. 6 (January/February 1978), p. 12.
140. James Ramsey and Merl M. Hackbart, *Innovations in State Budgeting* (Lexington, Ky: Center for Public Affairs, University of Kentucky, 1977), pp. 1–10; Robert D. Lee, Jr. and Raymond J. Staffeldt, "Executive and Legislative

Use of Policy Analysis in the State Budgetary Process: Survey Results," *Policy Analysis* (Summer 1977), p. 397; Selma J. Mushkin, "Policy Analysis in State and Community," *Public Administration Review*, Vol. 37, No. 3 (May/June 1977), p. 245.

141. James T. Campbell and Frank K. Gibson, "Program Evaluation by States and Localities: Overview and Outlook," *GAO Review* (Spring 1982), p. 11.

142. Larry Polivka and Laurey T. Stryker, "Program Evaluation and the Policy Process in State Government: An Effective LInkage," *Public Administration Review*, Vol. 43, No. 3 (May/June, 1983), pp. 255–159; Office of Legislative Analyst of California, *Review of Sunset Concepts and Possible Alternatives for California* (Sacramento, 1977).

143. Department of Administration, *Manual for the Preparation of the Executive Operating and Capital Budgets, 1977–79 Biennium*, Madison, Wisc. 1976); Richard S. Morres, "An Analysis of the Texas Budget System" (Paper prepared for the New York State Temporary Commission on Management and Productivity in the Public Sector, April 1977); various internal memoranda on performance measurement in the New York State Division of the Budget, especially February 21, 1978 and July 6, 1980; Thomas W. Carroll, *A Legislative Initiative in Budgetary Reform: New York Key Item Reporting System*. (Albany, N.Y.: Rockefeller Institute of Government, State University of New York, 1984); Thomas Lauth, "Performance Evaluation in the Georgia Budgetary Process," *Public Budgeting and Finance*, Vol. 5, No. 1 (Spring 1985), pp. 67–79; State of Mich., Department of Administation, 1974), p. 15; Commonwealth of Pennsylvania, *Program Policy Guidelines for 1977–78* (Harrisburg, Penn.: Department of Administration, 1976); Polivaka and Stryker, "Program Evaluation"; Patrick J. Lucey, *Policy Papers, 1973–75* (Madison, Wisc.: Department of Administration, 1973); Michael J. Schering, *Performance Information Audit Manual* (Trenton, N.J.: State of New Jersey, Department of the Treasury, Division of Budget and Accounting, 1975), pp. 1–25.

144. Ramsey and Hackbart, *Innovations*, p. ix.

145. National Association for State Information Systems (NASIS), *Information Systems Technology in State Government* (Lexington, Ky: NASIS, 1984).

146. E. S. Savas and Sigmund G. Ginsburg, "The Civil Service: A Merit System," *The Public Interest*, Vol. 32, (Summer 1973), pp. 72–83.

147. Theodore H. Poister and Robert McGowan, "Use of Management Tools in Municipal Government: A National Survey," *Public Administration Review*, Vol. 44, No. 3 (May/June 1984), pp. 217–221; Lewis B. Friedman, *Budgeting Municipal Expenditures* (New York: Praeger, 1975), p. 184.

148. International City Managers Association, "Performance and Challenges," *Management Information Service*, April 1976; Committee on Management Analysis in State and Local Government, *Challenge to Management Analysis to Improve Government Performance* (Hartford: University of Connecticut Institute of Public Service, 1974), pp. 1–12, 55; *Public Administration Times*, November 1, 1985, p. 2.

149. GAO, *State and Local Government Productivity*, p. 12; Frederick O'R Hayes, *Productivity in Local Government*, (Lexington, Mass.: Lexington Books, 1977); Frederick O'R Hayers, "City and County Productivity Programs," *Public Administration Review*, Vol. 38, No. 1 (January/February 1978), pp. 15–17; The Urban Institute, *The Challenge of Productivity Diversity: Improving*

Local Government Productivity Measurement and Evaluation, Part IV (Washington, D.C.: The Urban Institute, 1972).

150. Richard E. Winne, *Results of Survey of Local Government Budgeting, Program Planning Analysis and Evaluation Efforts*, Working Paper 201-5, (Washington, D.C.: The Urban Institute, March 1972), pp. 2, 4, 51.

151. Herbert A. O'Keefe, Jr., *Performance Audits in Local Governments—Benefits, Problems and Challenges*, Management Information Service Report, Washington, D.C., International City Managers Association, April 1976, p. 6.

152. Edward A. Lehan, *Simplified Governmental Budgeting* (Chicago, Ill.: Municipal Finance Officers Association, 1981), pp. 15–16, 24–26.

153. John Leslie King and Kenneth L. Kraemer, "Information Systems and Intergovernmental Relations," in Miller, *Public Sector Performance*, pp. 106–111; King and Kraemer, *The Dynamics of Computing* (Irvine: University of California Public Policy Research Program, 1983).

154. Fisk et al.,——,*Private Provision of Public Services*, pp. 26–29.

155. Ibid., p. 26; E. S. Savas, "Making New York No. 1 Again: A Strategy Toward the Year 2000";——, *Privatizing the Public Sector* (Chatham, N.J.: Chatham House, 1982); John T. Marlin, ed., *Contracting Municipal Services: A Guide for Purchase from the Private Sector* (New York: John Wiley & Sons, 1984).

156. Fisk et al., *Private Provision of Public Services*, pp. 48, 63–64.

157. Savas, "Making New York No. 1," p. 57.

158. Fisk, *Provision*, p. 99.

159. Ibid., pp. 89–101.

160. Based in part on United Nations, *Handbook on the Improvement of Administrative Management in Public Administration* (New York, 1979), pp. 1, 6–10, 14–16; ——, *Enhancing Capabilities for Administrative Reform in Developing Countries* (New York, 1983), pp. 7–10.

161. United Nations, *Administrative Management*, p. 14; ——, *Report on Budget Management Techniques in Selected Developed Countries* (New York, 1978), pp. 60–63.

162. U.S.S.R. Academy of Sciences, *The Second Soviet-American Symposium on Local Government Problems* (Moscow, 1978).

163. United Nations, *Administrative Management*, p. 1.

164. Ibid., pp. 8, 13.

165. Abdullah Sanuse Ahmad, "Administrative Reforms for Development in Malaysia—Focus on Grass-Root Organizations." (Paper presented at meeting sponsored by the U.N. Asia and the Pacific Development Administration Center, New Delhi, September 1979.) The author had been Director General of MAMPU for several years. The writer validated many of the views in the article by personal observations in Malaysia from 1978 to 1980.)

166. United Nations, *Budget Management Techniques*, pp. 84–85. Also based on interviews in the British Treasury in August 1987.

167. United Nations, *Administrative Reform*, pp. 7–20.

168. Donald Axelrod, "Performance Audit for Development," in United Nations, *Public Auditing Techniques for Performance Improvement* (New York, 1980), pp. 61–82; Ernst Heuer, "Organizational Audit," ibid., pp. 44–45.

169. Sperry, "The Canadian Experience," pp. 28, 50–54; Keith E. Marvin, "Trends in Evaluation," *GAO Review* (Summer 1980), pp. 2–8; National Audit Board of Sweden, *Effectiveness Audit Guidelines* (Stockholm, 1977); Conference

of Asian Budget Directors, *Proceedings* (Kuala Lumpur, Malaysia: Ministry of Finance and the German Foundation for International Development, 1981), pp. 4–5.

≡ Section 4

1. Advisory Commission on Intergovernmental Relations (ACIR), *Significant Features of Fiscal Federalism, 1987 Edition,* (Washington, D.C., 1981), p. i.
2. U.S. Department of the Treasury, Office of State and Local Finance, *Federal-State-Local Fiscal Relations* (Washington, D.C.: USGPO, 1985), p. 153.
3. ACIR, *Fiscal Federalism, 1987,* p. 7. Based on ACIR estimates for 1986.
4. Ibid., pp. 8–11.
5. Ibid., p. 36.
6. Robert Gleason, "Federalism 1986–87: Signals of a New Era," *Intergovernmental Perspective,* Vol. 14, No. 1 (Winter 1988), p. 9.
7. *Budget of the United States Government, Fiscal Year 1989, Special Analyses,* "Special Analysis H, Federal Aid to State and Local Governments," (Washington, D.C.: OMB, 1988), p. H21.
8. Helen F. Ladd, "Federal Aid to State and Local Governments," in Gregory B. Mills and John L. Palmer, eds., *Federal Budget Policy in the 1980s* (Washington, D.C.: The Urban Institute Press, 1984), p. 194.
9. Paul L. Posner, "Block Grants: A Framework for Assessing Accountability" (Paper presented at the annual conference of the American Society for Public Administration, New York City, April 17, 1983).
10. Steven D. Gold, *State and Local Fiscal Relations in the Early 1980s* (Washington, D.C.: The Urban Institute Press, 1983), p. 3; George E. Hale and Marian L. Palley, "The Impact of Federal Funds in the State Budgetary Process," *National Civic Review,* Vol. 67 (November 1978).
11. George F. Break, "Fiscal Federalism in the United States: The First 200 Years, Evolution and Outlook" in Advisory Commission on Intergovernmental Relations, *Future of Federalism in the 1980s,* M-126 (Washington, D.C., 1981), pp. 39–66; David B. Walker, "Categorical Grants: Some Clarification and Continuing Concerns," *Intergovernmental Perspective,* Vol. 3, No. 2 (Spring 1977), pp. 14–19.
12. Advisory Commission on Intergovernmental Relations, *The Question of State Government Capability,* A-98 (Washington, D.C., 1985), p. 5.
13. ACIR, *A Catalog of Federal Grant-in-Aid Programs to State and Local Governments: Grants Funded FY 1987* (Washington, D.C., 1987).
14. *Budget of the United States Government, FY 1986,* "Special Analysis H," pp. 16–17, 22–23.
15. ACIR, *Catalog,* p. 3; ACIR, *The Federal Influence on State and Local Roles in the Federal System,* A-89 (Washington, D.C., 1981), p. 12; U.S. General Accounting Office (GAO), *Grant Formulas: A Catalog of Federal Aid to States and Localities* (Washington, D.C., 1987), pp. 10–11.
16. ACIR, *Block Grants: A Comparative Analysis,* A-60 (Washington, D.C., 1977), p. 57.
17. GAO, *Block Grants Brought Funding Changes and Adjustments to Program Priorities* (Washington, D.C., 1982), p. ii.

18. *Budget of the United States Government, FY 1989,* "Special Analysis H," p. H23.
19. Deil S. Wright, *Understanding Intergovernmental Relations* (Duxbury, Mass.: Duxbury Press, 19810, pp. 86–87.
20. Richard P. Nathan, Allen D. Manvel, Susannah E. Calkins et al., *Monitoring Revenue Sharing* (Washington, D.C.: The Brookings Institution, 1975), pp. 344–47.
21. Ibid., pp. 3–4.
22. U.S. Domestic Council, *History of Revenue Sharing* (Washington, D.C., 1971), pp. 1–4.
23. Deil S. Wright, *Understanding Intergovernmental Relations,* 2nd ed. (New York: Brooks/Cole, 1982), pp. 124–125.
24. Revenue Sharing Act of 1973; Domestic Council, *History,* p. 4; National Science Foundation, *Economic and Political Impact of General Revenue Sharing* (Washington, D.C., 1976), pp. 2–11.
25. Nathan et al., *Monitoring Revenue Sharing,* pp. 37–64.
26. Department of the Treasury, *Federal-State-Local Fiscal Relations,* p. 183.
27. Gleason, "Federalism 1986–87," p. 11.
28. Otto G. Stolz, *Revenue Sharing: Legal and Policy Analysis* (New York: Praeger, 1974), pp. 75–83, cited by Wright, *Understanding Intergovernmental Relations,* p. 90.
29. *Budget of the United States Government, FY 1986,* "Special Analysis H."
30. Nathan et al., *Monitoring Revenue Sharing,* pp. 92–96; R. P. Nathan, C. J. Adams, Jr. et al., *Revenue Sharing: The Second Round* (Washington, D.C.: The Brookings Institution, 1977), pp. 160–163; Gleason, "Federalism 1986–87," p. 12.
31. Nathan et al., *Monitoring,* p. 310; Nathan, *Second Round,* pp. 9–17; National Science Foundation, *Economic and Political Impact,* pp. 2–11.
32. Wright, *Understanding Intergovernmental Relations,* p. 98.
33. David B. Walker, *Toward a Functioning Federalism* (Cambridge, Mass.: Winthrop Publishers, Inc., 1981), pp. 84, 180–81; ACIR, *State Government Capability,* pp. 14–19.
34. *Budget of the United States Government, FY 1985,* "Special Analysis H," p. H22.
35. ACIR, *Catalog,* p. 2, George E. Peterson, Randall R. Bovbjerg, Barbara A. Davis, Walter G. Davis, Eugene C. Durman, Theresa A. Gullo, *The Reagan Block Grants* (Washington, D.C.: The Urban Institute Press, 1986), p. 35.
36. Department of the Treasury, *Federal-State-Local Fiscal Relations,* pp. xiii, 159.
37. GAO, *Proposed Changes in Federal Matching and Maintenance of Effort Requirements for State and Local Governments* (Washington, D.C., 1980), pp. 10–13.
38. Ibid., p. 78.
39. Congressional Budget Office (CBO), *The Federal Goverment in a Federal System* (Washington, D.C., 1983), p. 9.
40. GAO, *Proposed Changes,* p. 2.
41. Ibid., pp. 69–70.
42. Catherine Lovell and Charles Tobin, "The Mandate Issue," *Public Administration Review,* Vol. 41, No. 3 (May/June 1981), pp. 319–32.

43. Ibid., p. 326.
44. Thomas Muller and Michael Fix, *The Impact of Selected Federal Actions on Municipal Outlays*, Report for Joint Economic Committee of U.S. Congress (Washington, D.C., 1980), cited by Lovell and Tobin, pp. 320–322.
45. ACIR, *Intergovernmental Perspective*, Vol. 9, No. 1 (Winter 1982), pp. 8–11.
46. Walker, *Functioning Federalism*, p. 193; ACIR, *Regulatory Federalism*, A-95 (Washington, D.C., 1984), pp. 8–10; ACIR, *Intergovernmental Perspective*, Vol. 11, No. 1 (Winter 1985), pp. 14–17; Joseph F. Zimmerman, "Federalism and the Urban Fiscal System" (Paper presented at a conference in Cologne, West Germany on reforming the urban fiscal system, November 14, 1984).
47. ACIR, *Intergovernmental Perspective*, Vol. 11, No. 1 (Winter 1985), p. 13.
48. GAO, *Grant Formulas: A Catalog of Federal Aid to States and Localities* (Washington, D.C.: GAO, 1987), pp. 10–11.
49. Department of Treasury, *Federal-State-Local Fiscal Relations*, pp. 238–239.
50. Ibid., pp. 209–223.
51. *Intergovernmental Perspective*, Vol. 11, No. 2/3 (Spring/Summer 1985), p. 20; Department of Treasury *Federal-State-Local Fiscal Relations*, pp. 209–233.
52. Walker, *Functioning Federalism*, p. 87.
53. Donald Haider, *When Governments Come to Washington* (New York: The Free Press, 1974), ch. 1.
54. ACIR, *Intergovernmental Perspective* (Winter 1985), p. 43.
55. Stephen L. Schechter, "The State of American Federalism in the 1980s," in Robert S. Hawkins, ed., *American Federalism: A New Partnership for the Republic* (New Brunswick, N.J.: Transaction Books, 1981), p. 61; Lovell and Tobin, "The Mandate Issue," p. 318; Michael D. Reagan and John G. Sanzone, *The New Federalism*, 2nd ed. (New York: Oxford University Press, 1981).
56. ACIR, *State Government Capability*, p. 384.
57. CBO, *The Federal Government*, p. x.
58. ACIR, *State Government Capability*, p. 384; ACIR, *Summary and Concluding Observations*, A-62 (Washington, D.C., 1978), p. 131.
59. ACIR, *State Government Capability*, p. 384.
60. *Budget of the U.S. Government, FY 1980*, "Speical Analysis H," pp. 254–5.
61. ACIR, *State Government Capability*, p. 384.
62. Rochelle L. Stanfield, "State and Local Governments Favor the Pay-In-Advance Plan," *National Journal*, Vol. 9 (March 5, 1977), p. 348.
63. Robert S. Hawkins, "American Federalism: Again at the Crossroads," in Hawkins, *American Federalism*, p. 6.
64. Schechter, "American Federalism," p. 66.
65. Hawkins, "American Federalism," p. 4.
66. Jane Massey and Jeffrey D. Straussman, "Another Look at the Mandate Issue: Are Conditions-of-Aid Really So Burdensome?" *Public Administration Review*, Vol. 45, No. 2 (March/April 1985), pp. 298–9.
67. Break, "Fiscal Federalism," p. 45.
68. U.S. Commission on Organization of the Executive Branch of the Government, *Concluding Report; a Report to Congress* (Washington, D.C.: USGPO, 1947); ———, *Final Report to the Congress* (Washington, D.C.: USGPO, 1955).
69. Break, "Fiscal Federalism," pp. 42–3.

70. Wright, *Understanding Intergovernmental Relations*, p. 7.
71. Break, "Fiscal Federalism," pp. 49–53.
72. Foreword in John W. Ellwood, ed., *Reductions in U.S. Domestic Spending* (New Brunswick, N.J.: Transaction Books, 1984), pp. xiii-xxii.
73. R. P. Nathan, P. M. Dearborne, C. A. Goldman et al., "Initial Effect of the FY 1982 Reductions in Federal Domestic Spending," in Ellwood, pp. 315–319.
74. Richard P. Nathan and Fred C. Doolittle, *The Consequences of Cuts: The Effects of the Reagan Domestic Program on State and Local Governments* (Princeton, N.J.: Princeton University Urban and Regional Research Center, 1983.)
75. Jesse Burkhead, "Block Grants and Distributional Equity" (Paper delivered at the annual conference of the American Society for Public Administration, New York City, April 1983).
76. National Governors' Association, *Staff Papers to Governors' Commission on Executive Management and Fiscal Affairs* (Washington, D.C., October 6, 1981); *New York Times*, January 19, 1982, p. A11.
77. OMB, *Budget, FY 1986*, "Special Analysis H," pp. H2, 27–28. Studies by the Treasury Department asserted that state and local governments were in better fiscal shape than the federal government. See summary of studies in *New York Times*, November 25, 1984, p. A1; *New York Times*, January 3, 1985, p. A16.
78. Ibid., p. H-22; *Intergovernmental Perspective*, Vol. 8, No. 4 (Winter 1983), p. 5; *Public Administration Times*, July 1, 1982, p. 4; General Accounting Office, *A Study of the Joint Funding Simplification Act*, (Washington, D.C., 1978), pp. 2–3; Susan Golonka, "Whatever Happened to Federalism," *Intergovernmental Perspective*, Vol. 11, No. 1 (Winter 1985), p. 10; OMB, *Budget, FY 1986*, "Special Analysis H," pp. H23–24.
79. Wright, *Understanding Intergovernmental Relations*, p. 165.
80. U.S. Bureau of the Census, *Federal Expenditures by State for Fiscal Year 1984* (Washington, D.C., 1985), Table 1, p. 1.
81. Ibid., Table 8, p. 25.
82. Thanos Catsambas, *Regional Impacts of Federal Fiscal Policy* (Lexington, Mass.: Lexington Books, 1979), p. 93.
83. Michael Lawson, "The Flow of Federal Funds," *Intergovernmental Perspective*, Vol. 11, No. 2/3 (Spring/Summer 1985), pp. 18–19; Janet R. Pack, "The States' Scramble for Federal Funds: Who Wins, Who Loses," *Journal of Policy Analysis and Management*, Vol. 11, No. 2 (1982), p. 181.
84. Pack, p. 176; Wright, *Understanding Intergovernmental Relations*, pp. 167-8.
85. Pack, "The States' Scramble," p. 186.
86. Ibid., p. 179.
87. Ibid., p. 189.
88. ACIR, *Strengthening the Federal Revenue System*, A-97 (Washington, D.C., 1984), p. 37.
89. Ibid., p. 116–117. The Supreme Court came dangerously close to challenging the tax exemption of municipal bonds in *Westfall v. Erwin*, 108 S.Ct. 580, 98 L. Ed. 2d 619 (1988).
90. Ibid., p. 37; OMB, *Budget, FY 1987*, "Special Analysis H," p. H16.
91. OMB, Budget, *FY 1987*, "Special Analysis H," p. H15; *FY 1988*, pp. H18–19.
92. OMB, Budget, *FY 1988*, "Special Analysis H," p. H19.

93. OMB, *Budget, FY 1988, Special Analyses*, "Special Analysis F," p. F53.
94. Ibid.
95. National Association of State Budget Officers (NASBO), *Economic Recovery Plan: Impact on the States* (Washington, D.C., 1981), p. 10.
96. Ibid.,pp. 66–67.
97. Ibid., pp. 7–9; Steven D. Gold, "How the Federal Policies Adopted in 1981 Affect State Revenues Aside from the Direct Effects of the Reduction of Federal Aid" (Denver, Colo.: National Conference of State Legislatures, Intergovernmental Finance Project, October 11, 1981), pp. 1–5; Charles W. de Seve and Thomas E. Vasquez, "The Impact of Changes in the Federal Tax Code on State Tax Revenues," *National Tax Journal* (September 1984), pp. 393–409.
98. Carolyn D. Lynch, "The Impact of Federal Tax Reform on State Personal Income Taxes," *Intergovernmental Perspective*, Vol. 13, No. 1 (Winter 1987), pp. 37–39.
99. *Wall Street Journal*, March 16, 1987, p. 22.
100. Based on survey conducted by National Governors' Association and National Association of State Budget Officers in 1987, reported by the *New York Times*, October 4, 1987, p. 37.
101. E. F. Hutton, Municipal Research Department, "Internal Dynamics of State Revenue Structures: Sales Tax Outlook—Boom or Bust" (New York, 1987), cited by *Public Administration Times*, June 15, 1987, p. 3.
102. Department of the Treasury, *Federal-State-Local Fiscal Relations*, p. xix.
103. *Wall Street Journal*, January 22, 1982.
104. John Shannon, "Federal and State-Local Spenders Go Their Separate Ways" (Paper presented at the annual conference of the American Society for Public Administration, New York City, April 18, 1983).
105. ACIR, *Federal and State Capital Finance* (Washington, D.C., 1983), p. 3.
106. *Wall Street Journal*, January 24, 1982.
107. Congressional Budget Office, *Countercyclical Uses of Federal Grant Programs* (Washington, D.C., 1978), p. xx; Walker, *Functioning Federalism*, pp. 108–109; Carol S. Weissert, "Restraint and Reappraisal: Federalism in 1976," *Intergovernmental Perspective*, Vol. 3, No. 1 (Winter 1977), p. 11; U.S. General Accounting Office, *Impact of Anti-recession Assistance In 15 State Governments* (Washington, D.C., 1978), pp. 1–49; ———, *Impact of Anti-recession Assistance in 21 City Governments* (Washington, D.C., 1978), pp. 11–52; Department of the Treasury, *Federal-State-Local Fiscal Relations*, p. xix; "State and Local Government in Trouble," Special Report, *Business Week*, October 26, 1981, pp. 180–181.
108. Shannon, "Federal and State-Local Spenders," *New York Times*, June 14, 1987, p. 4; Peterson et al., *Block Grants*, p. xv.
109. Shannon, "Federal and State Local Spenders."
110. ACIR, *State Government Capability*, pp. 305, 379, 389; study by Council of State Governments, cited by *New York Times*, December 6, 1985, p. A19.
111. ACIR, *State Government Capability*, p. 313; ACIR, *Recent Trends in Federal and State Aid to Local Governments*, M-114 (Washington, D.C., 1980).
112. U.S. Bureau of the Census, *State Payments to Local Governments, 1982 Census of Governments* (Washington, D.C., 1984), Table 3, p. 3.
113. Gold, *State and Local Fiscal Relations*, p. 7.

114. ACIR, *Significant Features of Fiscal Federalism*, 1985–86 *Edition*, p. 31; ——, 1987 Edition,pp. 30–37.
115. ACIR, *Fiscal Federalism*, 1987 Edition, pp. 30–37.
116. Gold, *State and Local Fiscal Relations*, pp. 11–12.
117. ACIR, *Fiscal Federalism*, 1987 Edition, p. 59.
118. ACIR, *The State of State-Local Revenue Sharing*, M-121 (Washington, D.C., 1980), pp. 1–3, 6, 9, 49–58.
119. Gold, *State and Local Fiscal Relations*, p. 45.
120. Ibid., p. 46–51.
121. ACIR, *State Government Capability*, p. 296.
122. Ibid., p. 296.
123. Gold, *State and Local Fiscal Relations*, pp. 7–8.
124. ACIR, *Significant Features of Fiscal Federalism*, 1984 edition, Table 100, p. 162; *Intergovernmental Perspective* (Winter 1985), p. 28; ACIR, *State Mandates—An Update* (Washington, D.C., 1982).
125. *Intergovernmental Perspective* (Winter 1985), p. 28.
126. Gold, *State and Local Fiscal Relations*, p. 57.
127. Ibid., pp. 58–59.
128. Ibid., pp. 55–57.
129. ACIR, *State Government Capability*, pp. 327–28, 337.
130. Ibid., pp. 336, 338.
131. Ibid., pp. 337, 346, 382.
132. Roy Bahl, "The Design of Intergovernmental Transfers in Industrialized Countries," *Public Budgeting and Finance*, Vol. 6, No. 4 (Winter 1986), pp. 3–4.
133. Ibid., p. 14.
134. Ibid., p. 19.
135. ACIR, *Studies in Comparative Federalism: Canada*, M-127 (Washington, D.C., 1981), p. 39.
136. Ibid., p. 24; ACIR, *Studies in Comparative Federalism: Australia*, M-129 (Washington, D.C., 1981), pp. 45–47.
137. ACIR, *Australia*, pp. 15–33, 45–47; ACIR, *Studies in Comparative Federalism: West Germany*, M-128 (Washington, D.C., 1981), pp. 8–9.
138. ACIR, *West Germany*, p. 42.
139. Ibid., pp. 36–43; Kenneth Howard, "Similarities and Differences: Federalism in West Germany and the United States," *Intergovernmental Perspective*, Vol. 10, No. 2 (Spring 1984), p. 26.
140. Howard, "Similarities and Differences," p. 26; also based on interviews in the British Treasury in August 1987.
141. David N. King, *Fiscal Tiers: The Economics of Multi-Level Government* (London: Allen and Unwin, 1984), p. 43.
142. Howard, "Similarities and Differences," p. 28.
143. ACIR, *Intergovernmental Perspective*, Vol. 3, No. 3 (Summer 1976), pp. 13–14.
144. *New York Times*, January 31, 1981, p. A10.
145. T. F. Cripps and W. Godley, *Local Government Finance and Its Reform* (Cambridge University, 1976), pp. 18–19.
146. ACIR, *Australia*, pp. 8–13.
147. Verda Doss, *Impact of Planning on Central-State Financial Relations in India* (New Delhi: National, 1978), pp. 80–84, 164–169.
148. ACIR, *West Germany*, pp. 54–56.

Index